Charles Francis Keary, Eva Tindall

Norway and the Norwegians

Charles Francis Keary, Eva Tindall

Norway and the Norwegians

ISBN/EAN: 9783743338623

Manufactured in Europe, USA, Canada, Australia, Japa

Cover: Foto ©ninafisch / pixelio.de

Manufactured and distributed by brebook publishing software (www.brebook.com)

Charles Francis Keary, Eva Tindall

Norway and the Norwegians

CONTENTS

CHAPTER I.—THE LAND.

Recent Habitation of Norway—The Glacial Era and its Effects—The Island Rampart—The Hills—Remains of Ancient Glaciers—The Fjords—The 'Norwegian Canal'—General Conformation of the Country—Snowfields—Waterfalls—Forests, ... 1

CHAPTER II.—THE PEOPLE.

Theory of the Origin of the Aryans in Scandinavia—Traces of Prehistoric Life: Ship-building, House-building—Homesteads—Primitive Customs—The Midsummer Fire, 31

CHAPTER III.—SEAFARING.

Ship-building in the Viking Age—Rise of the Viking Age—The Norsemen in Ireland—The Vikings in Continental Europe—The Swedes in Russia, ... 60

CHAPTER IV.—THE EDDA AND ITS MYTHOLOGY.

Norse Colonies and Discoveries in the Faroes, in Iceland, in Greenland and America—The 'Greater Scandinavia' of the Ninth and Tenth Centuries—Origin of Scandinavian Literature—Old Teutonic Metre—The Eddic or Poetical Literature—The Mythology of the Edda—The Jötuns—Thor—Frey—Balder—Odin—The Valkyriur—Lesser Divinities, ... 83

CHAPTER V.—THE EDDA MYTHOLOGY (*continued*).

The Underworld—Conjuration of the Dead—Ragnarök: The Doom of the Gods—Heroic Lays and Court Poetry, . 107

CHAPTER VI.—THE SAGAS.

The Settlement of Iceland—Rise of the Saga—The Shorter and Longer Sagas—Character Studies from Saga Literature—Narrative—Quotation from *Njala*—The Book Age—Snorri Sturluson, ... 122

CHAPTER VII.—HISTORY.

Consolidation of Norway—Harald *Fairhair*—Battle of Hafirsfjord—Harald's Land Laws—Harald's Sons—Erik *Blódöx*—Hakon *the Good*—Lapp Magic—Gunhild—Hakon and the Sons of Erik and Gunhild—Battle of Frædarberg—Battle of Stordö—Death of Hakon—Harald *Greyskin*—Earl Hakon—Hakon and the Haralds of Denmark and Norway, ... 143

CHAPTER VIII.—HISTORY.

Olaf Tryggvason—His Legendary Youth—The Age of the two Olafs—Conversion of Olaf Tryggvason—Earl Hakon and the Joms-vikings—Battle in the Jörundfjord—Death of Earl Hakon—Succession of Olaf—Christianisation of Norway—Olaf and Kjartan—Olaf and Halfred *Vandraduskald*—Olaf and Svend, King of Denmark—Alliance against Olaf—The Battle of Svold—Death of Olaf Tryggvason, A.D. 1000, ... 167

CHAPTER IX.—HISTORY.

Norway under Earl Erik—Early Years of St. Olaf—Olaf acquires the Crown of Norway—His Government—The Spread of Christianity—Olaf of Norway and Olaf of Sweden—Character of St. Olaf—Opposition Party in Norway—Olaf and Cnut, King of Denmark—Olaf driven from Norway—His Return—Battle of Stiklestad and Death of St. Olaf, A.D. 1030, . . . 205

CHAPTER X.—HISTORY.

St. Olaf's Son Magnus (the *Good*) restored to the Throne of Norway—Magnus and Hardacnut, King of Denmark—Magnus in Vendland—Svend Estridsson and Magnus—Harald *Hardradi* at Stiklestad—In Russia—As Commander of the Varangian Guard—He returns to Norway and shares the Government with Magnus—Harald as sole King of Norway—Harald's Invasion of England—Battle of Stamford Bridge and Death of Harald *Hardradi* A.D. 1066—End of the Heroic Age—Picture of Norse Life in the Heroic Age, ... 238

CHAPTER XI.—HISTORY.

Magnus and Olaf (*Kyrri*) the Sons of Harald—Peaceful Era in Norse History—House-building—Inns - Building of Churches—Mediævalism in Norway—Death of Olaf Kyrri, A.D. 1093—Magnus Bareleg—His kingly saying—His Death, A.D. 1103—Magnus's Sons—Sigurd the Crusader (d. 1130)—Magnus (the Blind) and Harald *Gilli*—Beginning of the Civil War—Increase in the Power of the Aristocracy and of the Church—Elevation of Magnus Erlingsson (A.D. 1161)—The Power of the Church—Rise of the Birkibeinar—Sverri—Civil War between Magnus and Sverri—Defeat and Death of Magnus, A.D. 1184—Personal Government of Sverri—Hakon Hakonsson—Hakon's Expedition to Scotland and Death, A.D. 1263, ... 264

CHAPTER XII.—HISTORY.

Magnus, the Son of Hakon—His Constitutional Reforms—Fall of the Aristocracy—Norway united to Sweden—Union, at Calmar, of the Scandinavian Countries—Norway ceases to be an Independent State—Movements which affected the Three Scandinavian Countries—Trade—The Hansa—The Black Death—The Rivalries of Sweden and Denmark—The Sture Family—The Rise of the Vasas—The Reformation—Growth of the Russian Empire—Transition to Modern Times, . . . 297

CHAPTER XIII.—MODERN NORWAY.

The present Constitution of Norway—The Ministry—The Parliament (*Storthing*)—Internal Administration—Revenue—Liquor Laws—Religion—Religious Intolerance of Norwegians—Education, . . . 320

CHAPTER XIV.—MODERN NORWAY.

Land Tenure—Few traces of Feudal Tenures—Abolition of Titles of Nobility—Inheritance—Continual increase in the number of Landed Proprietors—Productive Industries of Norway—Fisheries—Agriculture—The *Sæter*—Forestry—Common Rights in the Forests—Life of the Wood-Cutters—Means of Transport—Physique of the Modern Norseman—National Costume—National Diet—Effect of Republican and Democratic Institutions as exemplified in Norway, ... 336

CHAPTER XV.—LITERATURE.

Rise of Modern Norse Literature—Syttendemai Poetry—Wergeland—Welhaven—A. Munch and J. Moe—Norse Antiquarians and Historians—P. A. Munch—Ibsen and Björnson—Björnson's Works—Influence on them of German Literature—Björnson's Character—His different manners—Novels of the Early and Middle Period—Dramas—Björnson's later manner—Ibsen—The greatest name in Norse Literature—Not to be judged by Social Dramas only—*Brand* and *Peer Gynt*—Ibsen's other Dramas—His Pessimistic Character—A. Kjelland and Jonas Lie, ... 370

CHAPTER XVI.—THE WILD FLOWERS OF NORWAY.

Peculiarities in the Distribution of the Norse Flora—Habitat of the principal Wild Flowers—Description of Wild Flowers, ... 380

GENEALOGICAL TABLES, ... 395

INDEX, ... 396

ILLUSTRATIONS.

Bergen in the Sixteenth Century,	*Frontispiece*
Ground-plans of Norse houses, showing development of the art of house-building in Norway,	43
Old house in Orkedal,	45
Stabbur or store-houses,	48
Ranunculus glacialis,	388
Gentiana purpurea,	393
Linnæa borealis,	394

MAPS.

HISTORIC NORWAY,	xvi
SCANDINAVIAN SETTLEMENTS IN N. EUROPE, TENTH AND ELEVENTH CENTURIES,	408

NORWAY AND THE NORWEGIANS

CHAPTER I

THE LAND

The Glacial Era and its remains—Islands—Mountains—Fjords—Valleys—Forests—Conformation of the Country.

The Scandinavian Peninsula may be called—according to the light in which we choose to regard it—either one of the youngest or one of the oldest lands in Europe.

In the lands to the south of it, more especially in what we are wont to speak of as the classical countries, it is almost impossible to dissociate nature from mankind. The villages which crown the hills of Italy, for example, and which the eye catches sight of one after another nestling among the Apennines, we cannot possibly imagine removed from the scene. If they were not there we should be in a different country. They transport our thoughts back at a bound to the Middle Ages, when they were as numerous, almost, and perhaps more prosperous, than they are to-day. And they may well transport us further back still,—to the days of ancient Rome; or to yet earlier times before Rome had grown to its full greatness: to a Saturnian age, while yet there was no fear of Jove, while Etruscan and Italic communities lived unthreatened by the increasing power of the city by the banks of the Tiber. In the plains below these mountain villages the records of an antique civilisation are only just hidden from sight. Scratch the ground, and you come upon traces of the dead, upon vases which have been maybe brought by traders from Greece, and been there manufactured in the days when Sophocles still lived, and when Phidias and Polycletus worked in marble. Everywhere, therefore, in lands such as these, the history of mankind has, we may say, worked itself into the very soil. It is impossible to dissociate man and nature, even in thought.

But leave Italy, and travel to the Scandinavian countries, and you find everything in as great contrast to this as possible. Here man appears like a new comer; his civilisation, his cultivation of the soil, seem to be still only attempts, only a beginning. Every thing that is human seems most temporary; man has not yet made himself at home with nature. This impression, which is stronger than anywhere else in Norway, is heightened by what are perhaps mere accidents. The houses in Norway and Sweden are not maybe really slighter or more quickly built than the cottages in many other countries: but they look much more so. At a distance they look like wooden toy-houses, scattered upon no fixed principle here and there over the landscape. At best they resemble more the wooden shanties which people put up in the backwoods of America or the colonies, than the cottages of other European countries.

The tilling of the ground, too, appears to our eyes wonderfully slight and accidental. It is at best not very scientific, and to our English eyes it appears much more casual than it is perhaps in reality, if we come to understand the principles upon which it is carried out. The meadows are beautiful in the eye of the traveller, for they are full of wild flowers; but they would not be beautiful in the eyes of a scientific farmer. Here they are a mass of harebells; a little further on pink campion (ragged robin), or, that with us rarer form of campion, the fly-catcher, colours them crimson. Over all wave the heads of dock sorrel their rich russet brown. Then, again, in the midst of the meadow you come, without any apparent rhyme or reason, upon a little patch of potatoes or barley. In a later chapter we shall speak again of these eccentricities in farming; for the present we have only to do with the impression they make upon the eye of the traveller. On the other side it must be admitted that, occasionally, we are surprised by the ingenuity with which the smallest opportunities have been seized upon. We may sometimes see the top of a flat rock, though not much bigger than a good-sized table, made to bear a crop of corn or potatoes. One instance of this I can especially well remember. It lies on the road between Grönaas and Hellesylt. All the side of that road, between it and the river, the ground is a mass of immense stones and boulders, the *débris* of glaciers and avalanches in past times. It seems a region given up to barrenness. But on one of these rocks, which, because it is quite flat, is suited to retain a layer of earth, there grows this little potato-patch, an oasis in a wilderness.

At the best, however, the cultivated lands throughout Norway bear but a small proportion to the uncultivated area of the country,—they seem of no account compared to the vast stretches of woodland, of rocky mountain, of lakes, of rivers, of glaciers. All these things combine to produce the same impression upon the mind, to the effect that man is still but a recent intruder upon the antique solitudes of nature. You might even fancy that nature is preparing summarily to eject him; that it needs but a slight convulsion—slight as an exercise of her power—to crush for ever those scattered houses which lie between the cliffs and the fjord; to sweep away the farm-houses on the mountain side, or bury them beneath a portion of a single glacier; then, that her ancient and majestic peace will be restored to the primeval land.

Looked at, therefore, in this light, it is the immense antiquity of the Scandinavian countries which is brought home to you. All the forces and the relics which are impressed upon your imagination are the forces of nature, the relics of her work. Waterfalls which fell as they fall to-day ages before man set foot upon the soil; glacial boulders, moraines, which have been left exactly where they now stand when some hundreds of thousands of years ago the Glacial Age came to an end.

And yet, even in the annals of Nature (strange though the assertion must sound), Scandinavia may be said to be a younger country than others in Europe. She is so precisely in virtue of the great share she has had in the Glacial Era of which we have just spoken. It is not, I imagine, unknown to the reader that there was a time—a time we can hardly reckon, however roundly by years, but one not so very remote in the category of geological ages—when the whole of northern

Europe was covered by an impenetrable sheet or sea of ice. When, for example, starting from close upon our most southern latitudes, there was not a green thing to be seen between those latitudes and the pole. The southern limit of this huge glacier would lie, for our islands, a little way from the southern coast of England; on the Continent, at about the latitude of Dresden or Cracow; eastward the snow region spread as far as Nijni Novgorod or as Voronej; westward it covered the whole bed of the North Sea, the whole of our islands (except the strip just spoken of) and pushed on into the Atlantic some little way beyond the present limits of the Hebrides and of Ireland. Then, in the course of Nature, the great ice-age slowly passed away. The glaciers began to melt and to transform themselves into the floods which have hollowed out the great river-beds of Northern Europe, until at last they remained only in the high lands. This change took place last in Scandinavia, which, therefore, longer than any country, retained its covering of ice.

After that in other lands life had begun; when lichens had begun to grow upon the rocks, and duckweed in the swamps; as these in course of time gave place to grass and herbs, and the herbs developed into trees, and animal life came to re-inhabit the awakened earth, in Scandinavia the awful stillness of the ice-fields remained—their utter solitude and deprivation of even the germs of life. This is what I mean when I say that, even in the annals of Nature, Norway and Sweden may be reckoned the youngest among the countries of Europe.

This history of Scandinavia in the glacial age is the

more worth remembering, because it accounts for some of the phenomena of the country which are most striking, even at the present day, some which would attract the attention of even the most casual tourist, and for others again which, though they are no longer so obvious, are always present and show themselves by their effects. It might be some time before the traveller quite realised the meaning, even of those characteristics which he saw, and it would be longer still, probably, before he divined their true cause, unless he happened to have already studied the subject. Let us try and describe some of these legacies from the Ice Age which Norway still keeps and shows to the traveller. I will suppose this traveller to come to Norway—as nine out of ten do—across the North Sea, from Hull, or Newcastle, or Leith, or it may be even from the Shetlands, arriving first, as in some of these cases he will do, possibly at Stavanger, but in any case passing immediately to Bergen. At this last place he is close to some of the grandest scenery which Norway produces. The two most celebrated fjords of Norway—the Hardanger and the Sogne—lie on either side of him. Twelve or fourteen hours' steam, in the one case to the north, in the other case to the south, will take him well into the inner parts of one of those fjords, where he will see hills towering skywards, and immense cliffs descending sheer down into the sea. In rainy weather, of which, unluckily, he must expect a fair amount, he will see the mountains quite losing themselves in the clouds, glaciers constantly gleaming among them. The streams have that opaque colour—almost the colour of opal—which we are familiar with in glacier water. These things belong to our ordinary experiences of a mountainous country, and at any rate the traveller who has been in Switzerland will be familiar enough with them; familiar, too, in some degree with the torrents and the waterfalls, from the sound of which, after his full entry into Norway, the traveller's ears will, perhaps for days or weeks, be never free; and familiar with the wonderful beauty and variety of the ferns and flowers which he finds among all this grandeur. These things, I say, are common to Switzerland and Norway, as more or less to all mountain regions. Norway and Switzerland, in fact, always associate themselves in the mind as two countries essentially similar in scenery, whose flora are closely allied, and so forth.

But there are other features of Norwegian scenery peculiar to that Switzerland of the north, that Switzerland by the sea.

The first of these which the traveller in his supposed tour catches sight of is the belt of islands which lies between the mainland and the ocean. On his way into Bergen, for example, or into Stavanger, he will first pass for some hours among these rocky islands. They are of various sizes and of various elevations; but they share the same general character. They have much the same general look that rocks have which have been worn down by long detrition of the sea, only in the case of these islands it is not water which has robbed them of all their sharp angles, as we shall see presently. Similar islands may be found off the western coast of Scotland, and they are not infrequent off the west coast of Ireland, but no other land of Europe has such a continuous belt of islands as has Norway. This is one of the special features of the country which the traveller should note when he first sees it. The island rampart protects the whole coast with the quite insignificant exception of a small district at the extreme south, between Lister and the mouth of the Stavanger Fjord, and another opposite the Lofoten Islands. *Skjærgaard*, or rock-rampart, is the collective name which this protecting belt receives in Norway.

The general appearance of these islands—of the larger as well as the lesser, the mere rocks—is, as I have said, as if they had been sea-worn. What seems at first sight stranger still, you will find, as soon as you have threaded the last of them and arrived at the main coast, that that too carries on the same effect. The hills are now much higher than the most lofty of the islands which you have passed through, certainly high enough (if there could be any doubt about the latter) to be, and to have always been, far out of reach of the sea; and yet these hills have, like the *Skjærgaard*, a rounded, billowy look, as if they too had been worn smooth by the action of water. Round Stavanger, the point on the Norwegian coast which the traveller from Hull first touches, this characteristic of Norwegian coast scenery is very marked. So much is this the case, that I have before now been doubtful when arriving at that port in the twilight whether the eminences which I saw between me and the eastern sky were really hills or clouds; the hills have so very much the look of dark clouds hanging on the horizon. At Bergen you see the same effect, not quite so marked. In the more northern fjords it is frequently absent, so far at least as regards the appearance of the land from the sea. In the Nordfjord, for example, a number of jagged peaks cut the sky-line almost as impressively as the peaks in Switzerland stand out against the horizon. But even this effect, produced by gazing straight up from below, in a way you seldom can do in Switzerland, would be lost if you could get a wider perspective. Taking the country as a whole, and anticipating for once the later experience of the traveller, we are bound to confess that the contour of the hills in Norway is far less grand than in Switzerland, or in the Apennines or Pyrenees. We miss that long succession of rugged peaks which are so impressive in mountain chains, such as that of Mont Blanc, of the Bernese Oberland, or any of the other well-known chains in Switzerland. Nay, it is often worse than this. The general rugged effect of a mountain country against the sky-line is often lost altogether. The hills of Norway seen in this way look puddingy. If we are close beneath the cliffs they look stupendous; but when we are far enough off to take in the effect of a whole range of hills, that effect is, it must be confessed, much inferior to what we receive in the other highland regions I have spoken of. This is the one disappointment which the tourist must expect in Norway, and it is pleasant to get rid of this as soon as possible. Very likely the reader has experienced something of the same disappointment when first travelling in the Scottish Highlands. He expected mountains, but from a little distance off, at anyrate, the mountains look mere hills or hillocks.

This effect is due to precisely the same causes in Scandinavia and in Scotland, namely, to that very glacial era of which we have already spoken. It has been the wear and tear of the superincumbent sea of ice which, going on through ages and ages, has rubbed down the tops of the hills, has destroyed their fine and jagged outlines, and has reduced them to that puddingy contour which we cannot but deplore. Of course, since the glacial age departed, atmospheric influences have come in and partly modified its effects. To these are due the return to rough and jagged outlines which we find on many of the cliff-sides. But these have not had the effect of altering the general contour of the Norwegian highlands. From the islands of the Skjær-gaard, or island barrier, to the highest of the eminences which enclose the fjords of Norway, the effects of this glacial rubbing may be detected. When the traveller has once been put upon the track he will easily distinguish the marks of the corroding glacier as it ground down the hill-sides. He will constantly detect on the rocks what are called the glacial striations, the scorings of the surface produced either by the ice itself, or more commonly by stones carried along in the ice and ground against the surface of the rock. He may study the effects which the glaciers of Norway are producing at this very moment, by going up to some of the branches of the Jostedalsbræ or the Folgefond, the two greatest glaciers of Norway (of which more anon). In some of these branches the glacier is actually advancing down the valley, and he will see trees which it is beginning to push over on its downward march. Such a branch is the Buarbræ branch of the Folgefond, near Odde. But in other places,—and these are the more instructive,—he will find receding branches, which, as they decrease, leave behind them the marks of what they have done, the faces of the rock worn down and scored by the ice and the stones which it carried with it. The Nigardsbræ, or the Gredungsbræ branches of the Jostedalsbræ I will mention for the sake of giving instances, or the Kjendalsbræ branch at Loen. Then, again, after he has long left the glacier behind him, our traveller will continue to mark exactly the same scoriations on the rocks in his path that he noticed when he was at the part from which the glacier had only recently retired. I will mention one place where I myself have remarked them in greatest quantities,—the walk between the Gradunasbræ and the *sæter*, near Gradunstol. But over all Norway they are to be found.

Only in some of the great mountain regions of the interior do we come to peaks which stand higher than the highest point to which the glaciers have reached. This is the case in many of the hills of the Dovrefjeld and the Jötunfjeld.

Thus the traveller will convince himself of how much may be due to the action of the immense ice-sheet when it rested upon the whole of Scandinavia, or when, through subsequent millenniums, it began to decrease and work its way down the mountain-sides towards the sea. Armed with this thought, he will begin to observe how many of the greater hill-sides have the same kind of rubbed and smoothed appearance which he first detected in the rocks,—a smoothness varied by scoriations just such as the lesser rocks have. Even where, now-a-days, the hill is covered by vegetation, this general effect of its contour is very noticeable when once we have had our attention directed to it. I would take the Hardanger Fjord as a good instance in point. During all his first day's sail from Bergen to Eide (say) the traveller will notice these smoothed yet rocky hill-sides stretching down to the fjord on either hand: and recalling to mind the appearance of the hills of Norway as he first saw them at Stavanger, he will see how these things, too, are the outcome of the glacial age.

If, so far, these effects of the glacial era have been rather injurious to the beauty of Norwegian scenery, amends have surely been made in the burrowing out of the fjords. For that, too, is the work of glaciers. I have already, by anticipation, carried the reader into some of the fjords; but we have now to speak more particularly of this feature of the country. I take the things in order of our experience of them; first the *Skjærgaard*, or island belt, next the hills, and now, more decidedly unique than either of the preceding, the fjords. I say advisedly the most distinctly unique of the three. The reader who has never been to Norway, and has formed his judgment chiefly from maps, will perhaps hardly understand the statement. Fjord, so far as its etymology goes, is simply firth; and firth is the Scottish term generally used for the estuary of a river. Any one who had never been to Norway might be expected to interpret the word simply in this sense, and to look for river-mouths or estuaries of essentially the same kind that he would find in England or Scotland. In reality, however, the fjord is a natural feature peculiar to Scandinavia, as the tourist will soon begin to discover.

The two fjords which the traveller is likely first

to visit are those of which I have already spoken, lying on either side of Bergen,—the Hardanger and Sogne Fjords,—the one some sixty miles' sail to the south, the mouth of the other more than a hundred miles to the north. These are the two longest fjords of Norway; the Hardanger is sixty-eight miles long, the Sogne a hundred and six miles. In either case a day's steam from Bergen suffices to take one into either fjord. From Bergen to Eide, for example, well at the back of the Hardanger, is a matter of some twelve hours; to Odde, the extreme point of the same fjord, about twenty-one hours. You can get from Bergen to Vadheim, one of the first stopping-places in the Sogne, in eight or ten hours; to Lærdalsören or Aardal, the stations at the end, it takes about twenty hours. But the times of the steamers vary immensely, according to their class and to the number of places at which they stop *en route*. Each fjord has its own characteristics. The Hardanger has wide reaches enclosed by hills, high, indeed, but well clothed with vegetation, and, as a rule, sloping towards the water in the way I have already described. The branches of the Sogne are much the narrower,—the sides of them the most precipitous and bare. Sometimes these lesser branches are enclosed by walls so towering and close that they seem to shut out all sunlight, and, in fact, there are places on which for a very large portion of the year the sun never shines. Each of these smaller branches of the fjord is the continuation of a valley, narrow or broad according to the breadth of the estuary; and as down each valley of Norway runs a stream, these narrower fjords at any rate seem at first glance quite to answer to the common idea of a firth or river-mouth. But neither the lesser branches nor the greater fjords do so in reality, for reasons which I will now point out.

One way in which the fjords are distinguished from ordinary estuaries and river-mouths we have already spoken of—and this is the first peculiarity which the traveller to the Hardanger or the Sogne will notice—namely, by the island-belt which separates the fjord mouth from the open sea. In most countries the river mouths form the only harbours of the country. Where the firths afford safe anchorage, this is due, as a rule, to the formation of the estuary itself; and the advantage which is derived from protection from winds and waves is to a certain extent neutralised by the complications of tides and river-currents. But with Norway the whole sea-coast may be spoken of as one vast harbour; for all the force of the sea is kept out by the island rampart.

And let me pause at this point a moment to point out how this protected character of the Norwegian fjord should make us modify some of the views with which we probably have become imbued before ever we came to Norway. We are always thinking of the hardy Norsemen venturing forth to battle with the wild Northern seas, to wring his livelihood from their death-dealing waters, and in this struggle with Nature learning those arts of navigation which created the indomitable race of Vikings or Sea-rovers, and made the Scandinavian people the greatest seafarers and the greatest pirates of the early middle ages. This picture is partly true and partly false. I shall speak hereafter of the Vikings and their origin, and tell something of their history. It is enough to say at present that, in the first place, the earliest Scandinavian navigators probably learnt their art not on any portion of the coast which faces the north Atlantic, but in the comparatively safe waters of the Baltic, just as the Greeks learnt their art of seafaring in the enclosed waters of the Ægean. This in the first place; and secondly, that even the navigators of the North Atlantic coasts had for their first essays these protected fjords shut off from the outer ocean by the wall of the *skjærgaard*; and that it was because they had this protected region to experiment in, because they could gradually improve upon the rude boats with which they first began and did not need until they had had time for long practice and long development to venture forth into the open sea, that the forefathers of modern navigation became the great sailors which they did become. No doubt the men of Norway did venture out at last and battle with the elements, with the wildest of Atlantic storms, when, through the course of ages, they had learnt to make their ships fit for the contest.

And now we return to the description of the fjord. The fjord is not like a true firth, because, for one thing, there is no single great river current sweeping down it, fighting against the influx of the tide, as there is in the firth of Forth or Clyde, as there is in all great river mouths. Nor, on the other hand, can the fjord be at all justly compared to an ordinary bay.

Other bays, surrounded by high cliffs, have almost always a deposit of some kind at the foot of the rock, a beach of some sort between the cliff and the sea. Howsoever steep and high may be the surrounding rocks, the beach itself slopes gradually into the sea. This must be the case in the natural course of circumstances. Through the ages fragments must detach themselves from the rock and roll down to its base to be in time ground to sand and pebbles by the action of the tides. And if the fjords were like other bays we should see the same phenomena here. The reason why we do not see them springs from the main distinction between the fjord and all other firths or bays, the most remarkable one of all, though one which does not, as a rule, come under the eye of the tourist. The fjords are much deeper than the outside sea. We may say that, as a rule, the water which lies between the outer island belt and the land, into which it runs in creeks and fjords, is very much deeper than the sea some way outside the *skjærgaard*. In many cases the area of greater depth runs a considerable way beyond the *skjærgaard*. The difference is often very striking. Now, here we have certainly a most striking peculiarity in the fjords of Scandinavia, and one which distinguishes them from all other estuaries, bays, and river-mouths that we are likely to meet with in our travels. The cause of this peculiarity is precisely the same as the cause of the peculiarity of the rounded mountain tops of Norway, namely, the huge glacier which once lay upon the whole peninsula.

It was this vast sheet of ice which, pushing by its weight always down towards the sea, scraped out wherever the ground was softest the deep valleys of Norway; and when it got to the water's edge continued, as it were, the bed of these valleys into the sea, and hollowed out the vast depths of the fjords.

"The grandest display of ice-action which we could

wish to see," writes Mr. James Geikie, "is that which the fjords and valleys of Norway present. The smoothed and mammillated mountain-tops, the rounded islets that peer above the level of the sea like great whales, the glistening and highly-polished surfaces of the rocks that sweep right down into deep water, the great perched blocks ranged like sentinels on jutting points and ledges, the huge mounds of moraine *débris* at the heads of the valleys, and the wild disorder of crags and boulders scattered over the former paths of glaciers combine to make a picture which no after amount of sight-seeing is likely to cause a geologist to forget."

The action of the rivers of ice, as we may call them, which hollowed out the valleys and the fjord-beds did not always follow the bend of the surface of the soil. We can understand how the great pressure of the ice sheet may have forced the ice lying on the surface to pass over elevations and across small valleys. Thus we find that many of the rock-scoriations travel across moderate valleys and go up and down hill. On the same principle it is believed that, beside the ice-rivers which ran down the chief valleys, there was a lower ice-stream which took a direction at right angles to their direction, and that it was due to the action of this lower river of ice—lying at the edge of and outside the streams which were working down the valleys—that we have the extraordinary phenomenon of a deep channel running all along a great part of the Norwegian coast and following the line of that coast.

This submarine channel is called the Norwegian canal. The canal spreads all round the south-west ledge of Norway, and travels far up its western coast. It begins in the Christiania Fjord, a little to the west of Christiania itself. Its deepest point lies in the Skagerrak, between Arendal in Norway and the Scaw, the extreme northern peak of Jutland. Here it is upwards of 400 fathoms deep. Off Lister it has a depth of 200 fathoms. Off the Bömmelö, opposite the mouth of the Hardanger Fjord, it is 120 fathoms deep; and this is its shallowest part. It begins to increase in depth as we pass farther north. Off the Sogne Fjord it is again more than 200 fathoms deep, and it continues to deepen until, by the Cape Stad, it debouches into the deep channel of the North Atlantic Ocean.

There is, as the reader probably knows, a great submarine bank beneath the waters of the North Sea which unites Denmark with the British Isles, and which stretches out some little way beyond the west coasts of Scotland and of Ireland. To the east this bank stretches as far to the north as Cape Stad, or Statt, the most westerly point of the Norwegian mainland. Therefore, when the Norwegian canal has passed Cape Stad, the bank beside it suddenly dips down to the channel of the North Atlantic, and the canal is merged in the deep sea.

When the Great Glacier had disappeared from the face of the country, or rather when it had shrunk into those fragments which we now find lying on the high lands of Norway, the territory which it laid bare was the peninsula of Scandinavia which we have to-day. It is a territory which, in the extreme north, is almost a plain—an extremely sad-looking barren and rocky plain, with but stunted birch bushes instead of trees. But as you travel southward the trees grow higher, firs and pines appear, and, at the same time, the land begins to rise up, and then forms a sort of crest like the crest of a wave, or like a backbone ; or, for another simile, we may take that implied in the name which is given to it by the Norwegians themselves, Kjölen, the Keel. The most important part of this Keel begins about 69° north latitude, in the diocese of Tromsö, and reaches to 63°, the southern part of the diocese of Throndhjem. It rises in its course into certain special elevations, or groups of mountains, such as Sulitelma.

Some way south of the Trondhjem Fjord this ridge turns westward nearly parallel with the trend of the coast in that direction. And at the same time it spreads out into a series of highland countries, the most important of which are the Dovrefjeld, the Jötunfjeld (which adjoins the celebrated Jostedal glacier) and the Hardanger Vidde. These three groups of hills give a peculiarly rugged character to all the country which lies between them and the coast,—that is to say, to the great fjord district containing the Hardanger and Sogne Fjords, whereas the country to the north of them is lower-lying and more fertile.

Before the 'Keel' reaches the south of the peninsula it gradually subsides, so that from about latitude 62° the rivers, which have hitherto always run either east or west, begin to run due south. Still their course is very rapid, and we get nothing approaching level land until we come to Lake Mjösen, which lies chiefly south of latitude 61°. It is this region falling away from the Keel, till we get to a more level country, that is known in early Norse history as the Upland; and the inhabitants of it play an important part in this history. South of Mjösen, and along the coast of the Skagerrak, and the beginning of the Cattegat, is the flattest and most fertile part of Norway; the district which was earliest inhabited, and which is historically the most important in the whole country.

It must be borne in mind that most of the land of Norway,—even where no special range of hills is distinguishable,—lies, as compared with the sea-coast, at a very considerable elevation: and that this great table-land, which is the essential Norway, is everywhere intersected, when we get near the coast, by valleys or fjords that run far into it, and by the beds of rivers which have a steep fall and a very rapid course. Some of the larger valleys in the interior are very celebrated, as are the Romsdal and the Gudbrandsdal. Even the lower lands approaching the Christiania Fjord are far from level; the rivers which run through them have, for the most part, too precipitous a course to allow of their navigation.

The whole history of Norway is suggested by the character of the country which these formations bring about. It is, in the first place, a country facing two ways: looking out in one direction (as its rivers flow) towards Denmark, towards the Baltic, which is the sea uniting all the Scandinavian countries; looking out in the other direction towards the wild North Atlantic, towards the British Islands, and beyond them to the boundless west. Then, again, it is a country cut up by its formation into many different parts, into the bare, flat Finmark in the extreme north; into the rocky Halogaland (now Nordlandsamt and Tromsöamt) lower down, a district particularly rich in its fisheries; into the fertile Throndhjem region (Nordre- and Sordre-Throndhjemsamt) always throughout Norse history strong in virtue of its substantial yeomen (*bænder*, bonders), the backbone of the Norse nation, and independent beyond any other district of Norway; into the two long valleys, the Osterdal and the Gudbrandsdal, which the Dovrefjeld separates from the Throndhjem country and the Uplands, which lie alongside of them; into the fjord district (Northern and Southern Bergenhus, or in history Hördaland and Sogn)—to which we may add Sondre-Möre and Romsdal—a region which, we have seen, is cut off from the Gudbrandsdal by mountain ranges; into the barren, uneven country of the southern bulge of the peninsula Rogaland, Agder, Thelemarken; and finally, into the more fertile region which lies to the south of Lake Mjösen, where the Uplands cease.

These last are the divisions most often mentioned in Norse history—East Agder, Grænland, Westfold to the west of the Christiania Fjord, Vingelmark to the east. And just behind these regions, between them and the true uplands, lie Ringariki, Römariki, and Hedemark.

Add to these divisions by hill and valley the vast forests which still cover the inner slopes of the country, and of which the traveller who goes by rail from Christiania to Throndhjem gains some idea, and we see how difficult a country Norway must have been to unite into one whole. We understand how rival forces may march and countermarch in such a country without ever coming in sight of one another; and we are in a position to understand the tale of constant wars and factious rivalries which make up the history of Norway.

For when we come to the coast the same features meet us. The innumerable fjords and bays by which the coast is cut up; the countless islands which lie outside it, make it as easy for one of two rival fleets to avoid an engagement—or, on the other hand, to obtain a surprise—as the varied character of the interior makes it easy for two rival armies to do so.

Here, then, is the true history of Norway told in a moment. A land whose sons have done great things abroad, and formed a heroic character at home. But a country likewise, it must be owned, which has had scarcely any political history of importance. No other country, save Ireland, has had such a turbulent domestic history as Norway has had, or been more constantly the theatre for the struggles of rival factions. Thanks to the unrivalled beauty of the northern saga literature (an Icelandic literature rather than a Norse), some of the makers of Norse history, Hakon the Good, Olaf Tryggvason, Olaf the Saint, stand out in a heroic guise before us. But we must not make the mistake of thinking that this glamour which literature has cast over the history of Norway makes that country great, as in political matters we estimate greatness. It is great in beauty, but not politically important; as the land of Norway is to-day. For the very causes, which have kept the country so long divided, and have left it so little opportunity for great national movements for a wide culture or for the creation of great monuments, such, for example, as the architecture with which the Middle Ages covered other European countries, is precisely the cause of the exceeding attraction of the country to the traveller of to-day, who is tired of seeing on every side of him the signs of a too solid material prosperity from which the reign of nature seems quite shut out.

In our country life, even, the signs of wealth and luxury meet us on every hand. But here we may wander for days seeing nothing more civilised than tiny wooden houses; and though Norway is every year getting more overrun by tourists, we may still pass from valley to mountain and see no signs but of a primitive and simple life, which has been unchanged for centuries.

And now to give a few statistics which may show the proportion of valleys and hills and higher mountain peaks in Norway.

20·5 per cent. of the area of Norway lies between the sea level and 500 ft. above it.

22·6	,,	between	500	and	1000
26·0	,,	,,	1000	,,	2000
16·8	,,	,,	2000	,,	3000
9·1	,,	,,	3000	,,	4000
3·8	,,	,,	4000	,,	5000
1·0	,,	,,	5000	,,	6000
0·2	,,	,,	6000	,,	7000
0·02	,,	over			7000

We see from these figures that the amount of territory which rises above the height of 7000 feet is extremely insignificant. There are, in fact, no very high mountains in Norway. The Galdhöpig, in the Jötunheim, which is the highest of the Norwegian mountains, is only 8400 feet in altitude. This does not seem much beside the 15,784 feet of Mont Blanc, or the 15,217 feet of Monte Rosa. About five per cent. of the area of Norway lies above 4000 feet from the sea level,—that is to say, above the highest point to which the Scandinavian glacier ever reached. These hills, therefore, which consist of the higher portions of the Jötunfjeld, the Dovrefjeld, and Kjölen, and of certain isolated peaks scattered about these districts, are quite free from the effect of glacial action. Some of them are exceedingly precipitous in shape and imposing in appearance, more so than most of the mountain ranges in Switzerland. What we have said, therefore, of the disappointment which the traveller experiences in comparing mountainous Norway, as a whole, with mountainous Switzerland, must not be taken to apply to these exceptional ranges.

It will be seen from the above statistics that more than one-third of the area of the country lies above 2000 feet from the sea-level. And owing to a peculiar character of Norwegian scenery, and the degree in which all the light soil has been carried into the valleys, this means, practically, that this area of the country is not cultivable. At best it only affords some mountain pastures for cattle and sheep. But of the area of Norway under cultivation, and of the character of the farming which obtains there, we shall have to speak in a later chapter of this volume. This is enough of statistics for the present.

What Norway shares with other mountainous countries, its hills, its cliffs, its everlasting waterfalls, its moist hill-sides carpeted with flowers, it owes to geological conditions such as they have undergone; such as produced Switzerland, for example, and its bordering highlands between the plains of France and Lombardy. But that which is most characteristic of Norway, its rounded hill-tops and its deep fjords, it owes to glacial conditions almost peculiar to this country. This is why I have paused to dwell upon them, and why the tourist may well bear them in mind.

And now to these two products of the glacial era in Scandinavia let us add a third, which, however, is not so much a result of the Ice Age as a continuation of it, —I mean the immense glaciers which still remain in Norway. The line of perpetual snow in Norway is, as we might expect, far lower than in Switzerland. In some places it is as low as 3000 feet above the sea level. It is not merely the northern situation of the country which produces the great snow fields and glaciers of Norway. Their presence is partly due to the smoothness of the hill-tops which I have already spoken of. Thus it might be said that the glaciers of Norway are so huge to-day, because they were so much vaster in former ages.

It is not, by the way, easy to persuade those who have never travelled in Norway of the size of her glaciers; the Swiss glaciers are so much the most celebrated that their reputation overshadows that of the ice-fields of Norway. In speaking of the Jostedalsbræ as the largest glacier in Europe, I have so often met with the response, 'You mean after the great Swiss glaciers,' that it may be worth while to give the reader an idea of the comparative areas of these different ice-sheets. The largest glacier in Switzerland is the Aletsch glacier: it is not more than a sixth of the Jostedalsbræ, with its 350 square miles, nearly half as large again as the county of Middlesex. Even the next largest glacier, the Folgefond, has an area of over 120 square miles,—that is to say, it is nearly as large as Rutlandshire. For the reasons which I have already given, the Norwegian glaciers lie much lower than those of Switzerland, and are, therefore, more easy to reach. The task of crossing the huge Jostedalsbræ, which is very narrow in proportion to its length, is not beyond the compass of a third or fourth rate mountaineer. Every year one or two ladies perform the feat, and have the pleasure of boasting that they have crossed the largest ice-sheet in our quarter of the globe.[1] These two glaciers belong to the two fjords of which I have already spoken several times; the Folgeford overlooks the Hardanger, and may be seen from almost any point on that fjord. The Jostedalsbræ, in like fashion, lies close to three of the branches of the Sognefjord, the Lysterfjord, the Sogndalsfjord, and the Fjärlefjord, and generally lies along a portion of the watershed between the Sognefjord and the next great fjord north of it, the Nordfjord.

The Skjærgaard, or island-belt round the coast, the fjords and the mountains which immediately enclose them, the snow-fields and glaciers which rest above, and the streams and waterfalls which descend thence into the fjords and into the sea, these things we have spoken of; they sum up all the principal features of the country with which nine out of any ten travellers in Norway come in contact. For the travellers in, or, say, the visitors to, Norway may be divided into three classes. First, those who come for sport—which here is almost exclusively fishing—these usually settle themselves for the whole time of their stay not far from the mouth of one of the salmon rivers of the country. The scenery which they get a glimpse of is the scenery of the fjords and the river-lakes near the coast. Another set are those who come either in private yachts, or on what are called now-a-days yacht-steamers, and scarcely

[1] Save one in Iceland.

ever leave the coast during the whole time they are in Norway. They steam from fjord to fjord; occasionally they may go for a day's drive over some neck of land, but their knowledge of the country is like that of the sportsman, entirely confined to the coast region. Lastly, there are the regular travellers in the country; but even these travel little in the interior. One cross-country route is a good deal frequented. It is that from Christiania down the Gudbrandsdal, ending with the magnificent Romsdal. There is good reason for this exclusiveness in Norwegian travel. The coast scenery is far the finest which the country has to show, and is, in truth, so magnificent that I shall not attempt to find language fit to describe its beauties. The constant juxtaposition of mountain and fjord gives this scenery its peculiar charm. Add to this the moist and warm summer climate which produces a vegetation of unequalled richness and beauty, the quantity of melting snow which feeds an endless succession of waterfalls and torrents. Nowhere are waterfalls so numerous as in this land. You may travel for days and yet the sound of them be never out of your ears. I have counted as many as four-and-twenty, standing in one spot. To the flowers of Norway a special chapter at the end of the volume is dedicated. I will not say that the meadows here are richer than I have seen them in Switzerland in the spring, but they are as rich. And there is one feature about the flora of Norway incidental to a country with a short summer of long days of sunshine, which, at midsummer time, even in the southern half of the country, lasts from two, or half-past, in the morning, to half-past nine or ten at night:

this feature is the rapidity with which the flowers come to maturity, so that we see—what seems so strange to us—blooming side by side the flowers of spring and of late summer. While you find the ditches still yellow with golans, you see the wild rose-trees in full bloom, the meadows full of harebells, and the foxgloves out in the woods and on the hill-sides.

Such are some of the beauties of Norway, and these, as I have said, belong chiefly to the fjord districts. Then, again, these fjords are so numerous, the distances in Norway are so great, that there is little danger for the traveller that he will exhaust the beauties to be seen in these regions, supposing it were really possible to exhaust the beauties of nature. Far be it from me to suggest that such is possible: but still, taking the average tourist as we find him, it must be owned that it would be far easier for him to *do* Switzerland than to *do* Norway.

It is, therefore, reasonable that the average traveller should confine himself almost exclusively to the fjord district, but by so doing he hardly gets an idea of the character of Norwegian scenery as a whole. The effect of seeing Norway only from the sea is something like the effect of seeing the Rhine-land only from the Rhine. In the latter case we get an impression of passing through almost a mountainous country; but if we clamber up to the top of these hills we find we are on a vast table-land, and that it is the deep bed of the river which produced the illusion of hills. So, in the case of Norway, it is the sudden cutting off of the table-land of the country which is accountable for the greater part of the effects which we witness from the fjordside.

But Norway, as we have said above, is not merely a table-land. In many places it breaks into real mountain scenery, as in the Dovrefjeld and the Jötunheim; and in almost every case the table-land continues to rise in elevation toward that great back-bone of Scandinavia, the Keel, which runs nearly parallel with the Norwegian coast. Any one who has never visited this interior portion can have no notion of what the pine-forests of Norway are like in their grandeur.

The traveller, therefore, should not leave the country without seeing these back parts of it, or travelling somewhere near the Keel; and in the present day, by the spread of the railway system, this is not difficult to do. The railway from Throndhjem to Christiania begins near the southern end of the Keel, and at first the line continues to ascend till it attains a considerable elevation. At Röraas we see the country in its bleakest aspect; when we reach Koppang we find the forests in their perfection. We are now hanging upon the lower skirts of the Keel, and well in that country known as the Upland. At either Röraas or Koppang we can, if we choose, leave the train and travel for a while inland by road on foot or by kariole. We have a still more interesting experience as we mount the old road from the Throndhjem Fjord leading straight across into Sweden. We travel continually uphill, getting splendid views of the fjord in many windings and branches—just such a view, in fact, as St. Olaf saw a few days before his death, as we shall narrate hereafter, and fancied he was looking over the whole world. The road rises from the neighbourhood of Verdal. At first the country is very rich, as all the Throndhjem district is.

We see fields of rye waving before us (and this may remind the historian of another story of King Olaf the Saint). Then gradually we ascend into the deep pine-woods; and at last, by a steep but well-made road, we reach the plateau on which runs the dividing line between Norway and Sweden. If we continue our walk we should find ourselves in Jemteland, another district which figures often in early Norse history. It is now a district of Sweden. The large farms on the route afford us hospitality. There are no inns.

Of quite recent years a railway has been made taking rather a different route; and it may be presumed the road is very much less used now than it formerly was.

CHAPTER II

THE PEOPLE

Traces of Prehistoric Life in Modern Norway

WHEN the great glacial era came to an end, and the ice-sheets retired to as it were entrench themselves in mountain fastnesses, as in the Swiss mountains or in the Pyrenees, or else in the colder lands to the north, certain animals which, in those conditions of Arctic climate, had ranged freely over Europe, but could not stand the change to conditions more temperate, retired with the ice-sheet. The chamois was one of these. He took refuge in the highlands of Southern Europe. The reindeer was another. He retired to the north of Scandinavia. Some anthropologists believe that glacial man,—that is to say, the man who lived in Southern Europe while the great glacier covered all the north, and who, therefore, for generations upon generations had grown habituated to an Arctic climate, was obliged in like manner to migrate northwards after the rein-deer; and that he fixed his home in Scandinavia, and continued there the earlier European race, while a new race of men from the south or from the east came in to occupy the countries farther south which he had abandoned. It was in the cold conditions to which for hundreds nay, thousands of years it had been subjected (so say these anthropologists) that the fair-haired, light-skinned type of mankind was formed. They imagine these fair-haired people continuing, after their forced migration northwards, through hundreds or thousands of years, and they point out that it is only in the southern Scandinavian countries, in Denmark and South Sweden, that we have traces of the presence of man, apparently so continuous as to bridge over the time between his earliest remains (in what is called the First Stone Age) and his later remains of the Second Stone Age. Thus, for a time—a period not estimable in years, and in an unspeakably remote past, measuring by historical standards—there lived on in the north these fair people of the north, and in Central and Southern Europe a different race of darker people, more allied to the dark races of Asia or Africa. At last the fair people migrated southwards, conquered the dark races, mingled with them, and imposed, it may be, their language upon them. Out of this mixed race sprang all those different European peoples, which are, we know, allied to each other in language, as well as those other races of Persia and India, whose language likewise shows them descended from the same stock as the Europeans. The supporters of this theory point out among other things how many of the dominant races among the people of antiquity prided themselves upon their fair hair—among the Greeks, for example, and the ancient Persians — whereas it is not common to find a fair-haired man among their modern representatives; and they take this as evidence of the conquest by the fair-haired race from the north of the Southern

European peoples; analogous to the conquest which took place thousands of years later of the Roman races by the Goths and Lombards and Franks from Germany. And though all this is mere speculation, or not much more than that, what is not mere speculation is that out of the Teutonic races of a later time, among those very conquering Goths and Lombards of whom we have just spoken, and others of the people who rose upon the fall of Rome, a very large number believed themselves to have come at some very remote era from the Scandinavian countries.

Whether or not in times indefinitely remote, long before the dawning of the historic era in any part of Europe, a Scandinavian people had played the important part which this theory assigns to them, it is certain that (except maybe in some half-forgotten tradition) they had been long lost sight of by the nations of the south, and that when the day of history broke upon these, the people of the north were left still in darkness.

It was, we know, in the basin of the Mediterranean that all the civilisation of the west took its rise, beginning on the eastern side, on the Ægean or on the Asiatic coast, with the Phœnicians and the Greeks, and then passing westward to Sicily and Italy, to Northern Africa, and on to Spain and to Southern Gaul. One slender thread of this stream, it is thought by some, made its way northward. There seems some trace of a trade route starting from the Greek seas and passing by the Black Sea up the Dnieper (a river which the Greeks knew well, and named the Borysthenes) up to the western parts of what is now Russia: by another

river, the Dwina or the Vistula, it found its way down
again to the Baltic. There seem to be some traces of
this thin uniting thread of trade between the south and
the north; and some think that the earliest northern
alphabet — the well-known *runic* alphabet, which
belonged to the Scandinavians and the North Germans
— found along this route its way from Greece to the
Baltic countries; but of this connection between the
north and the south no written record now remains.
No Greek traveller has told us how the Baltic countries
presented themselves to his eyes.[1] The Greeks did,
we know, talk of a land of the Hyperboreans — a land
to the back of the north wind, but they meant by that
no region so far away as Scandinavia. What they
meant by this land at the back of the north wind was
simply the territory in which no longer blew a certain
wind which daily blows down the Ægean Sea; so that
their land of Hyperboreans would lie but a little to the
north of the Greek Sea, say in Thrace, or on the other
side of Mount Hæmus, the Balkans, *i.e.* in modern
Bulgaria — far enough removed from the Baltic lands.

But when we have travelled down the stream of time
till the days of the Roman Empire, until after the
beginning of our era, then we do find the Scandinavian
lands beginning, as it were, to dawn on the general
knowledge of mankind. A certain knight in the reign

---

[1] The only Greek traveller who got at all near to these regions and left
any record of his travels was Pytheas, a merchant of Marseilles. Some
commentators have thought from his descriptions that he passed beyond
the Cimbric Chersonese (Jutland) to within the Baltic. But the best
authorities are agreed that he never saw any of the Scandinavian
countries, save, maybe, Denmark, and of that only the western coast of
Jutland.

of Nero is said to have been the first Roman who actually gazed upon the Baltic Sea. It is Pliny the Elder who tells us this; and the words in which Tacitus, writing about the end of the first century, speaks of the Scandinavian countries are worth remembering—the first recorded glimpse of any worth into this remote world by the eye of a Roman.

It is after he has finished describing the people of Northern Germany, who lay along the southern shore of the Baltic, that Tacitus goes on to speak of what lies beyond. The Romans, as yet, knew only the southern bulge of the Scandinavian Peninsula, and therefore did not know but that this was an island in the midst of the Northern Ocean. Wherefore the Baltic is for them but a portion of the great ocean which lies round the north-western coasts of the European continent, round Frisia, round Jutland (the Cimbric Chersonese), and round the north of Germany. Tacitus, however, does make a distinction between this Northern Sea south of the Scandinavian 'island,' and the Arctic Sea on the other side of it. He speaks first of the land of the Suiones (*i.e.* the Swedes), which lies in the Northern Sea opposite the coasts of Germany. We must take this land to be the southern bulge of Sweden, part of which is to-day called Skane, or Skönen. Scania, Scandia, Scanzia, Scandinavia were the names by which the country was known to the Romans. Of his land of the Suiones, all that Tacitus tells us is that it is rich in arms and ships and men; and then he goes on to say that 'beyond the land of the Suiones is another sea (*i.e.* the Arctic Sea), sluggish or almost stagnant, which, we may believe, girdles and encloses the whole earth. For here ['in the Suiones' land'] the light of the setting sun lingers on till sunrise bright enough to dim the light of the stars. More than that, it is asserted that the sound of his rising is to be heard, and the forms of the gods and the glory round his head may be seen. Only thus far—and here rumour seems truth—does the world extend.'

Here, is indeed, a picture which might excite the imagination of a Roman of those days. We have reached the very edge of the world, so near the place where the sun goes down for his night's rest or emerges again to make the day, that his light still hovers about the place all night, and it is said (the paragraph is a little obscure) that you get so near the blazing chariot that you can distinguish the figure of the godlike charioteer, and that the sound of his rising is to be heard. Beyond this is the part where the earth seems but half created out of the primal chaos in which there was no distinction between land and sea. The sea is sluggish or almost stagnant, and this is, like the Oceanus of Homer's verse, the stream which encircles the whole earth. One would say that the travellers who brought back to Rome this picture of the north, and reported how the light of sunset lingered on till dawn could have been there only in summer weather. And yet in this almost stagnant sea there seems to linger a picture of the frozen, or half-frozen, ocean in winter time. Perhaps the two most remarkable features of the north, the twenty-four hours' day of midsummer and the frozen sea of midwinter are here confounded in the account of Tacitus.

Here, at anyrate, is a beam, though a faint one, of

recording history breaking over the lands of the north. And, strange to say, in the above-quoted passage our author places on record one of the things by which the north was destined to make itself most famous in the history of the world. These Suiones (Swedes) were, we see, already a seafaring people 'rich in ships.' Nay, we have other independent proof that, for as many as five hundred years before Christ, six hundred years before Tacitus put on record what he had gathered concerning Scandinavia, there was an art of shipbuilding known in these countries. Let the traveller who has leisure, and desires in his travels to see all kinds of Scandinavian scenery, if he has begun his tour by going first to Sweden, and has explored its placid beauties before turning to the more exciting ones of Norway, turn aside to visit one of the countries in the southern bulge of Sweden, just that part which escapes the notice of the great majority of travellers. This is Bohuslän, which lies between Götteborg and Christiania, and is passed by the steamers which ply between these ports. The country is flat and tame, but it is not unsought by the Scandinavians themselves, who think that there is something specially salubrious in the air of this coast. The flat scenery and the many windmills of this region remind one somewhat of Holland. To the historian the most interesting things in Bohuslän are the remains which lie scattered up and down it of a very remote antiquity. There are many Stone-Age chambered tombs in this region; and more interesting than all remains of this kind are certain carvings on rocks which the northern antiquaries pronounce to date from an age not less remote than B.C. 500. The majority of

these representations are concerned with ships; we may
believe that some of them are representations of sea-
fights, like the sea-fights of the Vikings in the ninth or
tenth centuries of our era. And rude as the drawings
are, they do allow us to gather some notion of the kind
of vessels employed in that very remote age: which, it
may be said at once, correspond in the principal features
not only with what we gather were the kind of boats
used in Tacitus's day, but save in one point of great importance, with what we know were the kind of vessels
used by the Vikings. That is to say, these ships of the
rock-carvings were row-boats with very high carved
prows or stern posts, and steered not by a rudder behind but by an oar at the side. This last practice long
continued, and has given us our word starboard, *i.e.*
steerboard, to signify the right-hand side of the vessel.
But where the Viking ship differed from the vessels of
Tacitus's time, and those still earlier ones which are
displayed upon the rock-carvings of Tanum or Brestad
in Bohuslän, is that they possessed sails, which the two
previous orders of vessels were quite without. They
were still rowing boats, but with the addition of a sail
which could be hoisted when required. This new
device,—new to them,—the northern people had learnt
more or less directly from the Romans. For our word
sail, and its equivalents in other Teutonic languages,
segel, *segl*, *seil*, are all derived from the Latin word
sagulum.[1]

So much for the northern lands as they presented
themselves to the imagination of a Roman of the first

---

[1] A short cloak originally much worn by the Gauls; afterwards the word was applied to a sail.

century. We who travel in the north shall, most of us, like the Romans, see the country only in its summer aspect. We shall see often enough the phenomenon which struck the Roman travellers as so wonderful as to be a proof that they had got near the borders of the earth—the light of sunset lingering on bright enough to dim the light of the stars. But what their imagination likewise saw, the forms of the gods and the glory round the head of the sun-god, that is lost to us for ever, not less than the sight of Proteus rising from the sea or Triton blowing his wreathed horn.

Let the traveller, in passing among the rocky islands and fjords of Norway, note those heavy boats with high prows and squared sails which he will see here and there lying among more modern-looking craft. They have an indescribable air of antiquity about their build, and at once contrast with the numerous boats, of the build that we are accustomed to in our coasting vessels and fishing smacks, which we shall see beside them. For, now-a-days, this more modern species of craft is much the commonest, and the heavy square-sailed boats which I have been describing are getting rarer day by day. In an experience extending over only seven years, I can notice a marked decline in them. In the cod-fishing,—especially that of the north,—vessels of this build, but still more like the old Viking ships (in that they have pointed sterns), are still used. The voyager to the North Cape will encounter many of them. But the average tourist may not see many. These old-fashioned boats are a link between us and the remotest past of Scandinavia, a link with the Scandinavia of Tacitus's day, with the still earlier

Scandinavia of the rock-carvings in Bohuslän. When I come to speak more particularly of the Viking boats, of which examples are extant in the museums, I shall point out the *difference* between the modern craft which I have described and the Viking ships and the ships which preceded them. But despite the differences which exist, there remains enough likeness to make this existing boat a real link between us and the remotest past.

Other links between us and the past are the houses of Scandinavia, especially those of Norway, many of which keep the form which was given to them in the most primitive days. Most houses, we know, have grown by *accretion*; what are now the different rooms of a house were different buildings added on as age followed age and people became more refined and exacting in their tastes. The primitive element, what we may call the kernel of the English house, is really the hall; and that is why the word 'hall' has come to have such a wide and varied significance in our language. In old-fashioned houses even of to-day, and in houses which, like modern country houses, try and imitate the architecture of an earlier time, the hall with its wide fireplace is simply the largest room in the house: the other rooms seem to have gathered round it. What we might call the two essential constituents in a house of the Middle Ages are the 'hall' and the 'bower,' so often brought into connection and contrast in our ballad poetry. 'Bower,' it may be said, has no connection with boughs, and means nothing in the nature of an arbour, though many people have a sort of notion that it does. It is really the 'building,'[1] in other words, the building on to the hall; and hall and bower stand connected or contrasted really as the men's and women's parts of the house, or, if you like, the men's and women's houses built together.

Just the same is the *essential* character of the Greek house as it stands revealed to us in Homer. The chief room, the hall of that house was called μέγαρον, 'the great,' simply, but it meant the great room; or say great house, at a time when all other rooms were simply other houses built round. To the bower of our old poetry corresponded the woman's apartment, the θάλαμος. When the Greek house has become more elaborated (as we see it, for example, in the Pompeian house) these two essential divisions have expanded into two *groups* of rooms, each group surrounding a court, the men's quarter (ἀνδρωνῖτις) and the women's quarter (γυναικωνῖτις). Such is the chronicle and brief abstract of the art of house-building in the west.

In Norway we may still (even in this year of grace) go back to the primitive condition of things, where, what would be only a room of a house of the modern kind, is here a separate building, and sometimes the separate buildings seem in themselves to preserve all the characteristics of the most primitive house-architecture. The modern traveller,—especially the traveller who keeps close to the coast regions,—is only likely to find examples of this in the *sæters*, those temporary summer settlements lying generally on a small piece of table-land some way up a mountain, whither the Norwegians bring their cattle during the summer months to feed upon the moist rich pastures of these high lands:

---

[1] German *bauen*, to build and to cultivate.

where they themselves live as in a sort of encampment. It is the temporary character of the life led in the *sæters*, combined with the fact that the months passed there are all summer months, which has kept the houses built in them more primitive in form than the houses in the valley.

But, as I have said, in the interior likewise, in parts of Norway where wood is most plentiful, and where there has been consequently less temptation to depart from the ancient fashion, there may be found still more striking examples of the early method of building. In the Gudbrandsdal, which many Norwegian travellers pass down on the route from Christiania to the Romsdal, there are some good examples of this multiplication of small houses in place of a multiplication of rooms. One example given by Eilert Sundt, who has devoted a work to the subject of the peasants' houses in Norway, shows as many as thirty-three of these separate buildings.

Many houses in Norway have attached to them a sort of smoke-house or wash-house. It is called *Ildhus* or *Röghus*; or, at any rate, these used to be the names of it. These houses are not very common now-a-days in the more civilised parts of Norway. There used to be one at Vossevangen. The house is simply a square building, with a fire in the centre of it, on an open stone hearth. There is no chimney, but a hole (*ljore*) in the roof through which the smoke may escape. When it is shut, the apartment becomes full of smoke, and these smoke-houses are used for smoking the meat which the Norwegians preserve dried for a long period. The only other opening to the room besides the *ljore* is the door.

This smoke-house, according to Eilert Sundt, gives us the type of the earliest form of Norwegian house. Only, of course, in days when the building was used as a house it would be furnished with table, seat, and bed (board, bench, and bed), as in the accompanying woodblock (Fig. A) the Nos. 1, 2, 3 in this figure, as in the other two, represent table, bench, and bed. The bench is always a fixed part of the house; it always runs round some part of the walls, and this appears to have been

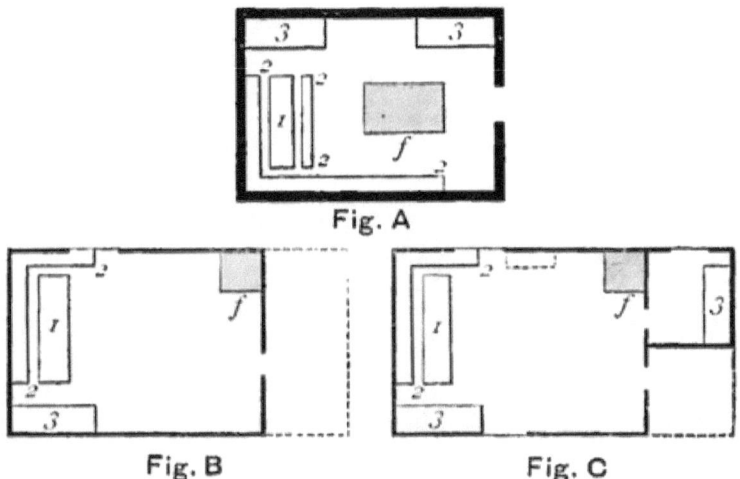

Fig. A

Fig. B Fig. C

the case in the old Saga-days just as it is to-day in many houses in Norway and Sweden.

In a dwelling-house of a similar structure, consisting of but one oblong room, we should see the fireplace (f) upon the ground, or only raised above it by a low hearth of stone. A kettle hangs over the fire, supported by a pulley from the roof; there is no chimney, and the smoke escapes from a hole in the roof. I have seen such a thing in the *sæter* houses.[1] The place

[1] The *sæter* house almost always has behind and united to it a small dairy. But the living-house often consists of one room only.

was full of pungent wood-smoke. Not seldom this opening in the roof serves as window as well as chimney. It must be close-able, to give protection against the weather; and, if it is closed suddenly, the room must get absolutely choking with wood smoke, which can then only find its way out at the door. When the fire has burnt to glowing ashes, so that there is little or no smoke coming from it, it is usual to shut up this opening in the roof in order to preserve as much heat as possible in the room. Probably in the old Saga-days most of the people in the house slept on the benches which went along the walls. But there were generally one or more separate beds, which the chief people occupied. They were sometimes partitioned off from the room, and are then spoken of in the Sagas as closed beds. The table was not always fixed, but brought in when the feast was laid. It stood apparently between the bench and the fire, which in large halls did not lie, as in our illustration, on a single hearthstone in the middle of the room, but ran all down the hall. The ale was handed to the people sitting on the benches 'across the fire,' as we are expressly told. That gave it some sort of blessing, no doubt. It was not until about A.D. 1100 that this custom was given up.

It is probable that at this date, too, the fire itself was removed to one side or to one corner of the hall. And that would lead very soon to the use of chimneys to carry away the smoke. Fig. B represents a small house which follows this plan. The fire (now-a-days the stove, *f*), stands, we see, in the corner of the room instead of in the centre. And there are windows as well as a door to the house (for the ground-plans given in our figures A, B, C are taken from existing buildings, not merely from imagination). The Old Norse name for the most primitive form of house (A) would be *bur*. Another word *stofa* (modern Norse, *stuva*), is etymologically the same as our *store*, and like the German *stube*, means a room with a fire in it. Fig. C represents a third and more developed type of house, which has an additional chamber and a porch.

The earliest houses built in Norway were, no doubt, in the strict sense of the word log-houses. There-

fore, if the traveller is on the search for a primitive form, he will do well to look out especially for buildings of this sort; for to-day wooden houses in Norway and Sweden are not usually built of undressed logs, but of boards. In the house given on the accompanying block we have an example of perhaps one of the oldest wooden houses actually standing in Norway. It stands, or stood at Uv in Rennebo in Orkedal. We see that it has been built of rough logs, but in spite of its primitive structure, some of the love of beauty which distinguished the middle ages has crept into the ornamentation of its porch.

This Rennebo house would perhaps be an intermediate form between the ground-plans B and C. We might have given this intermediate form, but it will easily suggest itself to the reader. The small plain quadrangular one-roomed building has only this of distinctiveness about it, that it has some form of protecting chamber, or at least portico before the door of the house.[1] This is rendered necessary by the severity of the weather, when snow may be piled up high against the door, and without some protection would melt there and run over the floor of the room within. This protecting fore-room, fore-hall may be simply a sort of portico; the roof carried forward a little and resting upon pillars. Among places where I have myself chiefly noticed this form of building, I will mention the well-known Romsdal; and I would advise the traveller who passes up that lovely valley to take note of the few scattered huts which he will see upon his way, and of their overhanging eaves resting upon two wooden pillars in front of the door. In some cases this portico has further decayed to be a mere overhanging of the eaves, or practically disappeared altogether; the *sæter* cottages show it in this state, for they, as I have said, are houses for summer only. But in a very large number of cases the same portico has developed into a closed-in room, a sort of vestibule to the house. A typical sort of house now-a-days (which is still built upon old lines) has a hall preceded by this vestibule, and running down the middle of the house,

---

[1] Suggested by the dotted square in Fig. B, p. 43.

with one room on each side of it, each the length of the central hall. Or it may be that these two side rooms have been again sub-divided to make two each. A house of this kind shows us really a building-on of the side rooms on either hand of the hall. You recognise the hall as the nucleus of the whole by the large fireplace which it contains.

I use such words as hall and vestibule for the sake of characterising the different sections of the house. But let the reader understand that the house itself and its divisions are supposed on a small scale. I ought, perhaps, to use the words cottage, hut, rather than house for some of the places which I have in mind; but words of this kind imply that the dwelling-place is abominably small, whereas these houses of Norway are really the original and primitive form of house; those that are larger (except when quite modern influences have come in) have become so (as has already been pointed out) by the growing together of several of these primitive buildings.

Among the buildings of the lower lands, beside the ordinary house, stands nearly always a separate single-roomed building for a store-house—in the Norse *stabur* or *stabbur*—properly *stav-bur*, stave-house. This, as the name implies, is a store-house raised upon props. Sometimes the houses themselves are raised in the same way. It is partly to avoid floods, partly to remove the stores out of the way of vermin that this principle is adopted; we see something of the same kind in Switzerland.

The accompanying wood-block gives a view of two of these *stabur*. They look like buildings still more primitive than the houses—more like covered wagons that have been deposited there on props when their wheels were removed; and in looking at them our thoughts are irresistibly carried back to the picture which the Roman writers give us of the ancient Goths during the days of their migrations; of how they lived in covered vans or wooden houses upon wheels, and in these travelled slowly and heavily from place to place. I do not say but that this association of ideas may be

partly fanciful; but I believe that these propped dwellings give us as near a representative of the house on wheels of the ancient Goths as any which could be found standing in this year of grace.

I have seemed, perhaps, to dwell too long upon the Norwegian houses, considering their primitive and simple structure; but it appears to me that there is an interest attaching to relics of the past such as these, as soon as we learn to understand them, scarcely less than belongs to more imposing monuments. The cathedrals, the walls, the towers, and Rath-houses of Germany carry us back to the middle ages. Half the towns in Germany have only just awoke from the sleep into which they were thrown at the beginning of the fifteenth century. Unfortunately, now they have awaked, and we must anticipate a day not distant when Lüneburg and Lübeck, Hildesheim and Dantzig; when Nuremberg and Heilbronn and Innsprück will preserve as little of the past (they can never lose all trace of it) as Cologne now does—Cologne which we can, most of us, remember while it was still in great part surrounded by its walls. Norway possesses few such monuments of antiquity; of what she does possess I shall speak hereafter when we come to that period of her history; but there is an antiquity of a much vaster stretch suggested by ships like the Norse ships, which have still so much in common with the vessels which navigated the Baltic five hundred years before Christ; with houses like the Norse ones, which seem to bring us back to the very beginning of the art of house-architecture, or which make us think of the ambulant dwellings of the Goths; of those great wagons in which they made their migrations over Europe, and which seem now to have only stayed for a moment on their wanderings.

From the house we pass to the group of houses forming a homestead or a village. There are some special peculiarities of Norwegian country life, and of the settlement of the country, which distinguish that land even from Sweden, and, indeed, from the other countries of Northern Europe. It is not, I dare say, unknown to the reader how much the social constitution of Germany and of England seems to point back to a time when the separate communities—call them tribes if you will—who occupied the locality and formed their houses into a *village*, constituted within the limits of that village a sort of commonwealth, and held their lands, or a portion of them, in common. The *village community*, as it has been styled, formed a unit in the constitution of almost every Teutonic nationality in primitive days. This form of community existed among all the nations on the shores of the Baltic, not the North Germans alone, but the Swedes and Danes likewise. But there is much less trace of it in Norway. The greater portion of that land seems to have been settled by individual emigrants in much the same way that the Western States of America have been and are being settled in our day. Some sturdy emigrant made his way into the unknown land, taking his family, his servants, his household gods, it may be, with him, and he settled down in a farm of his own, choosing a spot which promised well; other houses grew up round his—his own being many houses—occupied by his dependants; but the land on which he dwelt was his own, not common land, but held by free and allodial title. This settler was in his way an aristocrat. He had his own servants, but he served no man. His descendant, the modern peasant proprietor, is still the most genuine and ancient aristocrat of Norway. The times of trouble, of external war and Viking expeditions, raised up another and more military aristocracy in the country; but behind this class always stood the class of freehold peasants, *bondis*, bonders (*bønder*), yeomen, as we should call them, the descendants of the original settlers of the country. The representatives of this class are the great peasant proprietor class of Norway.

The immense majority of the landholdings in the country are what we should call quite small holdings. For instance, properties which are called there of a moderate size, are what with us would be considered very small farms. Farms that are capable of supporting some 2 horses, 15 head of cattle, and from 30 to 40 sheep; of yielding an annual produce of some 250 bushels of cereals, and 500 bushels of potatoes, occupy 59 per cent. of the cultivated area of the kingdom, and constitute one quarter of the total number of landed properties in the country. Below these come the very small holdings, whose owners have other means of subsistence, and are (generally) either labourers, artisans, or fishermen; these occupy 33 per cent. of the remaining land, and constitute three-quarters of the total number of properties. For really large estates only one per cent. of the properties is left, and only eight per cent. of the cultivated area of the kingdom.

What is so interesting to us in travelling in the country is to find the names of localities frequently taken from the names of quite small proprietors, men whom we should call mere peasants, who yet have the proud consciousness that they have bestowed a name upon a farm, a valley, or a mountain. Their ancestor may have been the first settler in the district, and the local names have been taken from him, for this seems not infrequently to have been the case. In other instances the name of the family has been derived from the locality, as with families 'of that ilk' in Scotland or England.

Thus, in Scandinavia, we may still find specimens, both of which appear to be as primitive as any we are likely to meet with in any country, of the village whose history dates back to the days of the village community, and of settlements, farms, or gaards, which belong to a system of landholding in which the village community has scarcely played any part. The former belong to Sweden and to some parts of the interior of Norway. It is not a little interesting to see these Swedish villages with their red houses (for in Sweden the majority of the wooden houses are painted red) scattered wide apart over a considerable plain. It is a village very different from our English idea of one, where the houses stand for the most part close together or touching each other, and 'dressed' like two lines of soldiers, facing inwards on either side the long village street. We may see much more irregular villages than this English type in Germany; but none where the houses stand so scattered as they do in most of the Swedish, and in a certain number of Norwegian villages. In looking at these we are at once brought back to the words of Tacitus in describing the way the Germans lived in his day : 'It is well known,' says the author (in a passage with which the reader no doubt is familiar enough), 'that the Germans do not dwell in towns. They do not even suffer their habitations to stand close together; but live apart and scattered, each one choosing his own home by stream, or grove, or plot of open ground.'

In large districts of Norway (I have already said) no

such villages are to be found. The traveller, however, need not go much out of his track to come to regions very sparsely inhabited, where the life is still most primitive, and where he may go on for days without finding anything but a succession of the gaards or homesteads of which I have spoken. I will take one district, which the traveller may easily visit if he choose. Thelemarken, which lies at the back, so to say, of Odde on the Hardanger Fjord. There is a fast route from Odde to Kongsberg, and from Kongsberg you get into civilisation again, for you get upon one of the few railways in Norway, and can travel by it to Christiania. Unfortunately, the living and accommodation are so rough that not many people are tempted to make the expedition through Thelemarken for the sake of a good specimen of primitive Norway.

Some primitive customs, too, relics of bygone superstitions, and even of pre-Christian religions, are better preserved in Scandinavia than in any other of the countries of Northern Europe, though even here, it must be said with regret, they are rapidly dying out. Of these, the one which the traveller has most chance of seeing some example of is the keeping up of the Midsummer, or St. John's Day fires; what in Germany are called, or used to be called, the Johannisfeuer, and in France Feu de S. Jean. There is scarcely a country of Europe which used not to celebrate this festival of Midsummer, which the Swedes and Norwegians still keep up under the name of the Sankt Hans. The time for the festival is the eve of St. John's day, and St. John the Baptist is the patron of it. But there can be no doubt that it springs from religious rites earlier than

Christianity,—that it is a festival to the sun, held on the sun's highest day. Sun-worship, and the worship of fire, are things intimately connected, the fire being supposed (naturally enough) a sort of image of the sun: this we see especially in the old Mazdean religion of Persia. It can hardly be said that this feast of the summer is peculiarly Teutonic or peculiarly Celtic. It rather seems to belong to a very primitive faith common to the ancestors of Germans and Celts alike. The festival, I have said, used to be kept up in all the countries of Christendom.

Strutt, in his *Sports and Pastimes*, says that it was usual in country places, on the Vigil of St. John the Baptist, commonly called Midsummer Eve, for the people, old and young, to meet together and make merry by the side of a large fire made in the middle of the street, or in some open and convenient place, over which the young men frequently leapt by way of frolic, and also exercised themselves with various sports and pastimes.

In the heathen times in the north, as we see by the Icelandic Sagas, the two great festivals of the year were Yule-tide and Midsummer, and both were celebrated by the lighting of great fires. So that we may assume that, in the festival as we witness it to-day, we are stepping back at once into the religious observances of heathen times.

Brand, in his *Popular Antiquities* (pp. 169-199) cites a number of authorities who refer to the custom of lighting these Midsummer fires in different parts of England and Ireland. Of the latter country a writer in the *Gentleman's Magazine* of 1795 says, ' I was so fortunate, in the summer of 1782, as to have my curiosity gratified by the sight of this ceremony to (over) a very great extent of country. At the house where I was entertained it was told me that we should see at midnight the most singular sight in Iceland, which was *the lighting of fires in honour of the sun.* Accordingly, exactly at midnight, the fires began to appear, and taking the advantage of going up to the leads of the house, which had a widely extended view, I saw on a radius of thirty miles all round the fires burning on every eminence which the country afforded. I had the further advantage of learning, on undoubted authority, that the people *danced round the fires,* and at the close went through these fires, and made their sons and daughters, together with their cattle, pass through the fire, and the whole was conducted with religious solemnity.'

This is a description of the ceremony in its most elaborate form, such as, even at that date, I suspect, was hardly to be found in England. Stow speaks of the custom of hanging garlands of lucky herbs over the doors, and among these garlands placing blazing lamps which burn all night. Among the herbs which were considered to give a blessing if thus employed, or according to other customs if thrown into the midsummer fire, St. John's wort is one that preserves the memory of this custom. Fennel, marjoram, green birch, are others of those magical herbs mentioned by different writers. In Sweden, besides lighting the midsummer fire, they in most places raise, or used a year or two ago to raise, a pole like a Maypole, and this was hung with garlands, which were no doubt originally, if they are not still, made up of these magical herbs. We read in some accounts of garlands plaited of nine sorts of flowers, and nine is a mystic number in the old Scandinavian mythology.

Souvestre, in his account of Brittany (ed. by Cambray), gives a description of the midsummer fires, which correspond very closely with the account of the ceremony in Iceland just cited. 'Cries of joy,' he says, 'are heard from every side. Every promontory, every rock, every mountain is alight. A thousand fires are burning in the open air, and from afar you may descry the shadow-like figures moving round the fire; in their dancing one might fancy it a dance of *courils* (fairies). The fires are often lighted by the priests, who make procession through the villages with consecrated tapers.' The ceremony of leaping through the flame, which some writers mention, must, one thinks, be the far-off reflex of the sacrifice of children by passing them through the fire. The ordeal by fire is itself a reflex of this custom. On the same principle that Abraham's readiness to sacrifice Isaac was accounted to him for righteousness: so is the readiness of an accused person to offer himself as a sacrifice to the deity supposed to show his innocence; and, as in the case of Isaac, the divinity is expected to intervene to prevent the completion of the sacrifice.

It would not be safe to affirm that the simple practice of jumping over the ashes of the fire, when it has burnt low, which we see the boys and young men do to-day in Sweden and Norway, is in its turn a relic of the more ceremonial custom of jumping through the fire when it was in full blaze. But, of course, it may easily be so.

Grimm, in his German Mythology (*Deutsche Mytho-*

logie), cites numberless authorities for the custom of lighting the *Johannisfeuer* in different parts of Germany. One of the most curious customs is related of a town Konz, on the Moselle (French in those days by nationality, but German by blood and tradition), where the members of each household had to carry up a truss of straw to the hill above the river. There a huge wheel was made and completely wrapped round in straw. A pole was passed through an axle, and the wheel was lighted with ceremony, and by the aid of the pole was rolled down hill into the Moselle. If it kept alight till it got into the river it foretold a good vintage.

In Sweden these fires still blaze on many a hill and headland, by the side of the lakes. In Norway they were more prevalent seven years ago than they are now; though in many places much visited by tourists, they are kept up as much, perhaps, for their sake as for that of the inhabitants. The ceremony generally begins with a mock wedding. A child or young girl is dressed up as a bride with the Norwegian bridal crown, and followed by a procession of other girls, a fiddler (as is always the case in a real Norwegian marriage) fiddling at the head. She corresponds to the May Queen in our English May-day festivities, such as still remain with us. In the evening the fire is lighted and dancing round it is kept up—the services of the fiddler again put into requisition—all through the undarkened night. When this takes place in a village by the side of a fjord, a headland looking far over the water is often selected for the scene of the fire (provided it present a sufficiently flat surface for dancing), and it is a very beautiful sight to see the boats stealing over the water from smaller villages or from solitary farms, each bringing its contingent of young men and girls dressed in holiday costume to take part in the festival.

No land seems more suited as a home for the creatures of popular superstition than this land; and till the other day almost, we may believe (from the Folk-Tales that have been handed down to us) these frowning cliffs and sequestered valleys were still for the peasant inhabited by the beings who figure in most Teutonic mythologies; that on the hills dwelt *Thursar* (Monsters) or Trolls; in the valleys or beneath the earth dwelt *Ælfar*, elves, and fairies. The celebrated Swedish waterfall Trollhättan (the Troll's hat) is a reminiscence of the belief in this race of giants and witches; so are the well-known Trolltinder (the Trold's needles) which are the most remarkable feature of the Romsdal in Norway. And there are many other places which bear names compounded of Troll or Trold. Troldvand, near one of the arms of the Jostedal glacier, surrounded by rocky walls, and reached through a deep and gloomy ravine, is one of the many lakes at the bottom of which a witch-woman dwells or dwelt, and to which heroes have been known to descend for the sake of fighting with the ogress. There are one or two more place-names confounded with 'trold' in this neighbourhood, *i.e.* close to the Jostedalsbræ. Troldkirketind, one of the scenes of the Witches' Sabbath of the Norwegians, overlooks the Norddalsfjord and the Slyngsfjord. Besides the Trolltinder before mentioned, there is a Troldstol (witches' chair) and another Troldvand (witches' lake) in this same neighbourhood; that is to say, we pass them on our journey from Molde to the Romsdal. Many other places compounded with the name may be mentioned, such as Trollabrug, near Throndhjem, and the Troldfjord high up the coast by the Lofotens. All these names witness to the deep-seated beliefs of past times. The hills above Bergen were among the chief places in Europe which popular superstition fixed upon as the scenes for the celebrated Witches' Sabbath, which was held on the eve of the first of May.

About fifty years ago two Norwegians, Asbjörnsen and Moe, one a man of letters and a poet, the other a bishop, set to work to do what the brothers Grimm had done for Germany, to collect the popular tales and legends which lingered in the mouths of the peasantry of their day. Their collection of stories has been translated into English, under the title *Popular Tales from the Norse*, and from these the reader can get some picture of the legendary superstition of the people about half a century ago. There is no such marked peculiarity in these stories as compared with the German popular tales of the brothers Grimm (*Kinder-u-Hausmärchen*) that it can be characterised in a sentence.

But since the days of Asbjörnsen and Moe, when passengers no longer row from homestead to homestead, but where steamers are found plying on all the Norwegian waters—when, too, primary education has reached a point of great excellence in the country— these popular beliefs and legends have been rapidly dying out; we may expect them to disappear altogether in a few years.

CHAPTER III

SEAFARING

The Vikings

The sight which we spoke of in the last chapter, of the boats on festival days or Sundays making from the lesser villages or from solitary farmhouses towards some trysting-place, is an exceedingly beautiful one, and is suggestive of much. It is curious to see how the boats appear to start out of the precipitous walls of the fjord, though they really come from some bay hidden from sight. The place where you are standing is rock-girt; no other houses are visible but those of your own village; behind you there stretches, may be, one road, or perhaps only a mountain path towards the interior of the country; in front lies the fjord. You feel as if you were standing at the end of the habitable earth, cut off from communication with the rest of the world. Then suddenly, one by one, these boats appear in sight, as if they had risen up from the water, or, as we have said, had sprung out of the rock itself. It is the water of the fjord which constitutes the road, the connecting link, between the farms and villages upon its banks, the safest imaginable way, and the easiest traversed. It is in this wise, by sights such as these, that we come to realise how, among a people situated as the Norse folk have been, the sea, from very early days, became their one road, and the people was a predestined race of navigators and explorers.

The bays and creeks of the Baltic, of Denmark and Sweden, afford the same facilities for navigation that do the fjords of Norway, with their protecting island guard; and, with the Norse Sea cut off by the narrow passage of the belt, and with the numberless islands of Denmark, this sea, too, is as protected as one could wish, so that the other Scandinavian peoples, the Swedes and Danes, have had equal opportunities with the Norsemen of becoming great navigators. It is, in truth, in the Baltic Sea, including therewith the channel which leads to it, Skaggerrak and Cattegat, rather than on the western coast of Norway, that we must look for the growth of that art of navigation which ushered in the great era in the history of Scandinavia, the Age of the Vikings. As we saw, it is Bohuslän, one of the southern provinces of Sweden, and abutting on the Baltic, which, in its rock-carvings, contains the earliest record of the use of ships and the knowledge of navigation to be found in the north.

We also saw that, so far as it is possible to judge, the shipbuilding of the early times represented by the rock-carvings, had not very materially changed when, a thousand years later, arose the Viking Age, in which these northern ships were to become known almost to every country in Europe.

In the Museum at Christiania (at the back of the University) we find two relics of the art of shipbuilding in the Viking Age, or near it. These two ships may

very well stand as specimens of the whole class. One
of them was found at Tune, which is the same as Tunsberg, so far as we can tell, the earliest of the towns of
Norway. The other boat, a beautifully preserved specimen, which stands in the house especially built for it
beside the Museum, was discovered at Gokstad in the
Christiania Fjord. It must be said that the latest use
to which this Gokstad ship has been placed has been
for the purposes of burial: that is to say, it has been
employed as an immense coffin. The custom long remained among the Scandinavian people of interring
men, presumably great leaders, in ships; and this was
done in the days when the bodies of men were burnt
as well as those in which they were buried.

In the former time the pyre was lighted on the ship,
and the ship was pushed out to sea; in the latter case
it was, like this Gokstad vessel, used as a huge coffin
and buried in the earth. It is because the Gokstad
ship has been buried in this fashion that it has been so
well preserved.[1]

This Christiania boat is sixty feet along her flat keel,
and seventy-five feet measured at her greatest length.
She is pointed at either end, and has high stem- and
stern-posts, like the boats represented in the Bohuslän
carvings. She is shallow, her depth at the broadest
part being little more than three and a half feet; her
gunwale rises as she grows narrower towards either end.
She was not decked, but may have had a sort of sloping

---

[1] So far as regards the names of the Norse vessels, the general name
skip applied to all. Battle-ships are often called 'dragons,' because of the
custom of ornamenting their prows with dragons' heads. They are also
called long-ships (*langskip*). The words *snekkja* and *skuta*, which likewise
occur, denote small, swift-rowing boats.

roof of planks over one end, possibly over the whole length, except a little bit of deck fore and aft. As a rule, in these boats, the men sat under awnings or tents, which were struck before they came into action. On the short piece of deck fore and aft there stood a group of the foremost fighting men; others, no doubt, stood round the side and made some sort of protection for the rowers. Very frequently there ran a gangway connecting the fore and aft decks, the forecastle (in old Norse *ausn*) and the poop (*lipting*). The Christiania boat had sixteen rowers a-side. The sizes of the boats of which we read descriptions in the Norse Sagas are always reckoned by the number of seats or benches of rowers they contained; and this Christiania boat would be called a boat of sixteen benches. These benches would accommodate from four to eight men; and it is probable that, in most of the war-vessels, the number of people they contained was almost six times as many as the number of benches, so that the Christiania boat in question would contain about a hundred men. This is, if anything, an inside reckoning. This Christiania boat is a fair average size for a boat of this period; we read of boats which had thirty and more 'benches,' but they are always spoken of as something exceptional.

A picturesque appearance was given to the Vikings' ships by the coloured square sails—often they were painted in stripes of colour; and by the coloured round shields, painted red, or black, or white, which hung outside the gunwale; and, finally, by the beautifully-carved and painted figure-heads and stern-posts.

The shallowness of these vessels made them very useful in the Viking days for lying in small creeks, or passing up rivers far into the interior of a country; but they could not have been good seafaring vessels, and doubtless many of them were lost. Among the specimens of old Norse poetry which have come down to us, and of which we shall speak in another chapter, there is one beautiful piece in which the author laments over the death by drowning of his favourite son. It may stand to us for a symbol of many thousands of laments which must have been uttered by fathers, mothers, wives, children over the men who were lost in in the same way. The boats had no regular tiller, but were steered by an oar from the side, the right side generally; and it is from this custom that the right side of a vessel has received the name steer-board—starboard.

We have spoken of the heavy square-sailed ships, with high curving prows, which are still to be met with all along the coast of Norway. These have generally square sterns; but in some places (off the Lofotens, for instance, if the traveller should go so far north) another sort of boat is used, almost exactly like these in build, but pointed both stem and stern. This is almost an exact copy of the Gokstad ship, that is to say, of the old Viking ship. Something the same shape is preserved in the smaller rowing-boats which are used on the fjords or island lakes. But these are too small, and too rarely hoist a sail to give the reader adequate means for realising the appearance of a Viking ship. We must then keep the high-prowed coasting or fishing vessels in our mind's eye if we want to get a picture of the sight which, towards the end of the eighth century, began to strike at first with surprise and then with terror all the dwellers on the coasts of Christian Europe.

It must not be supposed that the depredations of the northern warriors had gone on from time immemorial. There is a very definite date at which begins the Viking age, properly so called, the age of Viking voyages and depredations. This is in the year A.D. 789. And there can be no doubt that the one thing which, more than any other, led to this outbreak of piracy was the discovery of the use of sails by the Scandinavians. The Viking ships resembled those of the rock-carving of a thousand years earlier in almost every particular but one, that the earlier vessels had not, and the later had, sails; and there can be no doubt, while in other respects their art of boat-building was ancestral, that the northern people learnt the use of sails from the Romans. They began to use them probably some hundred years before their great era of adventure and piracy dawned. But for all that, it was this discovery more than any other which led to that era.

The first Scandinavian ships which harried any coast of *Christian* Europe were three vessels, which, in the summer of A.D. 789, appeared upon the Dorset coast. The officer in charge of the port—we are not told precisely to what harbour they had come—supposed them to be merchant-men, and rode down to demand the port-dues payable to the king. But he found to his cost that these were no merchants. The Vikings sprang to the shore, drew their swords and killed the port-reeve and his small following, then took plunder from the place and sailed away out to sea.

E

A custom obtained very much in the Christian Europe of those days for the pious, who raised monasteries in honour of God and the saints, to choose for the sites of these either islands in the sea or some promontory which was washed by the waves: it was done upon something of the same principle, it may be, which caused the Greeks to dedicate so many temples to Apollo (the most national of their gods) upon islands, or upon headlands along the coast. 'The high watches pleased him, and the rivers that run into the deep, and the shores stretching down to the sea, and the sea's harbours,' as the Homeric hymn to Apollo says.

And for the same reason, namely, that these places at the edge of all earthly kingdoms belonged especially to the god, were the early religious houses of Christendom so often built upon islands or by the sea-shore. In England one of the most famous of these establishments was Lindisfarne, or Holy Island, a foundation of St. Cuthbert. This was the next place attacked by a Viking fleet. The pirates slew or made captive all the monks, and the monastery itself was rifled and then burnt. This was in A.D. 793.

Then the pirates appeared on the south coast of Wales; and after that they sailed thence across to Ireland, and found another island monastery near to Dublin Bay, which they plundered and burnt, in the same way that their brother Vikings had plundered and burnt Lindisfarne. We soon find them sailing to Man; and next round to the west coast of Ireland, and plundering all that side of the island; or what seemed more impious still, sailing to the west coast of Scotland and plundering Iona, that famous foundation of St. Columba, indirectly the parent of almost all the monasteries of the English Church. All these attacks which I have spoken of had taken place before the ninth century had got into its teens. We see, therefore, how this new wave of plunder and destruction had, in the course of a few years, swept completely round the coasts of our islands.

Nor was it long before the pirates became as well known upon the Continent. The coast towns of what was then called Frisia, and is now called Holland, were the first to grow acquainted with the high-prowed, square-sailed vessels of the Northmen. Frisia was first attacked in the last year of the eighth century, 799. Another attack followed the next year; then a pause, and ten years later (A.D. 810) a very fierce and determined attack was organised by the King of Denmark. This king, whose name was Godfred, was at war with the mighty Charlemagne, who was at this time the Emperor of all Western Continental Christendom. Not much was to be feared from the Northmen as long as Charlemagne remained upon the throne. But there is a story told of this emperor which, if it is true, shows how well he appreciated the character of this new terror which was dawning upon Europe.

'Once,' the chronicler tells us, 'Charles arrived by chance at a certain maritime town of his dominions,[1] while he was sitting at dinner, and had not been recognised by the townspeople, some northern pirates

[1] The chronicler (the Monk of St. Gallen) makes it a town in the Mediterranean, a part to which the Vikings certainly never reached as early as the time of Charlemagne. It may be that the story really relates to quite a different sort of pirates—the Arab corsairs. For the Monk of St. Gallen is not quite to be relied upon.

came to carry on their depredations in that very port. When the ships were perceived, some thought they were Jewish merchants, some that they were Africans, some Bretons. But the wise king, knowing from the shape and swiftness of the vessels what sort of crews they carried, said to those about him, "These ships bear no merchandise, but cruel foes." At these words all the Franks rivalled each other in the speed with which they rushed to attack the boats. But it was useless. The Northmen hearing that *there* stood the man whom they were wont to call Charles the Hammer, were afraid lest all their fleet should be taken in the port, and should be broken in pieces; and their flight was so rapid, that they withdrew themselves, not only from the swords, but even from the eyes of those who wished to catch them. The religious Charles, however, seized by a holy fear, rose from the table, and looked out of the window towards the east, remaining long in that position, his face bathed in tears. No one ventured to question him: but turning to his followers he said, "Know ye why I weep? Truly, I fear not that these will injure *me*. But I am deeply grieved that in my lifetime they should have been so near landing on these shores, and I am overwhelmed with sorrow as I look forward and see what evils they will bring upon my offspring and their people."[1]

If this story is true, it shows that the great Emperor was a man of penetration. For few could have guessed from all that had yet been seen of the Vikings, some little fleet here and there outside a coast town, or near a monastery of England or the Low Countries, what a great flood of invasion was in the course of a few years to sweep upon western Europe, and almost to bring back this portion of Christendom into the reign of chaos, out of which it had emerged.

The earlier Viking piracies, of which we have given a slight sketch, proceeded, as would appear, rather from Denmark, or at any rate from the Baltic and its mouth, than from the western coasts of Norway. But it was not very long before another route was discovered for the pirate cruisers. This one led the way from the western fjords, probably straight across the North Sea to the Shetlands, and thence due south to the Orkneys and to the mainland of Scotland. The name of the county of Sutherland is a reminiscence of the settlement of the Northmen in these regions. For who but they could have named almost the most northern county of Scotland the southern land? In the same way they called the Hebrides the South Islands; south, that is to say, as compared to the Shetlands and the Orkneys, the islands in which the northern pirates first settled. The name South Islands—Sudreyar in Norse—became, as the reader most likely knows, corrupted into Sodor, and remains to this day in the title of the Bishop of Sodor and Man.

In these modern days a returning stream of invaders traverses in an opposite direction the route which the Vikings first laid open—the invading stream of tourists, many of whom come in steamers, which take this northern route from Scotland to the Orkneys and Shetland, and thence to Norway.

Other streams of northern pirates may have crossed the sea (in the opposite direction) along the route which is covered by the Hull and Bergen steamers of to-day.

But this was not at the beginning of the Viking age; for the first Vikings in northern England came from Denmark.

The two streams of Viking invasion of which we have spoken flowed all round the British isles; the Danish ascending from the south, having coasted round Frisia till they reached the English Channel, or in other cases sailed straight across the North Sea to the East Anglian or Northumbrian shore; the Norse stream descending from the north, generally by Scotland, to England or Ireland. Sometimes the two streams met in antagonistic currents, sometimes they combined and flowed in unison; they always ended by conquering and making settlements. We have no record of the Viking conquests in Scotland. But we know that, eventually, the settlements of the Norsemen in that country included the Orkneys and Shetlands, Caithness, a part of Sutherlandshire, and the Hebrides. For Ireland we have more details of the process of conquest; but the accounts of the wars of the foreigners[1] in Ireland are so confused that it is very hard to form out of them anything like a consistent picture. What we do see is, beside many lesser attacks, a great fleet coming about the year 832, led by a captain whose ambition was not satisfied by anything less than the conquest of one-half of the country. His name was Thorgisl. But this leader, this first real Viking king, as one may call him, did not reign long. He was captured by one of the Irish kings and

---

[1] Gaill, 'foreigners' simply, is the name usually applied to the invader from the north in the Irish chronicles. Another name is Lochlann, lake men (Fjord-men?). A third 'Gentiles.'

drowned; and his kingdom, the first Viking kingdom as it really was, was likewise the most ephemeral of all.

In the event, the presence of the Vikings in Ireland took the form of settlements made at certain fixed points, not of wide-extended conquests. These settlements, which covered no great area, were at last contracted into those so-called kingdoms of the Northmen, at Dublin, at Waterford, and at Limerick. The two lesser ones did not deserve the pretentious name of kingdoms; they were generally dependent upon the kings of Dublin. But these last were at one time people of no small power. They exercised, if not actual rule, a leadership—what the Greeks called a *hegemony*—among a group of other Scandinavian settlements in the west. The settlement in Man—kingdom of Man, as it was called, the kingdoms and earldoms in the western islands of Scotland were in a way subservient to the Irish kings of Dublin. They gave kings to the Danes and Norsemen in Northumbria; some, at any rate, of these kings reigning at the same time in Dublin and at York. And the great hero of Norwegian history, he who so greatly changed the position of Norway among the nations,—I mean Olaf Tryggvason (of whom we shall have to speak hereafter) was closely connected with the kings of Dublin. It is possible that he came from among the Dublin Norsemen.

These Dublin kings were (in the time of our Æthelred the Unready) the first rulers in Ireland who issued a coinage.

Cut off at last from intercourse with their fellow-countrymen, the Northmen of Dublin fell under the rule of the Irish kings; but they preserved no small amount of independence. Thus, when England was for the first time brought into close relations with the sister island, and Strongbow, Earl of Pembroke, went over to aid Dermot M'Murrough, King of Leinster, in winning back his kingdom, we find the chroniclers describing this Irish monarch as King of Leinster and the 'Danes.' 'Danes' is certainly not the right word to use here; it should be Norsemen. But the English had got in the way of calling all Scandinavians Danes. It is interesting to think that this Irish pale, which was the first foothold of the English in the sister island, was the territory, not so much of the native Celts as of the Northmen.

In earlier days, again, when Dublin and other of the Norse kingdoms in Ireland were in their most flourishing condition, they sent out bodies of invaders to the north-western parts of England, who possessed themselves of a considerable portion of what was then called the Strathclyde—all the region between the Clyde and the Dee. In Westmoreland, Cumberland, the north of Lancashire and the West Riding of Yorkshire, we find the largest traces of these Norse invaders, who came from Ireland. On the other side, in Northumberland and Durham, still more in the North and East Ridings of Yorkshire, and in Lincolnshire, the chief settlers were Danes, who had established a Danish kingdom in these parts, and had, in fact, turned the north of England into a Danish country, while another Danish kingdom, as we know, had by the treaties between Alfred the Great and Guthrum the Dane, been established in the eastern counties and the eastern midlands.

Scotland and Ireland, then, with a little strip off the north-west of England, we note as the chief spheres of

Norse influence (as opposed to Danish) in Christian Europe. As settlers of a more or less permanent kind, we see the Norsemen in the Shetlands, the Orkneys, the Hebrides, in Caithness, in Man, in the north-west of England, in several places round the Irish coast, especially Dublin.

There was a certain difference between the characters of the Norsemen and the Danes, who came as conquerors to our islands; consequently the influence of the two nationalities upon the people with whom they came in contact took different forms.

The Vikings of Norse blood were, so far as appears, of rather a different calibre from the Danish Vikings of the Continent and of the later invasions of England. While these last were filled with political ambitions, were colonisers and conquerors, *those* were imbued with commercial notions and were conquerors and traders. How significant in this light is the discovery of a Viking interment, which was made two or three years ago in the Hebrides! The man had been boat-buried after the heathen rites—though there were likewise some traces of Christian symbolism, crosses and so forth, on the tomb—and he had been a warrior who had doubtless died in his harness, which, with his sword, spear, and battle-axe, were placed by his side. His horse had been buried with him, and one of the big bones of the horse had been nearly cut in two by a sword or axe —no doubt in the hero's last battle. But along with all this war-gear, there was found buried with the Viking leader a pair of scales—curious type of the double nature of his life as a soldier and a tradesman! It was, as we have said above, the Norse Kings of Dublin who, about A.D. 1000, introduced the first native *coinage* into Ireland; till which date such a medium of exchange was almost unknown in this backward country.

There were other peculiarities which distinguished the history of the Norse conquerors. The only contact which these had with Christendom was in the form of contact with the Celtic populations of the west, almost exclusively with the Gaels or Goidhels, the Celts of the Scottish Highlands and of Ireland. Even the Norsemen in Strathclyde were in a country chiefly Celtic but British. From this contact between the Norsemen and the Celts there arose many consequences which we shall have to detail in the next chapter.

We shall have, too, in the next chapter, to trace the Norsemen in a new and somewhat different sphere of activity. But we will devote the rest of this chapter to following in brief outline the doings of the Vikings upon the Continent. These Vikings, we have already said, were chiefly Danes; and therefore their history has not so much concern with the history of Norway. But it would be impossible to leave out altogether the career of these Vikings on the Continent, which went on while the Norsemen were establishing their power in Scotland and in Ireland.

On the Continent—as no doubt the reader knows—the mighty empire of the Franks, founded by Charlemagne, embraced almost the whole of western Christendom of those days. It included the kingdoms of the East and West Franks, or what were beginning to be known as Francia (France) and Germania (Germany). The southern part of what is now France kept a separate name—its old Latin one, Provincia or Provence.

The kingdom of Italy, too, formed part of Charlemagne's empire. Spain was not Christian in those days, for it had been conquered by the Mohammedans; save, indeed, a little strip in the north, half of which belonged to the Franks, while the other half was independent. To whatever shore, therefore, the Vikings, coming from the Baltic, might direct their sail, unless they fell upon one or other of our islands, they were sure almost to come in contact with the subjects of the Frankish empire. As long as Charlemagne held this mighty power in his hands, the countries were safe from any serious harm; though, as we have seen, even Charlemagne had a foretaste of the evils of Viking invasion. Under Charlemagne's successor, Lewis, called the Debonair, or the Pious, the Frankish empire began to decay and fall to pieces; but even in this reign Christendom suffered little hurt from the northern pirates. It was after Lewis's death (A.D. 840) when his sons, who during the lifetime of their father had often been in rebellion against him, were now engaged in civil war one with another, that an opening was made for the Viking attacks.

While the rival armies of the imperial princes were manœuvring inland, the Viking fleets began to find their way to the mouths of the great rivers of Western Europe which emptied themselves into the North Sea, or into the Atlantic. The most eastern of these, and therefore the nearest to Denmark, was the Elbe. Near the mouth of it stood Hamburg, then a growing trading place and the See of an Archbishop. Next (to the westward) came the many mouths of the Rhine, which flowed through the country then called Frisia. On one of these mouths stood a city called Dorstad, which has now disappeared and hardly left a trace, but which was then quite the emporium for the north of Europe, carrying on a trade as far as the British Isles on the one side, and the Baltic countries on the other. Dorstad, which must have been known by reputation to the Vikings even before they came there, was one of the chief marks for their attacks, and was so frequently plundered, that by the middle of the ninth century its trade had almost entirely left it. A little further down the coast, after leaving the Rhine mouths, the Vikings came to the Scheldt, on which stood Antwerp, a city of some importance. Farther on still lay, at the mouth of the little river Canche, which empties itself into the English Channel near Calais, a town, Quentovic, which has now entirely decayed, but was then second only to Dorstad among the trading cities of the north. After they had left the Canche, the Vikings would come to the Somme, on which lay Amiens; and next to the far more important Seine, which in those days was rich in trading towns and in religious houses. Rouen lay not far from the mouth; and, when the Vikings had become adventurous enough to navigate some way inland, they came to Paris. Paris could not yet be described as the capital of France, but it was a city of growing importance. It was, too, full of sacred associations, on account of the many monasteries which surrounded it. The sieges of Paris by the Vikings are among the great events in the history of this century.

The next great river after the Seine was the Loire, only a little way up which lay the important town of Nantes. Nantes gave its name to the title of the count to whom was especially intrusted the guardianship of the Marches of Brittany. The Bretons were rebellious subjects of the Frankish empire; and it was in alliance with them that the first Vikings who came to the Loire made their attack upon the shores of that river and upon the town of Nantes. And higher up the river were two other places of great importance, Tours and Orleans. The former contained two famous abbeys, the most famous (perhaps) of all in Europe. This place was several times plundered by the pirates. Finally, after leaving the Loire, the Viking ships would come to the Garonne, up which they might sail as far as the old Roman-Gothic city of Toulouse, once the capital of the West-Goth kingdom in Southern France.

At the mouth of one after another of all these rivers the high-prowed, square-sailed Viking ships began to appear in numbers after the year 840. They were at first a strange sight to the inhabitants of Christendom. But we must remember that these lands were not less strange to the Northmen. Never before, probably, had the majority of these sailors ventured beyond the waters of the Baltic; not for hundreds of years had any of their ancestors done so. It was, therefore, a wondrous new life on which they were embarked. We cannot be surprised that, therefore, they proceeded with caution. The natural course for them would be to seize upon some one of the promontories at the river-mouth, the one which could be best guarded, or, safer still, upon an island, if there was one near the mouth of the river. For their Christian foes foolishly enough never provided themselves with strong fleets, and so the islands lay out of all danger of attack. The very first account we get of any organised Viking attack on any country shows the Northmen proceeding on these lines. We saw how they seized upon the island or promontory of Lindisfarne, for, like our St Michael's Mount or the French Mont. St. Michel, Lindisfarne was then only an island at high tide. And though the subsequent attacks of the Vikings on Northumbria were not successful, this beginning gave the pattern of their beginning in most of their other adventures. Their attacks on Ireland began with the seizure of an island near Dublin Bay; at the mouth of the Scheldt they made themselves masters of Walcheren; at the mouth of the Loire they took a little island called Noirmoutiers, and made it their depôt and their treasury.

When they were thus established, they seized their opportunity, and keeping as much out of sight as possible, they sped up the river under the woody banks. Their boats were constructed so as to draw very little water, and they could pass up much smaller streams and over much shallower places than might have been expected. The history of all these early attacks is much the same everywhere; only that sometimes we see the Vikings venturing quite alone, at other times (too often, alas!) we find them in alliance with some rebel part of the population, who no doubt furnished them with pilots to take them up the streams. In this wise, as we have already said, they first found their way up the Loire, took and plundered Nantes, killing a large number of the inhabitants, and among them the bishop of the place. By the same means they made their first expedition up the Garonne and plundered Toulouse. The earliest Viking expeditions up the Seine were more independent. On the first of these the Vikings sailed only as far as Rouen, which they plundered. The second time they sailed as far as Paris; and though the city itself was saved—by a miracle it was said—from their fury, some of the neighbouring monasteries were plundered. The same year that took place this first siege of Paris (A.D. 845), Hamburg was taken and plundered by another fleet of pirates sailing up the Elbe.

This gives us a picture of the earliest Viking attacks on Christendom, which were essentially summer expeditions and raids for plunder only. But in the middle year of the ninth century (850) we find the Northmen wintering for the first time in some of the countries which they attacked, and from this date onwards until the year 912 we may consider that the career of the Vikings in Christendom takes a new character. They became more and more settlers in the countries they have selected for plunder, and more and more cut off from the life of their countrymen at home. At first their settlement is no doubt a settlement only in entrenched camps, or other strong places: but gradually the idea comes to them of conquering or colonising great tracts of the enemies' countries. The first to whom this idea occurred seems to have been Thorgisl, the leader of the Norsemen in Ireland, of whom we have already spoken; but his attempt ended in failure. It was premature, for Thorgisl's death falls in A.D. 845.

Towards the end of the ninth century we see that large schemes of conquest are beginning to engage the thoughts of the Norsemen. The most extended of these schemes (the most extended that is estimated by its results) was the great invasion of England, which began in A.D. 866, and was only brought to an end after twelve years (A.D. 878) by the cession of half the land of England to the conquerors. This first Danish invasion of England—that of Sweyn and Canute at the beginning of the eleventh century being the second—is too familiar a portion of our national history to need dwelling upon here. But as our histories, especially our school and popular histories, were rather apt to tell it from the English point of view, and dwell exclusively on the efforts and achievements of Alfred, it is well to remember how successful a performance it was from the point of view of the invaders.

By the treaty between Alfred and the leader of the Danish army in the south, all of England north of the Thames, east of the Lea and of Watling Street (the great highway which ran, and still runs, between London and Wroxeter), and south of the Humber, was given up to form the kingdom of the Danish leader Guthrum, who became a Christian, and was baptized Æthelstan. But, meantime, all Northumbria, all England, and Lowland Scotland between the Humber and the Forth had been already subjected by another Viking leader, and this was constituted into a second Scandinavian kingdom in England.

The heathens from the north made great efforts to carry their conquests in France and Germany as far as they had carried them in England. One of their invading armies advanced up the Rhine as far as Coblenz. Another crossed the whole of France; but one town, Paris, held out for a year against a whole army of Vikings under a famous leader; and it may have been this obstinate resistance that saved France from a conquest as great as that which afflicted England.

None of these achievements were as lasting as they were impressive. The Northumbrian kingdom remained for some years; the other Danish settlements in England gradually diminished under Alfred's successors, Edward and Æthelstan. The invasions on the Continent were not lasting either; the result of them finally narrowed itself to the settlement of the Vikings, under their leader Hrolf, or Rolf, or Rollo, in the country which was then called Neustria, but which, from the Northmen, took the name of Normandy.

Before we close this chapter of the great age of northern conquest in Europe, and sum up the results thereof, which we must do in the succeeding chapter, let us take note of one other sphere of achievement on the part of the Scandinavians. This is Russia. While the Danes and the Norsemen were turning their ambition towards the west and south, their brother Scandinavians, the Swedes, were bent in an exactly opposite direction. They turned eastward, navigated the Gulf of Finland, and settled themselves in the province of Novgorod, a little to the south of Lake Ladoga. Thence they gradually extended their power, until they had founded a kingdom which in size was greater than the ancient kingdom of Sweden, and went by the name of Greater Suithiod—Greater Sweden. It extended from Lake Ladoga in the north as far as Kiev upon the Dnieper. By this last river, which afforded excellent navigation for their ships, the inhabitants of Greater Suithiod made their way down to the Black Sea, and eventually travelled as far as Constantinople and the islands of the Greek Archipelago. The emperors of the East (of the Byzantine Empire), who reigned at Constantinople, became familiar with these Russian Swedes, whose valour they esteemed so highly that the Byzantine Emperors came to form from their number a special bodyguard, which was known as the Varingian Guard.

This foundation of Russian Sweden, as we may call it, went on at the same time that the Norse and Danish Vikings were making their conquests and founding their kingdoms in the west. And if any detailed history of the doings of the eastern adventurers had been preserved, it would, perhaps, form almost as interesting a chapter in the history of the Scandinavian peoples as do the achievements of their western brothers.

CHAPTER IV

THE EDDA AND ITS MYTHOLOGY

Discovery of Iceland, Greenland, and America—Origin of Old Norse Poetry—The Mythology of the Edda.

THERE is a third chapter in the history of northern adventure different from the records of conquest of which we have just spoken, and deserving of a place to itself.

It would seem that, almost contemporarily with the coming of the Vikings to Great Britain, certain Irish or Scottish monks, adventuring without compass or chart into the North Sea, had found their way not only to the Shetlands, to the Faroes, but even as far as Iceland: nay, some think they got as far as America. It may have been that from some of the Celts whom they had conquered the Norsemen of Great Britain heard of these far lands. Certain it is that the settlement of the Northmen in our islands had not long taken place before there set in another stream, not now of conquest but rather of colonisation, towards these distant regions. The history of the first pioneers in this adventure is lost to us; but before very long people of consequence began to interest themselves in the matter, and soon the slender stream of emigration swelled almost into a flood.

There was a certain Norse King of Dublin named Olaf the White. His reign lasts from about A.D. 853 to A.D. 870. He was married to a wife called Aud, who gained the name of the Deeply Wise or Very Wise. This Aud was the daughter of a Norse King in the Hebrides called Ketil Flatnose: his nose had been cut off in battle, that is the origin of his name. By Olaf the White Aud had a son called Thorstein the Red, whom we catch sight of once in company with an Earl of the Orkneys marauding in Caithness. Thorstein was killed in Scotland, A.D. 875; and then his mother Aud, who, we see, had lost father, husband, son in three different parts of Great Britain, determined to seek a new home in those western islands to which the Norse stream of emigration had turned. She had with her several grand-daughters. She went first to the Orkneys, and while there she married one of her grand-daughters to the Earl of Orkney. Then she went on to the Faroes, and another of her grand-daughters she married to the chief Norseman in these islands. Finally, she made her way to Iceland, obtained there a large territory, and married other of her grand-daughters to the chief colonists of the country. These early colonists and their descendants were a distinguished class in the island—a sort of Mayflower emigrants, shall we say, or Knickerbockers? They were called 'the colonists' *par excellence—landnamamenn*; and about them was written the *Landnama-bók*: 'The Book of the Settlement.'

The stream of settlers in Iceland was to a large degree set flowing by the change in the history of Norway, which we shall have to relate in the next chapter. It is enough to say here that the celebrated

Harald Hárfagr had made himself sole King of Norway, and had driven out all the petty kings and chiefs who would not accommodate themselves to the new state of things. The kings who submitted Harald made earls in Norway; those who rebelled he drove away as outlaws. For some time these foes of the reigning dynasty in Norway maintained themselves in the western islands, in the Orkneys and Shetlands, in Scotland, in the Hebrides and Man; but eventually Harald sent a fleet to harry and subdue these places also, and his enemies had to escape to some still more distant land; so they found their way to Iceland.

Even this was not the end of the Scandinavian discoveries. Stirred up, we may believe, by rumours which had been handed down by the kin of the Celtic wanderers of the previous century, some of the Icelanders began to think of voyages still farther west. One of them named Ulf sighted land in this direction. Later on a powerful Icelander, Earl Erik the Red, who was banished from his native country, bethought him of fitting out an expedition to explore this new territory which Ulf had sighted. The result was that Erik came to Greenland, and made a settlement at the place which is now called Igaliko (an Eskimo settlement), and which was then called Brattalid; and from this discovery he won great fame. This took place about A.D. 986.

The son of one of Erik's fellow-voyagers who had been away in Norway at the time that his father sailed, on coming back to Iceland heard of the expedition, and set sail to follow his father; but he was caught in a fog and voyaged out of his course. The land he first sighted did not at all answer to the descriptions of Greenland which he had heard in Iceland. He saw land several times, but never put to shore, though his crew were anxious to do so. Leif, however, the son of Erik the Red, made an expedition in the same direction, and did land in one or two places. One of these, wherein he erected a little fort and did some trading and fighting with the natives—whom the account calls Skrælinger, the name which the Sagas also give to the natives of Greenland—he called Vinland—wine-land—because his men found grapes there. How the Icelanders recognised the grapes for what they were is explained by the fact that Leif had in his company a man called Tyrker, a native of the wine-growing parts of Germany. This Vinland is America; and there, on the American coast, we may leave for a while this most distant settlement of the northern race.

Now let us, remembering what was narrated in the previous chapter, take a glance at the map of Europe, say in the year A.D. 912, and see how wide an area was occupied by people of the Scandinavian race. They extended in a sort of arc, or, perhaps one should say, in two arcs, round the Christian nations, round the people who constituted the true Catholic Europe of the middle ages. Looking first to the east, we see them settled in their Greater Suithiod from Kiev to Novgorod. This place —their chief city and earliest settlement—they called Holmgaard. We do not quite know what settlements the Norsemen had in the Gulf of Finland, in Esthonia, and on the southern shore of the Baltic; but in the latter region there was one very celebrated little republic where lies modern Mecklenburg, whose capital was then called Jomsborg. The inhabitants, who were an exceedingly brave and independent race of freebooters, went by the name of the Joms Vikings. A certain Palnatoki is said to have been the founder of the republic of Jomsborg. He has been chosen as the hero of one of Björnson's plays. Then north and west of the Baltic lay the three ancient Scandinavian countries, Denmark, Sweden, and Norway; each of which (Norway the last) had before the end of the ninth century coalesced into a single kingdom.

Travel to the south of Denmark and we see that in this year, 912, the province of Neustria or Normandy has been handed over to Rolf (Rollo) and his Northmen. Then, again, in England, Northumbria and a large portion of the Midlands belong to the Danes and Norsemen. At this precise moment a certain Siegfrid, a Dane, of whom we know little, reigned in Northumbria. But a few years afterwards he was succeeded by a Regnald, formerly King of Waterford, and therefore a Norseman, not a Dane by descent. The kingdom of Northumbria must have consisted at this time both of Norsemen and Danes, or a Norse king would never have been chosen to reign over it. Of the Norse settlements in Ireland and Scotland we have already spoken, and need not speak again. Then, from the Orkneys and Shetlands we pass to the Faroes, and to Iceland; and in the course of the century the area of Norse rule and settlement extends to Greenland and to a fragment of America.

What an immense power was latent in this vast chain of nations stretching from the east to the west! Had there been political genius enough among the

Scandinavian race at this time to allow of their uniting into one vast confederacy, what might they not have effected! For one thing which is so interesting in this Greater Scandinavia is that its inhabitants, its whole manner of life had, within its limits, such a wonderful uniformity, and differed so markedly from the people and the life of Central Europe which it enclosed, of which unity of belief and of culture was gradually forming the Europe of the Middle Ages. The Northern People had not enough political genius, however, to combine together against Christian Europe. On the contrary, it is just when, at the beginning of the tenth century, the area of their conquests is nearly complete, that they begin to split up once more into separate and hostile fragments. Directly they ceased to win great territory from Christendom, they began to dispute among themselves for the possession of that which they had won. This change in the warlike bent of the Scandinavian peoples inaugurates a new era in their history; a saving change it was for the inhabitants of Christendom, a very fatal change it was for themselves. Viking expeditions still continued. But they were not, like the old ones, voyages of distant adventure directed against peoples with whom the plunderers had nothing in common. They were now more frequently directed by Danes against Norsemen, by Icelanders or Orkneymen against either, than by Scandinavians against the Christians of England or France.

As for the Northmen of Normandy—changing from being Northmen to being Normans—they almost from the first moment of their settlement began to separate themselves in ideas and habits (and very soon in speech) from the rest of their brother Scandinavians, and to take on the habits and thoughts and speech of their French neighbours.

It is this Second Viking age which is the great era of naval battles. Most of the Christian nations during the foregone century had possessed no navies. Our King Alfred was almost the only Christian ruler who had dared to meet the Northmen on their own element. Therefore, during the earlier Viking Age, naval engagements were very rare; the earlier Viking ships were almost exclusively vessels of transport. But when one seafaring nation began to turn its arms against another seafaring nation, then began the great age of naval battles, such as we find described in the Sagas, and the complete Viking war-ship sprang into existence. It is to this age that vessels such as that which lies in the Christiania Museum properly belong.

It might have been foretold that the effects of this great stir among the people of the north would not be exhausted by their conquests alone, nor by the change in the character of the populations of many countries which those conquests effected. For us the most speaking memorial of this age of change and adventure lies in the literature which it created. That is to say, the political effects of this era have been transmuted and absorbed in the passage of ages; but the remains of the literature which it created or awoke to new life are still with us undimmed by time.

The Scandinavian literature of the heroic age takes two forms,—poetic and prose; each one is very distinct from the other, more so even, I mean, than prose and poetry necessarily are. It is convenient as a distinction to speak of them respectively as the Edda and the Saga literature; for these names have long been in use. The rest of the present chapter we will devote to the poetic or Edda literature.

From times far more remote than we can exactly determine, the ancestors of all the Teutonic races must have fixed upon a certain form of poetry, which differs in most essential particulars from the forms of poetry which the classical nations affected; whether we take the hexameter metre which Homer made classical, or whether we take those early Latin metres, such as the Saturnian, which went out of fashion among the Romans when the Greek forms of poetry came in. The poetry of the Teutonic nations had little resemblance to any of these. On the other hand, there is a remarkable likeness in the form of the earliest German, English, or Scandinavian verse.

Let us take, for example, this little fragment, which is one of the very few relics we possess of verse composed in Germany while the Germans were still heathens. The fragment is now called 'Hildebrand and Hadubrand.' Its plot seems to be the same as that of the Persian legend of Sohrab and Rustem, which Mr. Matthew Arnold has enshrined in the most beautiful of his poems—a son unwittingly slain by his father. This is the passage where Hildebrand mourns over the son he has slain by his own hand. I mark by italics the letters on which the alliteration hangs:—

```
Welaga nu waltant got        wewurt skihit,
Ih wollota sumaro enti wintro   sehstic ur lante,
Dar man mih eo scerita          in folc sceotantero ;
So man mir at burg enigeru      banun ni gefasta.
Nu scal mih snasat chind        suertu hauwan.
```

Which we may translate, keeping the alliteration as well as may be—

Weladay now worthy [1] God	a woeful thing has fallen.
Sixty summers and winters [2]	have I strayed from home,
While arms I bore	with the king's warriors:
Yet never a burg	brought me my bane.
Now must I my own child	slay with the sword.

Here, again, is a fragment from one of the earliest, and certainly one of the finest, poems written in the English language. The celebrated poem *Beowulf* seems to have been derived, so far as its story goes, from Scandinavia, for its hero is a Swede. His great adventure is in the killing of a certain monster, call him a ghoul or a giant, which you will. His name is Grendel, and the passage which follows describes Grendel coming from his fastnesses among the moors and mountains to the king's palace, in order to seize the sleeping warriors and carry them off to devour in his den. This time I will give a translation only, and the text in a note:—

The grim guest was	Grendel clepen;
The mighty markstepper,	who kept the moors,
The fen and the fastness.	The fyfel-race's land
Held for a while	this wight accursed,
After the Creator	him had fashioned.
. . . .	. . . .
Forth he went to spy,	so soon as night had fallen,
At the high hall,	to see how the Ring-Danes
After the beer-bout	had ordered themselves.
There found he a host	of men of noble kin
Asleep after the feast;	no care knew they.[3]

---

[1] Properly, 'valiant.' [2] *i.e.* Thirty summers and thirty winters.
[3] *Wæs se grimma gæst   Grendel hátan*
    Mæra meorestapa;   se the morass heóld
    Fen and fæsten.   Fyfel-cynnes eard
    Wonsæleg wer   weardode hwile, etc.

In these translations I have imitated as closely as I could, though necessarily but roughly, the form and cadence of the originals. The peculiarities of the verse consist in the facts that it is not rhymed; that its cadence is nevertheless not measured by feet, but by beats or accents as in our English rhymed ballad metre of a much later date; and thirdly, that instead of by rhymes a certain satisfaction is produced to the ear by alliteration.

This form of verse, no doubt, was in use in Scandinavia at a pretty early period. It can hardly be, for instance, but that our Anglo-Saxon poem, Beowulf, had for its prototype another poem which was sung in Denmark or Sweden. Some of the Poetry which is classed under the head of Edda Poetry may belong to an age before the Viking expeditions began. But whatever may have existed before, it is quite certain that the writing of this verse among the Scandinavians took a great start about the end of that period which we have spoken of as the first or the Great Viking Age.

The scene of this new development of northern verse was not in any of the Scandinavian countries themselves, but rather in some one of those settlements which the Vikings made in the British Isles. Nay, we may say, almost for certain, that it had its origin either in the Scottish or Irish settlements. For it was among the Norsemen, and not among the Danes, that this new poetry began. We may attribute it in large measure to the contact of the Norsemen with the Celts, who were a poetic race, and had already their bards and poetasters forming a regular brotherhood among them, and whose verse had a form very closely resembling the

Teutonic form of verse. Vigfusson, who is the greatest scholar of Old Northern Literature which, perhaps, we have ever had, fixes upon the earldom of the Orkneys as the probable home of the class of poetry of which I am speaking, and which forms the body of what is generally known as Eddic Poetry. He points out how different the whole spirit of this poetry is from the northern prose literature which we know as Saga literature; and he thinks that the difference arises from the fact that the Eddic poetry has been the most deeply affected by the Celtic imagination.

The rest of this chapter and the next I will devote to a description of this early Norse poetry, and the mythology which it enshrines.

The Poetry of the Edda is not historical in any sense of the word; it is purely mythological. The chief part of it is concerned professedly with the northern gods. A certain number of poems deal with the achievements of heroes; but these beings too are not human,—they are a kind of gods.

It happens, unfortunately, that a writer, writing in Christian days, at a comparatively late date in Icelandic history, took upon himself to draw from these early northern poems, and from traditions which had come down to him, a system of Northern Mythology. He combined in this system many classical elements,— at any rate many things suggested by the mythology of the Greeks and Romans, with which he was undoubtedly familiar. The book which he compiled on this principle (which was in prose) has come to be known as the younger or prose Edda. Its proper name is the *Gylfaginning*. And ever since it was written—in the thirteenth century[1]—or rather ever since it was rediscovered by modern scholarship, it has been looked upon as the standard authority for the mythology of the north. People have re-read the old poems by the light of this commentary, and found in them much more than they really contained. Nay, many people have gone much further than that, and in the light of the organised system which was furnished them by Snorri Sturluson (for he is the author of the Younger Edda) they have proceeded to reconstruct the ancient beliefs of the Teutonic Nations—of the Germans of Germany and of our own ancestors—on the analogy of the system of Snorri.

It is very difficult for us now-a-days to think away all this; to take up the Edda poems, and read them with a fresh eye, so as to see the impression they directly produce. In the following short sketch of northern mythology I will endeavour to do this; will try to give an unbiased picture founded solely upon the ancient and authentic fragments of poetry which have come down to us.

But with these ancient fragments, which are really northern, I think we may group that Anglo-Saxon poem, *Beowulf*, whereof I spoke above, or rather the Scandinavian poem or poems from which it is derived. The poem of *Beowulf* has a motive very similar to that of many of the Edda poems. The most striking characteristic of it is the picture which it draws of the giant Grendel, the foe of man, who lives away from human habitations, and makes war upon mankind. The con-

---

[1] The Younger Edda is generally reckoned to contain three works, the *Gylfaginning*, the *Skáldskaparmál*, and the *Háttatal* (a poem). The first is the authority for the Eddic mythology.

ception of such a being as this, dwelling in the fen and the fastness, a haunter of the night, fits in exactly with the experiences of a northern people, in a country scantily inhabited and not fully explored, in a climate in which, if there were long summer days, there were long winter nights too, nights of darkness and bitter cold, seasons when all the ways were closed by snow and ice, or made dangerous by storms and floods. How naturally would such a northern people, pent in, by groups, within the limits of their villages and homesteads, conceive the notion of a vast and terrible outside world peopled by monsters such as the Grendel of *Beowulf*! It is this same imagery which forms the staple of the mythology of the Eddas.

The idea of a giant-haunted world is so engrained in the mythology of the German races that, even to our minds, it is one of the most familiar of mythic notions; though with us it has sunk down to a level with the nursery tales in which alone it survives. To our remote forefathers it was a very real and a very terrible idea. In the north the giant race was associated with the worst, the most inimical of the influences of Nature, with the frosts and snows which abounded in these countries. Thus, in the Edda, the giants—they are called giants, *jötuns, jötnar*, or monsters, *thursar*—are generally spoken of collectively as frost-monsters, *Hrím-Thursar*. This shows, it seems to me, that these beings, as they appear in the Edda poems, are essentially a Norse conception, and not at all Celtic. Some have, besides, horrible individual names which prove them to have been as terrible as the Grendel of *Beowulf*. One of the giants in the Edda, for instance, is called Corpse-devourer.

Some personify the ancient forming powers of the universe; some the world before it became formed, and was but a chaos, a gaping as of night. They are very ancient these giants, older than the gods; all human progress is a war upon them, for they are anterior to all human beginnings, and are for ever endeavouring to bring back the world to the state in which it was before change began.

Man would never alone be able to cope with these monsters—though now and then there arises an individual hero who, like Beowulf, is able to contend with a giant. But man in the north is under the protection of the great god Thor, the thunderer, whose peculiar mission it is to make war upon giants and wizards, whom he destroys with his wonderful hammer, the thunder-bolt.[1] Thor seems to have been the special god of the Scandinavian folk; and the number of names, both of persons and places, containing his name witness to the estimation in which he was held—Thorgeir, Thorstein, Thoralf, Thorulf, Thorketil, Thorgrim, Thorarin, Thorfinn, Thorleif, Thorhall, Thorgerda, Thorhild: it would be impossible to give them all. Then of places—Thursby, Thurston, Thurstanton, Thursfield, Thordal, Thorhus, Thorsborg, Thorshalla, Thorsnut, Thorvik, Thorstrand—are some in England and in Scandinavia.[2] In England, the place-names of this class occur chiefly in

---

[1] *Mjølnir*, the crusher.

[2] It is not always possible to distinguish with certainty in place-names between compounds of the word 'Thor' and of the word 'thurs,' a monster. In personal names, 'thurs' is hardly likely to form an ingredient. 'Thurso' is an example of a place containing the word 'thurs' (plural 'thursar'). It means the monsters' island—some giant, no doubt, having been supposed to have his dwelling there. In some Sagas it is called 'Thursa-skjær,' giants' rock.

those parts in which the Danes and Norsemen were settled; we may assume, therefore, that they were brought in by the Vikings, and were not Anglo-Saxon. Whereas the place-names compounded of the name of the greatest Saxon divinity, Woden, such as Wednesfield, Wednesbury, though these are far less numerous, occur in localities outside the sphere of Scandinavian influence.

In Scandinavia itself the proper names of persons or of places which contain the name of Odin (Odhinn, the northern equivalent of our Woden) are much less numerous than those which contain the name of Thor. Odensjö (Odin's lake), Odinshög (Odin's mound), are places that occur in the map of Sweden and Norway: the first two in Sweden. Odin itself occurs as a man's name, as does Thor. The local name Odnæs, and the proper names Odd, Oddrun, Oddny—these last two are women's names—are connected with a root *odd*, which means a 'point' of land or a 'head' of a family or of a troop. On the whole, the traces of the worship of Odin are much less conspicuous in Scandinavia than the traces of the worship of Thor—certainly among the Norsemen and Icelanders. Indeed, we may say that among the Norsemen and the Danes (we judge very much from the traces which these have left behind them in our country), Thor, though he was not originally the chief god of the Scandinavians—for *that* was Odin—was the most thought of and most often in men's mouths.

In the best description that has come down to us of a temple of the later days of heathendom, the description, namely, of a temple which stood at Upsala, and probably gave its name (Upp-salr, High Hall) to that place, Thor is spoken of as seated in the middle, and on either side of him Odin and Frey. And the same writer says that Thor rules the air, and governeth the thunder and lightning, and that Odin is the god of war, 'and his name signifieth madness. The third is Frey, who gives us peace and enjoyment, and is the god of generation.'

This description shows that a change had taken place in the characters of the Norse gods since the earliest days. For originally Odin was certainly the god of the air; and it is certain that originally it was Odin who was the chief god, the All-Father, the *Fimbul-tyr*, or chief god, of all the Scandinavian people; as indeed he was once of all the people of Teutonic race, of English and Germans (of our ancestors, and the ancestors of the Germans) as well as of the ancient Scandinavians. Of Odin we will speak more fully presently.

We saw in the above description mention made of a third god Frey or Fricco. Frey is rather specially a god of the Swedes. Then there is a fourth god, Tyr, who figures in the Edda poems, but not very conspicuously.

We may, perhaps, classify the three gods as above mentioned who stand next to Odin as follows:—

Thor is by far the most conspicuous and original a figure. He embodies the characteristics of the Norse people as they were—nay, as they are—to be studied in their native land. His adventures express the terror with which the Norsemen were inspired by the unknown forces of nature by which they were surrounded, by the cold and darkness, and by the great tracts of mountain and of heath, of barren unexplored territory. And at the same time he expresses the courage and resolution with which all these forces were met and confronted; and above all, he expresses the humour which was never far absent from the Norseman's mind even in the midst of the strangest surroundings and of the greatest dangers. There is no 'high falutin' about Thor. He sometimes fails conspicuously and makes himself ridiculous; but more frequently the laugh is upon his side. It has been said of Thor that, by the side of Odin, he is a somewhat rustic figure. He is essentially the god of the *bondi* or yeoman-farmer at home in Norway or in Iceland. He is not in an equal degree the god of the Viking, the seafarer and adventurer. Thor is a patron of agriculture as well as a constant fighter.

Frey is a great contrast to Thor in most particulars, though he resembles him in some. We know so little of the Swedes during this period that we cannot say whether Frey represents them as well as Thor represents the people of the Sagas; but if he does so they must have been a much more peaceful race than their brother Scandinavians. It is possible that this was the case. It seems to be a law of national growth that people are capable of exhausting their energy by great achievements, and that after these efforts they are condemned to a period of long repose. The Danes and Norsemen exhausted their energies by the immense vigour which they displayed during the ninth, tenth, and eleventh centuries. The Swedes, on the other hand, owe their chief title to fame to their achievements in the days of Gustavus-Adolphus and of Charles the Twelfth. If we assume that, during the earlier centuries of Scandinavian history, *they* were as much inferior in energy and spirit to the Danes and Norsemen as the Danes (for instance) were inferior to the Swedes in the days of Gustavus-Adolphus, we shall understand why the Swedish national god Frey is so different from the Norse god Thor. I say this may have been the case with the Swedes. True, there is the history of the conquest of Russia, of Greater Suithiod, which seems to negative that supposition. But then we have no details of this conquest. The country may have been very sparsely inhabited; in any case the danger of attacking it cannot have been as great, or seemed so great, as would in those days appear an attack upon the famous empire of the Franks or on the hardy English.

Frey is, of course, to some extent a warrior; no northern god could be otherwise. He is, like Thor, a patron of agriculture. And in his essence he is a god of peace. Men pray to him for good harvests and for peace. He is a god of spring-time; much more of what is called a Nature-god than any other god of the northern mythology. All the gods were in their origin embodiments of natural phenomena or natural forces. Thor, as we have said, was originally the thunder; Odin was the wind or the storm; Frey, the spring, or the early vegetation clothing the earth. But Frey alone still keeps his nature-being pretty conspicuously before our eyes. Odin and Thor have become idealised men and little else.

Another name of the god Frey is Yngvi, Yuge. Under this name he is the ancestor of the royal race of Sweden and of the first royal race of all Norway, the line of Harald Fairhair. This race was called the Ynglings. Certain feminine names which we meet with in Norse history, Ingeborg, Ingegerd, are perhaps derived from Yngvi-Frey.

Then Tyr; we need not pause to speak much of him. In times long past he had been the chief god of all the Teutonic races, and he is essentially one with the classic Zeus and Jupiter. But before the Norse mythology comes much into view he has sunk to be a secondary character. He is called the God of War. But in the Eddas Odin is really this. So we may speak of Tyr as having become a lesser Odin and no more.

Another god about whom we hear much in the Younger Edda, the Prose Edda of Snorri, but much less in the Edda lays which have come down to us, is Balder. Most readers know something of the story of this beautiful young god, who was slain by accident by his blind brother Höder, was carried to the under-world, with such universal grief that all nature, save one being only, wept to bring him back to earth. After Balder had been carried down to the kingdom of the dead, the gods sent a messenger to the regent of that kingdom, whose name was Hel,[1] to pray her to let the god come back to earth. She promised that she would do so if all things on earth, both living and dead, wept for him. And when the message was brought round, all things did weep, all living things, and earths and stones and trees and metals, 'just as thou hast no doubt seen these things weep when they are brought from a cold place into a hot one.' Only one person refused

---

[1] Our word Hell is, of course, identical with this word. But in the Norse mythology Hel appears not so often as the name for the kingdom of the dead, which is called Helheim, as for the queen of that region.

to shed a tear, an old crone named Thökk, who sang—

> Thökk will wail with dry tears
>   Over Balder's bale;
> Nor quick nor dead for the carl's son care I,
>   Let Hel hold her own.

And the old crone, it was thought, was none other but Loki in disguise; 'for Loki never ceased to work evil among the gods.' Such is the story of Balder's death. But we must not assume that this is a pure product of northern mythology; though evidently there has been a lay about it which is now lost, and therefore the story has as much a right to be considered ancient as any other in the poetic Edda. But all the Edda—all the northern mythology, almost—has in it a touch of Christianity; and in this story of Balder we have the strongest element of all.

It remains now to speak of the most important god of all, of Odin.

Odin was not a national god in the sense that Thor was a god of the Norsemen and of the Danes, and that Frey was especially a god of the Swedes. He has been sometimes spoken of as the god of the Vikings; but we must really consider him as the god of all the Teutonic nationalities, for we know that he was worshipped by our Anglo-Saxon ancestors; his name occurs in the genealogies of their kings, and there are a certain number of places in England which contain his name. In England he was called Woden. Among the continental Germans he was Wodan or Wuotan. He may have at one time been a sort of god of the heavens or of the sky. We know that he was called Allfather; and that is an epithet which religions very generally apply to a god of the sky. But the character in which the Norse Odin comes before us is certainly that of a god of the storm. So that, looked upon in this aspect, we may say that he and Thor divide between them the wilder phenomena of nature. Thor is the god of the thunderstorm; and his business is to fight against the embodiments of frost and snow, the giants who haunt the mountains and woods. Odin, as the storm wind, travels with unequalled swiftness over land and sea; his breath stirs up in men the excitement of battle, the love of carnage. We know that in every language the ideas of battle and of storm are confused; people talk of the storm of battle and the battle of the elements.

Thus much for the original character of Odin. It is quite natural that this being should have become the favourite god of the Vikings, who had so much to do with both kinds of storms. Thor might be supposed to stay at home in Norway, to fight with the frost-giants there, and to look after the interests of his special clients, the yeomen-farmers, at home. But that new race of adventurers, the Vikings, had a right, if any one had, to claim the protection of Odin. In their hands there grew up a more elaborate mythology concerning this god than had been known of before.

Let us realise once again the scenery in which the greater part of the Edda poetry and mythology took their final forms. The regions of immense mountains and of vast tracts of ice and snow had been left behind; and the descendants of the Vikings, who composed the later Edda poems, the most elaborate and most beautiful of the series, found themselves in the storm-vexed islands of the Orkneys or Shetlands. There are many passages and expressions in the Edda poems which must have been uttered amid surroundings of this kind. Then, again, the northmen had mingled with the Celts and had imbibed much of their spirit, nay, had inherited much of their blood. For it is remarkable, as Vigfusson has pointed out, how many of the celebrated northern bards are spoken of as dark men (having black hair and eyes), which argues an admixture of Celtic blood in their veins. Amid all these influences grew up what we may call the new mythology of the Norsemen.

All the interest of this mythology centres round the figure of Odin, who is surrounded by a sort of college of priestesses. Once these inspired women had been real priestesses of the great god, and had gained from him the power of divination. We see mention of such wise women among the German races, wherever they come before us in history. But in the new Edda mythology these priestesses have been transformed into a race of Amazons, who ride to battle with the god of the storm of battle; they, like a sort of houris, choose their favourites among mortal warriors, whose arms they bless, and whom, when they die, they are allowed to take with them to heaven. Valkyriur (sing. Valkyria) is the name of these maidens of Odin;[1] and some of the most exquisite passages of northern poetry are those which refer to them and to their relations with men. There is a fortified city where the gods dwell. Its name is Asgaard, the home of the Æsir (gods). (Such is the picture which later Eddic mythology draws for us.)

---

[1] 'Choosers of the slain;' the *Walküren* of Wagner's *Ring des Nibelungen*.

And in that Asgaard there has been prepared a special home for all heroes. It is called Valhöll, the hall of the chosen, the hall of the heroes, and is presided over by Odin and his Valkyriur, 'the choosers of the slain,' whose business it is from every battlefield to select the heroes who are worthy to go to Valhöll.

The imagination of the Norsemen did really behold that celestial company: Odin riding through the air on his eight-footed horse Sleipnir, the swiftest of steeds, and with him riding his troop of shield-maidens—'three nines of maidens,' as one poem says—mounted upon their horses, their bare-backed steeds. And the theory which lay at the root of all this business of choosing slain warriors and transporting them to Valhöll was that the powers of rude nature, the Giants and Trolls, were always ready to make war on the abode of the gods, and that one day they would all combine for one great assault upon it, the issue of which no man could foresee.

This is, in the language of sober prose, the myth of Odin and the Valkyriur, and of Valhöll (Walhalla). But prose is not the form in which it should be uttered. To appreciate it we have to look at it through the medium of the old northern poetry.

' Three troops of maidens, though one maid foremost rode,
 A white and helmed maid:
 Their horses shook themselves, and from their manes there fell
 Dew in the deep dales and on the high hills hail.'

Many other lesser gods are mentioned. Bragi is one, a god of poetry, and also in a manner a god of rash and boasting vows (whence our 'brag'). For it was the custom at feasts to hand round a cup called the Bragi-cup, over which men (being then half drunk) vowed to perform deeds which, in the cooler morning, they were often loath to set about. But Bragi is really only another name of Odin. Hermödhr (Battle-fury) also appears as one of the gods of Gods-burg (As-gaard). His name, too, is only another of Odin's names.

There is Skirnir (the Shiner), Frey's messenger, who is really his double. There is Œger, the god of the sea, from which is derived the word 'eager,' which is sometimes given to that tidal wave otherwise called the 'bore.' There is Niordhr, also a god of the sea. And more interesting than any of these there is Heimdal (Homedale), whose other name is Righ. He is a kind of universal ancestor, and appears as the fashioner of humankind. His second name Righ seems to be Celtic, not Scandinavian.

Then there are the goddesses. Frigg, the wife of Odin, is the chief of these. The name, compared to that of Frey, or Fricco, shows her to be really the feminine counterpart of that god—that is to say, a goddess of springtime, of peace and pleasure. There is, moreover, another being Freyja, who is called the sister of Frey. It is obvious that Frigg and Freyja are really one and the same. There is Nanna, the wife of Balder, who has scarcely any individuality; and Idun, a goddess of perpetual youth (the Hebe of the North). She, too, is probably identical with Freyja and Frigg.

Stranger than all of these is the devil-god, the mysterious inhabitant of the gods-burg, Loki. He, as we saw, 'ceases not to work evil among the Æsir.' Some writers of authority think him no more than an adaptation from the Lucifer of the Christians.

CHAPTER V

THE EDDA MYTHOLOGY (*continued*)

The Underworld

ALL that was described in the last chapter belonged to the present world, to the aspects of nature as they might be seen in Norway or Sweden, the birthplaces of the ancestral belief of the Norsemen; or as they might be seen in the storm-vexed lands to which the Vikings made their way, and which were the actual birthplaces of the Edda poetry that has come into our hands.

But the thoughts of our northern forefathers were very much concerned (as indeed are most mythologies) with the world beyond the grave—call it Underworld or Outerworld as you will—which was a place to be reached by a journey towards the bowels of the earth, or one to which the soul travelled by a long journey on the earth.

The contact of the Vikings with the Christians, who, of course, were full of thoughts and teachings concerning the future state, was sure to intensify the former's interest on these points. For, as a matter of fact, no one among the Christian nationalities was more concerned with speculations—ay, and *visions*—touching the future state than just that nationality with which the

Vikings came in contact—the Christian Celts. The many recorded visions which came out of Ireland and Scotland, and from Irish and Scottish monks, the visions of Furseus, of Drihthelm, of Adamnan, of Tundale, are a sufficient memorial of this fact.

Moreover, towards the year 1000, the hearts of all Christians in Europe began to beat with fear, or with hope. For the millennary of the first coming of Christ to earth was confidently fixed upon as the end of the rule of the powers of earth, the period of the return of Christ to reign in power and establish the millennium of the Church Triumphant. We may guess, from the fragments that have come down to us, how all these thoughts reacted on the imagination of the framers of the Edda lays.

By the side of the picture of the giants and the land of the giants given us in the Edda poetry, we have a picture of the underworld. This borders so closely on the giants' land, that the two cannot always be distinguished. But if I may venture on a conjecture, I should say that, as the cold Jötunheim (giant-home), the region of frost and snow, is characteristically Norse, the region of the underworld was originally chiefly Celtic; and that the confounding of these two places, to the extent that it occurs in the Edda, is really the mingling of two different mythologies.

The finest portions of the Edda poetry are those which bring us in contact one way or another with the underworld. They do this in various ways. Sometimes they speak of the summoning from his tomb or funeral mound of a dead man, some father or ancestor of the person who conjures him; more frequently a dead woman, some *Völva* or wise woman is summoned from her tomb. Other poems take us on a journey to the underworld. And finally we have a long poem, the most beautiful in the whole Edda, deeply imbued with Celtic-Christian mythology, which brings up all the beings of the underworld to join with the race of giants in a final battle against gods and men.

There are three Edda myths which tell almost the same story,—the visit of a god to the underworld. The first account comes from two lays, known as the Conjuring of Groa (*Grougaldr*), and the lay of Fiölsvinn (*Fjölsvissmál*), in which a certain god or hero Svipdag (day-swoop, daybreak) goes down to rescue a maiden who seems to be confined in the netherworld in a hall surrounded by flame. On his way he visits the tomb of his mother, Groa, and by incantations, we may believe, makes her arise from her tomb, and give him counsel before proceeding on his mission—

> 'Awake thou, Groa, awake sweet lady,
>   At the door of death I wake thee;
> Rememberest how thy son thou badest
>   Unto thy cairn to come.'

Then she awakes and cries—

> 'Why callest thou thy mother who is come to mould,
>   And gone from the world of men?'

After that she teaches him charms to keep him safe on his journey.

When he has reached the underworld or giant-land, for the two are not kept distinct here, the adventurer sees the house of the maiden—Menglöd is her name— and this house is encircled by fire. It is guarded by a monster—

> 'What monster is it within the fore-court standing,
> And hovering round the burning flame?'

And a little later he asks the same guardian giant—

> 'How name they this hall that is girt round
> With a certain flickering flame?'

The house girt round by flame occurs again in one of the poems belonging to what is called the Völsung Cycle,[1] because it tells the story of Sigurd or Sigröd, who corresponds to the Siegfried of the Niebelungen legend. In the lay I speak of, called the lay of Sigrdrifa, we find a maiden, Sigrdrifa,[2] who has been cast into a magic sleep, which is really the sleep of death, lying in a hall ringed about by fire; and through that fire Sigurd has to ride on his horse Grani to awaken her, or to rouse her to fresh life—

> 'I know that on the fell a war-maiden sleeps;
> Around her flickers the linden's bane;[3]
> With his sleep-thorn Odin has pierced the maiden,
> Who the god's chosen dared in battle to bring low.'

This act is the counterpart of Day-swoop's in bringing back the Lady of the Necklace.—That is the meaning of the name Menglöd.[4]

Now we come to a third story similar to the foregoing ones, a third Hell-ride told in the poem called Skirnir's Journey (Skirnisför). Skirnir is a lesser god, who is sent by Frey to woo for him a maiden called Gerd. Gerd, like Menglöd, lives either in the land of the giants, or under the earth in the land of the dead.

---

[1] The cycle of poems which tell the same story as is told by the late German poem the *Nibelunge-not*, and which to many modern readers will be best known through Wagner's opera cited above.

[2] Another name of Brynhild, apparently.   [3] Fire.

[4] And Menglöd is really Freyja.

Skirnir does not, like Svipdag, begin by a visit to a tomb. He borrows a horse from the god Frey, and that god's sword. He knows that he will have to ride through the flame which surrounds Gerd's home. 'Give me,' he says—

> 'Give me thy steed, then, that he may bear me through
> The murk flickering flame.'

From a fragment of poetry not actually included in the collection called Edda, but of just the same character as its poetry, we have another presentation of this fire, which always seems to surround the dead. This time it appears as if it flared out of the tomb itself, or the funeral mound. The fragment of poetry of which I speak is taken from the Saga of Hervör and Heidrek.[1] The story tells, among other things, of the visit made by a lady, Hervör, to the 'how'[2] of her father, Agantyr, which lies on an island in Sweden—much as Day-Swoop visits the tomb of Groa—in order to summon him from his death-sleep and learn from him the burial-place of a certain magic sword which is an heirloom. When she first comes to the island Hervör finds a shepherd, and asks the way to the mound. He answers—

> 'Who is this to the island come alone?
> Go hence straightway shelter to seek.'

Hervör repeats her question; but he supposes her to be a witch and runs away.

> 'Run we fast as our feet will carry us;
> All is awful for me to look upon:
> Fires are flickering, graves are gaping;
> Burn fold and fell. Let us run faster.'

[1] *Hervarar Saga ok Heidreks*, caps. iv. v.
[2] Funeral mound.

And she says—

> 'Be not we affrighted at such moaning;
> Though on all sides the island burns.
> Ajar lies hell-gate, the how is opened;
> Fire I behold all round the island.'

Then she awakes her father and he speaks to her.

There is one more hell-journey of which I have to speak. This is the most celebrated of them all, the famous ride of Odin, under the name of Vegtam, to the underworld.[1] Odin went to inquire what meant the portents which seemed to foretell harm to Balder, and which did, in fact, as we know, foretell his death.

Like so many other journeys to the underworld, this of the Sire of Gods and Men includes a visit to a tomb. It is the tomb of a sibyl; this time the tomb seems itself to stand within the world of shades, just outside the eastern gate of the city or citadel of Hel herself, the queen of the dead.

> 'Downward he rode towards Niflhel,[2]
> There met him the hell-hound from its cave coming:
> Bloody it was upon its breast;
> And it bayed and gaped wide
> At the sire of runic song.
>
> Onward rode Odin—the earth echoed—
> Till to the high Hel's home he came.
> Then rode the god to the eastern gate,
> Where he knew there was a vala's[3] grave.
> To the wise one began he his charms to chant,
> Till she uprose a-force, and the dead one spake:
>
> "Say what man of men to me unknown
> Trouble has made for me, and my rest destroyed.
> Snow has snowed o'er me, rain has rained upon me,
> Dew has bedewed me,—I have long been dead."'

---

[1] Well known through Gray's rendering: *The Descent of Odin.*
[2] Niflhel is a place—mist-hell.   [3] Vala or Völva, a Seeress.

It remains to speak of the rise of the infernal powers against the gods, the corollary, as we have called it, to the myth of Odin and the Heroes; and of the final battle which these are to wage with the giant race, the beings of Frost and Snow, with whom are allied beings of Darkness and Death. To the history of this great final battle—this Armageddon of the northern mythology—is dedicated one long poem of the Edda, which is perhaps the finest of them all. It is called *Völuspá*; or, 'The Wise One's Prophecy,' the prophecy being of the end of the world. In the old manuscript collection called Edda, from which all subsequent translations have been taken, this poem *Völuspá* stands the first. It is not, however, by any means the earliest in date of all the northern poems. We may surmise that it was composed a little before the year 1000, for then, we have said, the thoughts of Christian Europe were full of the expectation of the second coming of Christ to judge the world; full of expectation, of hope, but still more of dread; and I take it that this *Völuspá* poem is the reflection on the minds of the half-Christianized northmen in the Scottish islands of this same pre-occupation, of the same hope and dread. It is impossible to say how much the fancies of Celts and of Christians have mingled with genuine northern mythology to form this poem. Certainly the result achieved has an almost unrivalled beauty among creations of this order.

Völuspá, the prophecy of the völva or sibyl, begins with an account of the origin of all things; with descriptions of the different races of the earth; with some obscure hints of past history when the world was young. Then, about the middle of the poem, it passes from reminiscences of the far-away past to prophecies of a far-away future—namely, to the Last Day, as it presented itself to the northern mind. The end of the world is to begin with a terrible winter of three years' duration. All folk living on earth will perish in this cold. Only the immortal powers of good and evil—the gods from Asgaard, the City of the Gods, the heroes who have been translated thither, and dwell in the hall of the chosen Volhöll (Walhalla)—will be left to fight in this final battle.

> 'Swart grows the sunshine, and no summer after;
> All the winds are death-winds.'[1]

And then out of this darkness the Last Day dawns, as over graves:

> 'There on a how[2] sat, striking his harp,
> The giantess' watch, glad Egdir.
> Crowed to him from gallows'-wood
> A bright red cock that Fjalar hight.
> Crowed to the gods Gullinkambi;[3]
> And another crowed from beneath the earth,
> A dusk-red cock in the halls of Hel.
> Fiercely the hell-hound bays from the Gnipa-cave,
> Its fetter breaks, and the wolf runs free.
> How is it with the Æsir, how with the Alfar?[4]
> Jotunheim roars! The Æsir come to council;
> And the dwarfs are moaning before their stony doors.
> Know ye what that betokens?'

There are three great battles of this dooms-day—Ragnarök. Odin, the chief god, fights with a certain Fenrir, the hell-hound or hell-wolf, the son of Loki; Thor fights with another of Loki's children called

---

[1] Or winds from the dead, laden with pestilence.
[2] The funeral mound.   [3] Gold-comb.   [4] The elves.

Jörmungandr, the great earth-serpent who encircles the world. Frey fights with the fire-god, Surt.

> 'Surt from the south comes, the giant with the sword;
> The gods' sun shines reflected from his shield;
> Rocks are shaken; giantesses totter;
> Heroes fare to hell; and heaven is cleft in twain.'

When Odin has been killed by Fenrir he is revenged by Vidar, who strikes his sword into the heart of the wolf. Thor kills Jörmungandr; but, suffocated by the dragon's poisonous breath, he recoils nine paces and falls dead. Tyr and Garm (another hell-hound) slay one another. Last two of all, Loki, the embodiment of evil, and Heimdall, an ancient creator-god, fight: each kills the other. And now the Death-Flame (Surt) stalks unhindered over earth, and, spreading fire on every side, consumes it all.

> 'The sun darkens; the earth sinks into the sea.
> From heaven fall the bright stars.
> The Fire-wind storms round the all-nourishing tree;
> The flame assails high heaven itself.'

The original myth of Ragnarök perhaps ended here, drawing a veil over all things, plunging the earth again into darkness, as out of darkness it had emerged. As the old proverb said: 'Few can see farther forth than when Odin meets the wolf.' But the *Völuspá* does pass beyond this picture, and, influenced thereto by Christianity, lifts the veil again upon a new world, which rises out of the ocean of chaos, peopled by a new race of mankind, and a younger generation of Æsir. In a passage of the *Völuspá* of unrivalled beauty we are told how the prophetess, with an eye which pierces beyond Ragnarök,—

'Sees arise, a second time,
Earth from ocean, green again ;
Waters fall once more ; the eagle flies over,
And from the fell fishes for his prey.

The Æsir come together on Ida's plain ;
Of the earth-encircler, the mighty one, they speak.
Then to the mind are brought ancient words,
And the runes by Fimbultyr found.

Then will once more the wondrous
Golden tablets iu the grass be found,
Which in the ancient days the Æsir had,
The folk-ruling gods, and Fiölnir's race.

Unsown shall the fields bear fruit.
Evil shall depart ; Balder come back again ;
In Hropt's high hall dwell Balder and Höder,
The happy gods.

A hall I see brighter than the sun,
With gold adorned, on Gimil ;
There shall noble princes dwell,
And without end the earth possess.

Then rides the Mighty One, to the gods' doom going,
The Strong One from above who all things governs.
He strifes shall stay and dooms shall utter,
Holiness establish which shall ever be.

These are the chief elements in the mythology of the northern folk as it is given us in the Edda. The doings of the gods, however, occupy only a certain space in Norse poetry. Next (I do not mean next in point of time), after the lays, which are concerned with the gods and godesses, come the heroic lays or ballads which relate the doings of some great hero. These ballads are far less characteristically northern than is the pantheon of the Eddic gods. That it was a Scandinavian habit as much as a German one, among the

Germans whom Cæsar and Tacitus describe, to compose these heroic ballads we may be pretty sure. How otherwise than through some one or some collection of these could we English have obtained our poem Beowulf? But still the fact remains that the ballads of the Edda have to borrow from Germany for their principal figure. This personage is the Siegfried of the Nibelungen legend, who in these northern poems appears as Sigurd or Sigröd. The family to which Sigurd belongs is here called the Völsungs; in the German poem he is 'King of the Nibelungs.' But that the Siegfried legend is a tradition which has travelled to the north from Germany, and that it belongs to the time of the great German migrations, and of the fall of Rome, there can be no reasonable doubt. The German legend, even in the very late form which has come down to us, still preserves the names of some of the great heroes of the time of the German invasions, such as Theodoric the Goth, and Atila the Hun. Theodoric has in the German become Dietrich. Atila survives as Etzel; in the Scandinavian poems he figures as Atli. Another great personage of the same age also figures in the Scandinavian myths; Eormanrik, the Gothic king, who ruled in what is now Russia, and whose kingdom was destroyed by the Huns.

One might imagine that the old legend of Siegfried which lingered so long in Germany, and was finally put down in the ballad which we know as the *Nibelungen Lied*, was originally a Gothic legend; for we see that, taking all the forms in which it has come down to us, it preserves the names of two great Gothic heroes,— Eormanrik and Theodorik,—and of one man, the special foe of the Gothic race, Atila. And as the Goths were undoubtedly much more nearly related to the Scandinavians than were any other of the German peoples, this might account for the fact of the legend filtering back to the north.

Seeing that it did thus filter back, and that the northern ballad-mongers must have been full of the great deeds done by the Goths and other nations, cousins of the Scandinavians, in the fourth and fifth centuries, at the time Rome fell, we cannot but allow ourselves to speculate how far the thought of these deeds, the vague traditions of the riches and grandeur of the Roman empire, may have spurred the first Viking adventurers forth on their journeys, and to their attacks upon Christendom. And if we admit the possibility of this, may not we guess further, that a vague tradition of the kingdom of Eormanrik, the Goth, which was flourishing in the fourth century, may have enticed the first Swedish travellers into Russia in the early years of the ninth century?

The mythologic poems, then, and the heroic or legendary poems, form two divisions of the old northern verse. There is a third division, which in bulk is greater than either of the others—the *encomia* or laudatory ballads on living persons or persons just dead. These contain the only historic element in the poetry of the north.

It became the custom early in the history of the Earls of Orkney, and of the Kings of Norway and Sweden, for certain poets to attach themselves to the courts of these rulers. Generally they were warriors, too, who shared in the adventures of their masters, and sang them afterwards. But I dare say the king took the best care he could not to let his *rates sœur* run too great risks, lest he himself should go down to his long night unsung. We read, for example, of St. Olaf appointing a special guard (shield-burg) for his court-poet. The custom of having a poet at court was adopted by the northern kings from the Irish or the Highlanders,—it was a Celtic custom. We have a long series of poems of the historic era by the *skalds* (*i.e.* bards), as they were called, whose names, and something of whose character have been handed down to us. In its metre most of this court poetry differs in certain respects from the older mythological and heroic poetry.

Before it had come into vogue, moreover, the literary centre of the north had moved from the Western Islands to Iceland, so that most of these court poets are spoken of as Icelanders. But still the skalds were very often Irishmen by descent; as we have said, the descriptions of them represent them as dark-haired, dark-eyed men, for the most part, of a turbulent, adventurous, Celtic character. Almost the earliest of the encomiæ is the piece which was composed in memory of Erik Blödöx, the son of Harald Fairhair, a personage of whom we shall have hereafter to speak. And this is the most beautiful of them all. It begins by describing how Odin awakes from sleep, having dreamt that a host of dead heroes were on their way to Valhöll, and orders the benches and the mead-cups to be got ready for them. Presently they are heard approaching—

> 'What thunder is it, as if a thousand men were tramping,
>   Or a mighty host drew near?
> The walls are breaking,—as though 'twere Balder come
>   Again to Odin's hall.'

The best and earliest of the court poems are written in the old Eddic metre and spirit, the same as those in which the best of the mythological poems are written. But the regular race of court bards, who begin in the time of King Hakon (see Chapter VII.), write in a new metre, and in a style which, as the ages go on, grows more and more affected and *précieux*. We shall see quite late in the history of the kings of Norway this fashion of encomia or court-ballad dying down with the last embers of Norse adventure. The poets at the court of Hakon the Good, of Gunhild's sons, of Olaf Tryggvason, and of Olaf the Saint, were retained in order that they might be a sort of rhyming chroniclers of the deeds of these kings. And it is quite evident that many of the Kings' Lives, or Sagas of the Kings, on which our knowledge of Norse history is founded, have been chiefly made up from these long poems, of which, in most cases, fragments only remain to the present day. Thus, in the prose Sagas, we very frequently find a certain courtier taking a very conspicuous part in giving advice to the king, or help to him in battle. It puzzles us at first to understand why this individual, who does not appear to have been one of the first men in rank, should hold such a prominent place in the prose tale. The mystery is explained when we realise that he is the author of the poem on which the prose Saga is founded. It is natural that he should record at great length the events in which he himself bore a conspicuous part.

Among the more distinguished of these court bards —distinguished either by the excellence of their verse, by their achievements, or by their favour with the king

—may be cited Hornklofi, of the court of Hakon the Good; Glum Geirason, the bard of Harald Greyfell; Einar, Earl Hakon's poet; Halfred Vandrædaskald (the Troublesome Bard), who was a devoted friend of Olaf Tryggvason; and Sighvat, the poet of St. Olaf, who must have left a long poem describing all the achievements of that hero. Of most of the works of these court poets we have only very few remains, by comparison with what they may reasonably be conjectured to have written.

This later court poetry is genuinely Icelandic; most of the bards about the persons of the kings having been by birth Icelanders. The little Republic held a unique position among the Scandinavian nations for its literary achievements. But for all that this later court poetry is Icelandic in origin, the true power of Icelandic literature does not lie in the direction of poetry, but of prose. It is by the development of the prose tale, the Saga, that Iceland has won for herself a permanent and no mean place in the literary history of the world.

The growth and character of this literature deserve to be spoken of in a chapter to themselves.

CHAPTER VI

THE SAGAS

Let us go back to the foundation of the colony in Iceland. The earliest settlers in the island had gone thither, as would appear, from some portions of the British Islands, very largely, probably, from Ireland. For many Irish or Highland names are mentioned among those of the early settlers. A considerable number of these foreigners were brought to the country as thralls of the Norsemen. But there were also not a few who went thither as freemen, and took land alongside the Scandinavian settlers. One of the two heroes of the celebrated Saga called *Njála*, Gunnar of Litharendi, namely, was the third in descent from an Irish settler in Iceland. The other hero of the Saga (to which he has given his name) must have had some Irish parentage; for his name, Njál, is really Irish, not Scandinavian. It is the same as Niel in the family of O'Niel. And though the name became acclimatized in the Scandinavian countries, and has remained so to this day (whence the common Christian name Niels which we find in Iceland, in Norway or Sweden, and the numberless Nielsens, Nilssons, etc., among Scandinavian surnames), it exists only in virtue of acclimatization; and wherever found it betokens, we may feel sure, some Irish ancestor of the possessor, though he may be very remote. Of the Irish ancestors of the Scandinavians, whatever number there may have been, the largest proportion were probably to be found among the early settlers in Iceland.

It was in the south-west of Iceland, in the home of the earliest settlers, that arose Icelandic literature strictly so called. We cannot call the old Scandinavian *poetry* in any true sense Icelandic. But the *prose* literature, the literature of the Sagas, is so distinctly. And we may believe that, like the Edda poetry, though in a somewhat different fashion, this literature is the outcome of a fusion of the Celtic and the northern spirit.

How much of the literature of Europe at large may be due to fusion of a nature similar to this! As J. R. Green has said, there is something appropriate in the fact that our great national poet was born just upon the border line, where the population preponderantly Teutonic, English, runs into a population which is probably still by blood preponderantly Celtic. In French literature, again, we know that that which has carried the day, and decreed what was to be the ultimate form of the French language, has been the literature of northern France, of the *langue d'oïl*, not that of the southern *langue d'oc*; and it is in the north of France alone that there is any considerable infusion of Frankish (Teutonic) blood with the original Celtic. Goethe and Schiller were both born in that part of Germany which was Celtic before it was German: we cannot tell how large a Celtic element remains in it. And Dante—who can guess of what admixture of blood his may have been composed, made up of Etruscan, of Celtic, of Latin, and of Lombardic elements? So if the Icelandic literature has had an origin not dissimilar to that of so many other modern European ones, the fact certainly need not surprise us; but it is well worth noting.

For this Saga literature, though it cannot take rank with such great creations as we associate with the names of Shakespeare or Goethe or Dante, is far finer, and far more worthy of study than most men suppose.

We can partly trace, and partly surmise its growth. It sprang up, we have said, in the west of the island. The new settlers there, cut off from their old interests, and yet full of the energy which their past lives of adventure begat, threw themselves eagerly and vividly into their fresh life, so that small, and, as we should judge it, petty as that life really was, it became in their hands almost heroic; and under the imported influence of the Celtic bias that way it became fit for treatment in literary art.

Most people seem to have only a very vague and general idea of what the true Saga is. They confuse the Icelandic *Saga* with the German *Sage*, a tale, and fancy that the word may be applied to almost any Scandinavian story or history written at any period. But, properly speaking, the expression Saga Literature should be taken to denote a very distinct and a strictly prescribed outcome of the northern imagination. We will devote the rest of this chapter to an account of the birth and the development of the Icelandic Saga, and to a description of its peculiar characteristics.

The idea of this tale-telling was not native among the Icelanders. Tales, very like the northern Sagas, had been told in Ireland before ever the Northmen came thither. And whether it be that the northern settlers in Ireland learned the art of story-telling there, or that the Irish, among the early settlers in Iceland, brought with them the art into their new country, we must take this beginning of Icelandic literature to be a descendant of what may be called (by a sort of bull) the oral literature of the Irish.

The settlers in Iceland seem to have been a good deal self-centred. A great breadth of sea cut them off from the politics of that long chain of territories which we have called the Greater Scandinavia; and that Greater Scandinavia lay between them and the rest of Europe. Thus they preserved, with very minute care, the records of the early settlements in the island; the history of the families who were descended from these early settlers, who were a sort of Mayflower emigrants, and formed ultimately the aristocracy of the island. About the doings of all the chief men in these families stories, we may believe, were composed to be recited in winter days round the fire. Gradually there grew up a race of story-tellers, who worked upon a plan; so that the practice of Saga-making developed into a defined art. It is curious to trace the beginnings of a really great literature amid these petty surroundings and trivial interests. But it reminds us, to a certain extent, of the beginnings of other and still greater literatures. What the deeds of the Icelanders were, compared to the doings of the northern folk, in the native Scandinavian countries, or even in their settlements in our islands, such were the quarrels between two petty branches of the Pelasgic race compared to the wars which, at the same time, were raging between the mighty empires of

Egypt and Assyria, or between either and the great confederacy of the Hittites. Yet out of the petty quarrels between the Achæan-Pelasgians in the west and the Asiatic-Pelasgians in the east grew the Epic Poetry of Greece.

Making allowance for the difference between prose and poetry, the development of the Icelandic Saga is, probably, no bad reflex of the development of the Greek Epic. As in the earlier literature, a number of smaller ballads must have preceded the long poems which have come down to us, and must have, by a special art, been combined together to form these long poems; so in Iceland the short fireside stories have been combined to form the Sagas that we know; and a great deal of art has been used in making this combination. It seems extraordinary to us that such poems as the Homeric ones could ever have been committed to memory entire. We cannot be certain how far they were so, or how far the hand of the redactor is present, though concealed, in the written version. The Sagas present the same difficulty. They were, of course, eventually committed to writing; and how far the written form actually represents the narrated form we cannot be certain. On the whole, however, it seems to represent it pretty exactly, which is the same as saying that the long Sagas that we know were once preserved by oral tradition only.

It is thought that the full bloom of the Saga period dates from about the beginning of the eleventh century; that is to say, just after Iceland had become Christian, when the people were quieting down, and when, therefore, deeds such as those which the tales narrate were growing less frequent year by year. We can imagine how the Icelandic chiefs must have looked back with pride to the doings of their ancestors, and delighted to take part in them in imagination. And the picture of the Saga-maker, relating his story in their halls in the winter evenings, is very much the same as the picture of Homer or of the ballad-monger of the Homeric cycle singing his ballad to the descendants of the Argive chiefs.

The Sagas which have come down to us are of various lengths, and written in various styles.

If we accept the theory of Vigfusson and of Powell that the Sagas have their rise in the south-west of Iceland, we must place among the earliest extant ones the *Hardar Saga* or *Hólmsvega Saga*, as it is otherwise called, a story of adventure relating the deeds of a company of outlaws, who haunted the district of Iceland known as Hvalesfjord or Whalesfirth. Another of these south-western stories is the Saga of Hen Thori (*Hænsa Þoris Saga*), which tells of the rivalries of two Icelanders, Thori and Ketil, of whom the one in the end burns the other in his house—a very common ending of feuds in Iceland. The action of both these stories lies a little before the end of the tenth century. Another Saga which has the stamp of great antiquity is the Saga of another Thori, called Gold Thori (*Gull-Þoris S.*), and of this the action lies in the early part of the tenth century. This belongs, too, to the western side of Iceland. *Kormaks Saga* is another of early composition, though it does not belong to the birthplace of the Sagas, but to the north of the island. The hero of it has an Irish name (for Kormac, though it is common enough among Icelandic names, was, like Njal, an Irish name originally), and has, no doubt, a good deal of Irish blood in him. And the story of his courting of his mistress, Steingerda, is a curious half-real, half-magical tale, not unlike one of the stories told in the poetic Edda. It is in style and in treatment the nearest approach which we have to a link uniting the true Icelandic Saga and the Edda literature. Two other short Sagas well worth reading are the *Vatnsdæla Saga* and the *Vapnfirdhinga Saga*, the Sagas respectively of certain settlers in 'Waterdale' and 'Weaponfirth,' two districts in Iceland. Both are stories of blood feuds.

On the whole, it may be said that the plots of the Sagas turn mainly upon two subjects, either the rivalry of two heroes for the love of a woman, or a blood feud between two rival houses, and the duty which devolves (very often) on generation after generation of carrying it on. An incident in the narrative is frequently the outlawry of one or other of the parties to the quarrel; for outlawry was one of the chief weapons by which the law of Iceland struck offenders against the peace.

Other Sagas which may be mentioned, as containing a good deal of interesting matter, are *Hrafnkels Saga Freysgoda*, *Svarfdæla Saga*, *Vigu Glums Saga* (which contains some genuine and antique verses), *Þorsteins Saga Sidu Halls sonar*, the Saga of Thorstein, the son of Hall of Side. Hall o' Side had much to do with the first attempts to introduce Christianity into Iceland.

Gunnlaugs Saga Ormstungu (the Saga of Gunnlaug Snake-tongue), *Gisla Saga Súrssonar* (the Saga of Gisli Sur's son), are accessible to the reader in translations, the former by Messrs. Morris and Magnusson, the latter by Sir G. Dasent.

So far for the lesser Sagas—those which most nearly represent the original form of this work of art. But, as has been said, a time arrived when the narrators came to work out of the materials of the shorter tales long narratives which are almost epics. These often follow the history of many different families through several generations. As a matter of fact, they hover between the character of a chronicle and the character of an epic. These greater Sagas are the following—

Njala Saga, the story of Burnt Njal, the finest of them all.

Eyrbyggia Saga, the Saga of the inhabitants of Ere, between Broadfirth and Huna-floi, and their neighbours in the north-west of Iceland.

Laxdæla Saga, the Saga of the men of Laxdal, Salmon-dale, in the west of the country.

Egils Saga, a Saga whose story goes as far back as to the days of Harald Fairhair, king of Norway, but continues its history for about a hundred years. It is the history of the feud between the family of Egil and the descendants of Harald.

Grettis Saga, the story of Grettir the Strong. This is another outlaw's history.

Of these, the *Eyrbyggia Saga* approaches, perhaps, most nearly the chronicle form, while *Laxdæla Saga* is more like the old heroic epic, and is, in fact, practically a prose poem. It seems to have been affected by the legendary Volsung history. It professes to relate the story of some among the successors of that Aud the Wise of whom we have spoken. The *Njala*, or *Njáls Saga*, may be said to hold the mean between these two, and to present us with the Icelandic Saga in its very finest development.

The motives of these longer Sagas are not essentially different from those of the shorter ones. Loves and family feuds afford the staple of their material. They deal, in fact, in almost equal proportion with the two strongest passions of the human heart,—love and hate.

As a rule, the tale is a sad one. 'A sad tale is best for winter,' as Mamillius says in *The Winter's Tale*. Not seldom do we find that it is the least worthy man who wins. Literature here, as it generally does, shows that best part of its bias—a leaning to the losing side—such as we notice in Homer's picture of Hector, who far outshines in nobility his victorious rivals. So it is here. Hrafn gets the better of his nobler rival, Gunnlaug Snake-tongue; in the end both fall. Kjartan, in the Laxdæla Saga, is a finer and more interesting figure than Bolli, who gets the better of him and wins his love Godrun, just as Gunther gets the better of Siegfred in the Nibelungen story. The Njáls Saga tells of the slaying by the sword of the most brilliant man in Iceland, Gunnar, and the burning of the most stately and venerable man, Njal.

It must not be thought that though the Sagas deal chiefly in rivalries and slayings, that the picture of Iceland which they present is that of a purely anarchical country. On the contrary, we cannot but be astonished at the love of law and order which co-exists in the land along with this recognition of the duty of revenge. Certainly these northern republicans showed themselves well fitted for self-government. And alongside of their love of battle and adventure we see in them a reverence for law which is almost superstitious.

Of other superstition, or even of religious feeling, there

is little trace in the Sagas, and this is the most remarkable thing about them. Not, of course, that the ideas of magic or of ghosts are entirely absent,—that is not to be expected in such an age, and sometimes the magic intervenes in an odd way in most naturalistic story-telling. But the traces of the fundamental beliefs of old heathenism are very few. The *Svarfdæla Saga* is, perhaps, the most imbued with them. This peculiarity, which makes such a strong contrast between the Sagas and the Edda poetry, is an argument either that the Sagas, as they now stand, were written or composed after the conversion of Iceland; or else that, for some time previous to their conversion, the ancient creed had lost all hold on the people of the island. The latter is the most probable explanation. Ancient creeds, much less than modern ones, admit of a change of domicile. They are very largely rooted to the soil in which they have sprung up. And the fact that the Icelanders of the Saga age had so completely got rid of their ancestral beliefs is, I think, some evidence that the Edda mythology did really spring from Norse soil, and that it really does reflect, as it seems to do, the aspects of nature which belong to Scandinavia more than to any other country.

These Icelandic Sagas preserve the quintessence of the national character, and show it, moreover, not only in its heroic moments, but in the affairs of common life. We are irresistibly reminded in reading these accounts of the northern farmer, the Yorkshire farmer, say, as we know him to-day, the true descendant of the Scandinavian. Observe two men of this class meeting. They shake hands—in silence. Then, after a minute's pause, comes some commonplace greeting or commonplace observation.

'Fine day.'

'Ay, pretty well.'

Then another minute's pause.

'Will ye take summut?' and so forth.

All the while they know that they have met for a particular purpose. Each one is as well aware as his companion of the nature of the bargain or the business which has brought them together.

Compare with this picture from to-day the account of the negotiations for a marriage between two Icelandic families. It is Glum who, with his brother Thorarin, has come to demand the hand of Hallgerda, daughter of one Hauskuld, and niece of Hrut.

'They [Glum and Thorarin] gathered men together and rode off, ten in company, west to the dale, and came to Hauskuldstæde. Hauskuld gave them a hearty welcome, and they stayed there that night. But early next morning Hauskuld sends for Hrut, and he came thither at once; and Hauskuld was out of doors when Hrut rode into the farm. Then Hauskuld told Hrut what men had come thither.

'What may it be that they want?' says Hrut.

'As yet,' says Hauskuld, 'they have not let out to me that they have any business.'

'Still,' says Hrut, 'their business must be with thee. They will ask the hand of thy daughter Hallgerda. If they do, what answer wilt thou make?'

The family affection which exists among these men is a very pleasant feature of life in the Saga-age; though it has its antithesis in the awful persistence with which they exact vengeance for a slain kinsman and carry on a blood-feud through generations. In the Njal's Saga we find Njal, the famous law-giver, living peaceably with three grown sons in the house. Two of them were married and had farms of their own, but chose to live with their father and mother. The brothers Hauskuld and Hrut, whom we have just mentioned, though they were not always on such good terms, we find in every difficulty asking each other's advice, and consulting about family affairs.

And, when we get to the more exciting passages, few literatures have produced a more vivid style of narration than is to be found in the same Sagas. The framework of the stories is homely enough. We see the chief—and this again reminds us of the Homeric Epic—setting his men, his house-carls to work, and superintending their labours—watching his own hay cut, and going up upon the mountains to collect his sheep. But how vivid may be the narrative which accompanies these plain details let one quotation suffice to show us. It is taken from the *Njala*, perhaps the most poetic of all the Icelandic Sagas. The event which is here described is only an incident in the story, not its climax: but the fact that it is only an incidental touch causes the picturesqueness and vividness of the narration to stand out the more conspicuously.

There had been long a feud between the wives of two great friends—between Hallgerda, the wife of Gunnar, and Bergthora, the wife of Njal. Fortunately the two husbands swore that nothing that their wives could do should bring them to a quarrel; and this oath they kept till death. But as Hallgerda cannot stir up her husband to insult the family of Njal, or to avenge the slights which she conceives herself to have received from it, she casts about to find other instruments. One of these is Sigmund, an Easterling (Norwegian), who had come out to Iceland. 'He was a great voyager and a comely and courteous man, tall too, and strong. He was a man of proud spirit and a good skald (bard), and well trained in most feats of strength. He was noisy and boisterous, and given to gibes and mocking.' Hallgerda first egged on Sigmund to slay a servant of Njal, one Thord Freemansson. Then, when that business was pacified, and Gunnar had paid atonement for Thord, Hallgerda one day made Sigmund sing a mocking stanza on Njal and on his sons. Njal had no beard, so Hallgerda christened him 'the beardless carle;' and on hearing that he was casting dung over his land, she asked why he did not cast some over his beard. And to Njal's sons she straightway gave the name of dung-beardlings.

'And now do pray,' she said, 'give some stave about them, Sigmund, and let us get some good by thy gift of song.'

So Sigmund sang some satiric verses, which the gossips carried to the ears of Bergthora, the wife of Njal. Njal's sons were Skarphedinn, Grim, and Helgi. These three were the children of Bergthora; and Hauskuld was their bastard brother. The sons were all grown men, and two of them were married, but they stayed with their families in the house of their father and mother. They were all strong men. Skarphedinn, we are told, had dark crisp hair and fine eyes. But his face was ashen pale. Grim, too, had dark hair, but was comelier than his brother, and Helgi was very fair of face and had beautiful hair. These are the heroes of the adventure which follows.

The sons came in to their supper, and when they were sat down Bergthora spoke.

'Gifts have been given you, father and sons, and ye will be no true men unless ye repay them somehow.'

'What gifts are these?' asks Skarphedinn.

'You, my sons,' says Bergthora, 'have got one gift between you all. You are called "dung-beardlings"; but my husband is "the beardless carle."'

'Ours is no woman's nature,' says Skarphedinn, 'that we should fly into a rage at every little thing.'

'And yet Gunnar was wroth for your sakes,' says she, 'and he is thought to be good-tempered. But if ye do not take vengeance for this wrong, ye will avenge no shame.'

'The carline, our mother, thinks this fine sport,' says Skarphedinn, and smiled scornfully as he spake; but still the sweat burst out upon his brow, and red flecks came over his cheeks [his ashen pale cheeks] such as was not his wont. Grim was silent and bit his lip. Helgi made no sign, and he said never a word. Hauskuld went off with Bergthora. She came into the room again and fretted and fumed much.

Njal spoke and said, '"Slow and sure," says the proverb, mistress! and so it is with many things, though they try men's tempers, that there are always two sides to a story, even when vengeance is taken.'

But at even, when Njal was come into his bed, he heard that an axe came against the panel and rang loudly, and there was another shut bed, and there the shields were hung up, and he sees that they are away. He said, 'Who have taken down our shields?'

'Thy sons went out with them,' says Bergthora.

Njal pulled his shoes on his feet and went out at once, and round to the other side of the house, and sees that they are taking their course right up the slope. He said, 'Whither away, Skarphedinn?'

'To look after thy sheep,' he answers.

'You would not then be armed,' said Njal, 'if you meant that, and your errand must be something else.'

Then Skarphedinn said,—

'We shall fish for salmon, father.'

''Twould be well, then, if it turned out so that the prey does not get away from you.'

They went on their way, but Njal went to his bed, and he said to Bergthora,—'Thy sons were out of doors, all of them, with arms, and now thou must have egged them on to something.'

'I will give them my heartfelt thanks,' said Bergthora, 'if they tell me the slaying of Sigmund.'

Now they, Njal's sons, fare up to Fleetlithe, and were that night under the Lithe, and when the day began they came near to Lithend. That same morning both Sigmund and Skiolld rose up and meant to go to the stud-horses; they had bridles with them, and caught the horses that were in the farm-yard, and rode away on them. They found the stud-horses between two brooks. Skarphedinn caught sight of them; for Sigmund was in bright clothing. Skarphedinn said, 'See you now the red elf yonder, lads?' They looked that way and said they saw him.

Skarphedinn spoke again: 'Thou, Hauskuld, shalt

have nothing to do with it, for thou wilt often be sent
out alone without due heed. But I mean Sigmund
for myself; methinks that is like a man; but Grim and
Helgi shall try to slay Skiolld.'

Hauskuld sat him down, but they went till they
came up to them. Skarphedinn said to Sigmund,—

'Take thy weapons and defend thyself; that is more
needful now than to make mocking songs on me and
my brothers.'

Sigmund took up his weapons; but Skarphedinn
waited the while. Skiolld turned against Grim and
Helgi, and they fell hotly to fight. Sigmund had a
helm on his head and a shield at his side, and was girt
with a sword; his spear was in his hand; now he turns
against Skarphedinn, and thrust at once at him with
his spear, and the thrust came on his shield. Skarphedinn dashes the spearhaft in two, and lifts up his
axe and hews at Sigmund, and cleaves his shield down
to below the handle. Sigmund drew his sword and
cut at Skarphedinn, and the sword cuts into his shield,
so that it stuck fast. Skarphedinn gave the shield such
a quick twist that Sigmund let go his sword. Then
Skarphedinn hews at Sigmund with his axe, the 'Ogress
of War.' Sigmund had on a corselet; the axe came on
his shoulder. Skarphedinn cleft the shoulder-blade
right through, and at the same time pulled the axe
towards him. Sigmund fell down on his knees, but
sprang up again at once.

'Thou hast lilted low to me already,' says Skarphedinn. 'But still thou shalt fall upon thy mother's
bosom ere we two part.'

'Ill is that, then,' says Sigmund.

Skarphedinn gave him a blow on his helm, and after that dealt Sigmund his death-blow.

Grim cut off Skiolld's foot at the ankle-joint; but Helgi thrust him through with his spear, and he got his death there and then.

Skarphedinn saw Hallgerda's shepherd, just as he had hewn off Sigmund's head; he handed the head to the shepherd and bade him bear it to Hallgerda, and said she would know whether that head had made jeering songs about them, and with that he sang a mocking song on Hallgerda.

Other more exciting passages might be cited from the history of the Njals Saga, from which we have made these two extracts. But there is none in which the peculiar gifts of the narrator are better shown.

When we come to the kings' lives we shall give other extracts which display the same Saga manner, and serve further to illustrate this art of literature.

When the Saga-makers had become celebrated at home, they were naturally attracted to the courts of the greater northern chiefs in other lands. The Earls of the Orkneys had their Saga-men; and a series of histories of the Orkney Earls, known as Jarla-Sögur (Earls' Sagas) have been preserved. Probably the Norse kings of Dublin had theirs, for a fragment from their history has been preserved to us in the Icelandic Saga Njala. It tells of a celebrated battle which was fought in 1014 at Clontarf, between the kings of Dublin and their Norse allies on the one side, and the confederated Irish kings, under Brian-Boroo, on the other. The Irish had their Saga or history of the same battle. There are in the same way Sagas which relate the doings of the Joms Vikings.

The most interesting, historically, of the whole series of Sagas are those of which we have spoken above, called the Lives of the Kings,—that is to say, of the kings of Norway. At a later date, when writing had been well established, the literary men of Norway set to work, either simply to make copies and collections of the older prose Sagas as they stood, or else to write works in what we may call the 'Saga vein,' which were founded partly on extant prose tales and partly on fragments of verse. These latest and most elaborate productions of the Icelandic prose muse must not be confounded with the Sagas produced in the true Saga age. Albeit they are made up of elements which date from that era.

This is the second age of Icelandic literature, and, as distinguished from the true 'Saga era,' it may be called the book age; for, in point of fact, the word book (bók) now begins to be employed. The father of this second order of Icelandic literature—the true *literature*, if we use the word in its etymological sense—is Ari the Historian, Ari *Frodi*, as he was called by his countrymen. This Ari was a descendant of Aud the Wise, and of Olaf the White, king of Dublin, of whom we spoke in the last chapter. Ari's date is A.D. 1067-1148. He was, we see (at any rate we shall see when we come to the history of Norway), born the year after Harald Sigurdsson, or Harald Hardradi, fell in England. Three great works are attributed to this Ari *Frodi*, of which one has been preserved as he wrote it; the contents of another have been handed down to us, but not always separable from addenda of a later date; and of the third only an abridgment remains. These books are—

Landnama-bók, the Book of the Settlement of Iceland, of which we spoke on a previous page.

Konunga-bók, the Lives of the Kings of Norway. Ari's work is believed to be contained in the later and larger collection of 'Kings' Lives,' taken from older Sagas. It probably includes the kings' lives down to the accession of Olaf Tryggvason.

Islendinga-bók. This is the work which, in its original and expanded form, has perished.

Other names in the literary history of Norway, contemporary with or subsequent to Ari, are—

Sæmund, also called *hinn Froði*, the Wise or Learned. It is to him that the Poetic Edda was ascribed, but without foundation. Sæmund had a great reputation among his contemporaries, as he was thought to be a magician. We have no extant works which can with certainty be ascribed to him, and it is very likely that he did not write in the vernacular, but in Latin.

Kolskegg Asbjornsson. He, too, has the appellation *Froði*. He was a contemporary of Ari, and assisted the latter in compiling the Landnama.

Brand, called the Prior or Bishop.

Later in Norse history, after the heroic age has quite passed, we have—

Erik Oddsson, who wrote lives of two rivals for the throne of Norway, Harald Gilli and Sigurd Slembidjakn.

Karl Jonsson wrote the life of King Sverri, of whom we shall speak in a later chapter.

Odd, the monk, and Gunnlang the monk, were authors of Latin lives of the two Olafs—Olaf Tryggvason and Olaf the Saint.

Then arose the greatest figure in Icelandic literature. This is Snorri Sturluson (A.D. 1178-1241). His age is, in Norse history, the age of the end of the Civil War, when (as we shall see in Chapter XI.) the long disputes of rival dynasties were closed by the elevation of Hakon Hakonsson (Hakon IV.) to the Norwegian throne, and the suppression of his rivals. Snorri was much in Norway, and took an active part in Norwegian politics. For the politics of Iceland hung close upon the politics of Norway in those days; the rival parties in the northern kingdom being associated with rival parties in the daughter republic. Snorri sided against Hakon and with Earl Skuli, Hakon's rival. Skuli fell in 1240, and, at the instigation of Hakon, Snorri was murdered in Iceland the following year. This opened the way for the formal annexation of the republic to the Norse kingdom (see Chapter XI.).

Snorri's great work has always been supposed to be the *Heimskringla Saga*, one of the compilations of the Kings' Lives (of which there are variants) which is considered the most trustworthy. There is but small external evidence to support this attribution; but the internal evidence for it is strong, and has convinced those best able to form an opinion. We must consider the later lives, from Olaf Tryggvason to the death of Sigurd Jorsalfari (see Chapters VIII.-X.), as actually Snorri's work; the earlier Sagas as abridgements only.

The *Prose Edda*, which consists of three parts; first, the *Gylfaginning* (see Chapter IV.); secondly, the

Skáldskaparmál, a poetical gradus; and thirdly, the *Háttatal* (list of metres), a collection of specimens of all the different metres used in Icelandic verse. This is the second considerable work ascribed to Snorri.

Icelandic literature may be said to end with Sturla Thordsson, the author of the Islendinga Saga and the Thorgils Saga. To him have been attributed the whole mass of Sagas known under the head of Sturlunga Saga or Sögur. But it is probable that only two out of the collection are the work of Sturla. He was a member of the great Sturlung family, and a nephew of Snorri Sturluson. He was born A.D. 1214 and died 1284.

In the later period, when the Sagas of the kings of Norway began to be collected, some other collections of Sagas were made, which are now known under their collective names, as, for example—

Orkneyinga Saga. The history of the Earls of Orkney.

Færeyinga Saga. The history of the Farö Islands, especially of the Christianization of them.

Skjoldunga Saga. The history of the royal family of Denmark (the Skjoldungs).

Jomsvikinga Saga, of which we have spoken as the history of the Joms-Vikings of Mecklenburg.

When we read these Sagas of the kings, etc., it becomes obvious that the compilers of them did not always avail themselves of prose records only. Snorri, for instance, seems to have been very largely indebted to the court ballad poetry, of which we spoke in the last chapter.

CHAPTER VII

HISTORY

Harald Fairhair—Hakon—Gunhild's Sons. (*Circ.* A.D. 867-969.)

A NATION of small land-owners, each a little chief in his own way; for he has the sons of his house under him, his nephews, may be, and his nephews' and his sons' sons; and his servants, not perhaps precisely thralls nor *adscripti glebæ*, but what is next door to that; for they have little or no chance of livelihood, save upon the estate on which they have been born. Then, superior to these yeomen, these peasant proprietors, are certain *hersar*,[1] who are their leaders in war; and over these hersar, again, stand the earls or the petty kings. This is the nationality of Norway at the dawn of her historical period. But that which makes all the people, not of the whole of Norway, but those living in each considerable district of the country into a single nationality, is not the unity of its government, of its executive, but rather the unity of its legislature (though this is to some extent executive also),—that is to say, its general assembly of freemen, which was called the *Thing*. These Things were of many kinds and of various degrees of importance. There were

---
[1] Sing. *hersir* (*hersi*).

smaller local Things. But there were also larger ones, of which the ones most spoken of in the Sagas seem to have been four. The Borgar Thing was held at Sarpsborg, on the river Glommen, not far from the modern Christiania. Its jurisdiction took in all the coast which lies round the Skagerrak and Cattegat. In those days Norway extended as far as the Göta River, now in Sweden, so that its coast-line stretched along both the Skagerrak and Cattegat; and this coast district was generally known as Viken, or the Bay. The western portion of it was also called Westfold. Behind this coast district, higher up the country, towards Lake Mjösen, there was another fertile district, which ended in what is called the Upland,—that is to say, the country reaching back to the great back-bone of Scandinavia, which the Norsemen called the Keel. This district had another Thing for itself: it was at Eidesvold, not far from Lake Mjösen. Round to the west there was a Thing district, which included the two great fjords—the Hardanger and the Sogne: these were comprised in the district of the Gola Thing. And after that we come to the Trondhjem district; its assembly was called the Frosta Thing. All the region of the extreme south (Thelemarken, for instance, and the still wilder Sätersdal) seems to have no special electorate of its own. Probably these districts were very thinly inhabited; as, indeed, they still are. And we read of no great Thing belonging to the northern part, Halogaland.

Among the districts of these four Things, the Viken district and the Trondhjem district were by far the most fertile and the most thickly inhabited. The traveller in Norway to-day will notice this characteristic of them. Of the Christiania country, this almost goes without saying, seeing that the capital of Norway lies there. It need hardly be said that in heathen days there was no such town as Christiania. In those days the chief, or the only town, of the Vik country seems to have been Tuna, the modern Tönsberg. In the early days, however, of Norway's existence as a single kingdom, the seat of monarchy rather lay in the Throndhjem country. For there was held another Thing called the Öre Thing, which was always convoked for the purpose of bestowing the crown on each fresh successor to it, but for no other purpose. We can hardly speak of the capital of the country lying at Throndhjem, for there was no town in the country. Öre, at the mouth of the Throndhjems fjord, was the place of meeting for the Öre Thing, and nothing more. This Throndhjem country is, like that of Christiania, fairly level and very fertile, and forms, on the whole, a striking contrast to the great fjord districts—the Hardanger and the Sogne country, which probably the traveller will have first beheld. When we get up to the Throndhjem Fjord, the rough cliffs and snow-capped mountains have retreated or disappeared, and we find ourselves in a district of fertile hills and valleys. This country must have been very early inhabited by a hardy race of yeomen-farmers, for the Throndhjem people play a very conspicuous part in the history of Norway.

It may, in truth, be said that Norway is divided by Nature, and by the character of its inhabitants, into three districts, and that this division is very noticeable in reading early Norse history. The people who lived in Viken lived opposite Denmark, and close to Sweden (the southern part of Sweden then was a part of Denmark); and it would appear that the Viken people were among the earliest to take part in the piratical expeditions of the Viking age. For the very word Viking as it was used by the Norsemen or Icelanders of a later date, is probably derived from this word Vik; so that Viking means only 'man of the Vik.' The people of the Vik belonged to the Baltic; they took part in the same expeditions in which shared the Danes of Jutland, or of the islands, or of southern Sweden. But the men of the fjords of the extreme west lay far away from the Baltic, and opposite the Shetlands; and so it was from the fjord country that there issued that stream of adventurers whom we have described as passing down from the Shetlands to the Orkneys, to Scotland, and Ireland. These form two of the three great divisions of Norway. Thirdly, there was the Throndhjem region which, perhaps, was less concerned with the Viking life than either of the other two, whose inhabitants were, therefore, less thinned by the draining off of adventurers to take part in that life. The Throndhjem people seem, when we first catch sight of them, to have been a settled race of farmers, steady, well-to-do men, and, though fearing no man, contented enough with their life at home. The Throndheimers were, therefore, the most conservative among the people; not so prepared to resist a sudden attack as were the fjord men, they were yet more difficult to keep under. For they had not acquired those habits of loyalty to their chiefs which a life of adventure tends to produce. Norway, as we have described it, was, when we first catch sight of it in history, divided up among a great number of little kings and earls. Agder, Westfold, Raumariki, Vingulmark, Hördaland (modern Horland), Sogn, North and South Möre are some of these kingdoms. Some of these districts preserve their ancient names little changed. The beautiful Gudbrandsdal was called after a certain Hersir Gudbrand, who lived in the time of Halfdan the Black, father of Harald Fairhair. The Throndhjem country had then for its chief place Lade (Hladir)—for the town of Throndhjem was not yet built. North of Throndhjem country lay Halogaland.

In being cut up in this way among petty rulers, Norway was, at first, only in the same condition as the other Scandinavian kingdoms. Suithiod (the Upsala country), East and West Gothland, were originally all separate kingdoms in Sweden. Denmark had kings in both North and South Jutland. A third division, the Kingdom of Leire, consisted of the Danish isles, Zealand and the rest, and the southern extremity of Sweden, what are now the provinces of Småland, Bkeling, Halland, and Skåne. Eventually the kingdom of Leire swallowed up the Jutland kingdoms. For towards the end of the ninth century Sweden and Denmark began to coalesce. Gorm the Old made himself the sole king of Denmark; and Erik the king of the Upsala country made himself master of the rest of Sweden. What more natural, therefore, than that some one of the small kings of Norway should dream of doing the same thing in that land? And we might prophesy that the accomplishment of such a task would fall to the king in Viken, seeing that he ruled in not only a thickly-inhabited district, and in one which had already taken the lead in inaugurating the life of adventure of the

Viking age; but likewise because that country had been long in closer communication with Denmark and Sweden than any other part of Norway, so that it was more likely to follow the example of these states.

The first king of Viken or Westfold, who emerges out of the mythological age, is Halfdan the Black. The family to which he belonged claimed to be a branch of the famous Ynglinga line—descended from the God Frey—which gave likewise kings to Sweden. Of Halfdan the Black we know very little. He may have been the Philip of this Macedon, and prepared the way for the son who was to follow him. This son, this Alexander, was Harald. We need not repeat the legend, how the taunt of a maiden, Gyda, first inspired Harald with the idea that he should make himself sole king of Norway; how he swore that his hair should grow unkempt till he had accomplished his vow. The notion is more likely to have been instilled into his mind by his father Halfdan or by his mother Ragnhild, daughter of one of the petty kings, who, through her mother, claimed a famous descent. In any case, Harald did have this ambition; and soon after he came to the throne he applied himself to the task of subduing, one after another, his petty brother kings in Norway. The number of these is far too great for us to keep count of; though the saga tells us the names of those whom Harald subdued one after another. Some submitted voluntarily and became the king's earls. And Harald had already made himself master of the two most important divisions of the country, Viken, or Westfold, his patrimonial kingship, and the Throndhjem district, including North and South Möre, when the remaining kings leagued themselves together for the purpose of resisting his further encroachments.

The district which he had not subdued was just that one which, as we have said, had most connection with the Viking route to the British Isles; and it is quite certain that the allied kings, in their opposition to Harald, obtained the assistance of a large number of Viking leaders from England and Scotland and the other west countries. The allies assembled a large fleet, which was under the command of three kings, Kjötvi the Rich, king of Agder, Sulki, king of Rogaland, and Erik, king of the Hardanger district. King Harald was at this time lying with the fleet in Hafirsfjord. This fjord lies just to the south of Stavanger; and the traveller who has leisure may well turn aside from this point to visit it, historically one of the most interesting spots in Norway. He will find at the mouth of the fjord a little group of low islands called Jæderens Ref (reef), a reef of rounded ice-worn rocks. Here the allied fleet assembled. The rocks hide the fjord so completely that Harald's fleet may very well have lain there without being seen; and they, on their side, might have stolen close to the mouth of the fjord unobserved. The fleets engaged, and the battle was a severe one. Two of the allied leaders, the Kings Sulki and Erik, were killed, and the third, Kiötvi, took to flight. This battle of Hafirsfirth practically settled the fate of Norway. The opposition was annihilated; and Harald reigned as sole monarch of the kingdom, dressing his locks now that his vow was accomplished, and becoming Harald Fair-hair (*Hárfagr*) for his subjects and for all history.

It is always reckoned that Norse history begins with this substitution by Harald of a single rule for that of the numerous petty kings of a former time, with the loose tie of the Things (A.D. 867?). And if Harald had had political sagacity enough to lend all his efforts towards consolidating this rule and ensuring the position of his dynasty, it would, indeed, have been a momentous epoch in the history of the country, and might have led, who knows, to what supremacy of Norway among the Scandinavian nations, who knows to what power of the Scandinavian nations themselves in Europe? But Harald attempted too much.

In the step which the new sole King of Norway next took we seem to see a reflection of the difference between Viken and the rest of Norway. We have already pointed out how different from the beginning was the character of land-holding in Norway from that which obtained in the other Teutonic countries of Europe. Only in the regions near Viken are there traces of the primitive Teutonic village which other countries possessed; which, in fact, formed the unit of life to all the other Teutonic countries. Now, the primitive village developed by a natural process into something like the mediæval manor, that is to say, into the germ of the feudal system of land-holding.

Not feudalism itself, but what we may call the foundations of feudalism, had been laid in the Christian countries of Europe by the end of the ninth century, and the nearest heathen ones had probably gained some idea of it. Denmark, for instance, though heathen still, was not always in a condition of hostility to the neighbouring Christian states. Some of the kings of Southern

Denmark had been very favourably disposed towards some of the Christian prelates of North Germany; more especially to the celebrated Archbishop of Hamburg, Saint Ansgar; and by the intercourse which arose between the peoples, the ideas of the Christians on secular as well as on religious matters filtered into Denmark. The Danish kings established a system of land-holding which was more or less feudal in character; and as the kings of Viken were such near neighbours to Denmark, and as Harald himself was allied to the royal line of that country, we can easily understand how he, too, may have adopted the same ideas.

What is certain is, that Harald, as soon as his power was firmly established, set himself to dispossess the landowners of Norway from their freehold-, or, as it is called, their udal-tenure, and to make himself nominally owner of the whole land of the country, turning the former freeholders into his tenants or vassals. This was a most momentous change, and one which had a lasting influence; for it transferred all the waste lands to the possession of the crown. But in what it designed to effect, the change of the freehold tenants into vassals, it was much too sweeping, much too impolitic; as a matter of fact, Harald utterly failed to enforce it; and his action in this matter of land-tenure led to the fall of his own dynasty. In truth Harald, like many innovators, was not consistent in his policy. If he had sought to make himself the feudal monarch of all Norway, he ought to have abolished, in respect to his own crown, the old Norse laws of succession, which gave all sons, legitimate or bastard, an equal claim upon the property of their father, and to have established the succession upon a fixed rule of primogeniture. He did not do this, and the result was that the monarchy which he had founded began at his death to crumble away.

The ill effects of his policy were not seen till after Harald's death, which took place about A.D. 933, when the king had reached a venerable age. He was buried at Hauge, in the Karmtsund, the sound between Karmö Island and the mainland. Karmö the steamers pass after leaving Stavanger for Bergen, and so sail close by Harald's grave. It lay, we see, close to the scene of his great triumph at Hafirsfjord. Harald had many wives and concubines, and a number of children, whole or half-brothers to one another. The favourite of them all was Erik, son of the chief among Harald's wives, the daughter of the Swedish King. This Erik got the name of Erik Blódöx, *i.e.* Bloody Axe, on account of his fierce and war-like disposition. He was a great favourite with his father, and even during his father's lifetime he attained to something like kingly power. During his father's lifetime, too, he compassed the death of several of his brothers, and after his father's death he killed, one after another, most of those who remained. The mound of one of them, Björn, is still to be seen under the name of the Seaman's Mound, at Seim, near Tönsberg, on the Christiania Fjord. The youngest of Harald's sons, Hakon, had, however, long left the country. He had been sent into England to be fostered by the King of England, Athelstan, and, naturally enough, had been brought up in this country as a Christian. When his father Harald died, and Erik began, by fair means or foul, to make himself as much master of the country as Harald Fairhair had been, Athelstan furnished Hakon with a fleet and with troops in order that he might prosecute his claim of succession to a portion, at any rate, of the kingdom. Hakon sailed to the Throndhjem district, and there the people at once rose in his favour.

The Throndhjem people were brought over to Hakon's side chiefly by the promises which the new-comer held out, that he would restore to them their old freehold tenure. There was a very powerful family who ruled as earls of the Throndhjem district ; the earls of Lade they were generally called. Lade (Hladir) their estate lay close to where the town of Throndhjem now stands. The representative of the family at this moment was Earl Sigurd, and he declared himself for King Hakon. The defection of the Throndhjem people was followed by that of the people of what were called the Uplands, that is to say, the eastern part of Norway. The people of the Vik district followed suit, so that now Erik's kingdom was confined to the fjord district in the centre. Finding himself no match for his younger brother, Erik at last abandoned this also, set sail westward, and eventually became king of Northumbria, as a vassal of King Athelstan. It is said that he became a Christian there, but that seems doubtful. Erik's wife, Gunhild, at any rate, could hardly have done so, for we have quoted from the remains of that beautiful poem or dirge, composed by command of his widow after the death of King Erik, in which it is described how Odin makes preparation for the coming to his halls of this mighty warrior.

Though Erik thus continued his adventurous career in the west, after he had left his native country, he made no attempt to regain the crown of Norway. On the death of Athelstan he fell into disfavour with Edmund, the succeeding English King, and had to leave Northumbria. He first steered to Ireland; afterwards, as would appear, he made an effort to regain his kingdom of Northumbria, and died in the attempt.

On first leaving Norway Erik had sailed to the Orkneys, which was a fief of the Norwegian crown, and it would seem that he left his wife and some of his children in that country. This wife, Gunhild, was in the Orkneys at the time that she heard of Erik's death. She is a strange figure, who had a great influence on Norwegian history, and the story of her first acquaintance with Erik is worth telling.

The position which the Lapps occupy in the pages of the early Norse Sagas reminds us precisely of the position which the Jötuns and Trolls occupy in the Edda mythology. They are the masters of the art of magic, and they play upon Norwegians, high and low, the same sort of tricks which the Jötuns and Trolls were for ever playing on the Scandinavian gods. A king is sitting at table at the Yule feast; suddenly the table and all that it contains disappear, like the table set before King Alonso in the *Tempest*. The guests return home amazed. The king finds a Lapp lingering about the place, has him seized and tortured, but can gain nothing from him; and Harald, this king's son (for it is of Halfdan the Black that this story is told, and his son is Harald Fairhair) helps the imprisoned Laplander to escape, and escapes with him to the north. They travel till they reach the house of a Lapland chief, and there they stay all the winter. One day in the spring the Lapland chief says to Harald, with the grim humour which forms such a delightful feature of the Norse sagas: 'Thy father took it very ill last Yule because I helped myself to some of his provisions; but now I will return you good for this evil: the good piece of news, namely, that your father is dead.'

Harald was destined to meet the Lapp whom he had rescued once again; and in a manner which still more closely affected his own future. One winter towards the end of his reign Harald was staying with one of his subjects in Upland, at Tofta, in fact, a farm which still stands at the top of the Gudbrandsdal, close to a country which was in those days uninhabited, almost unexplored up to the Swedish border. This event, too, happened at Yule-tide. On the evening of the Yule feast came one Svasi and sent a message to ask the king to come out and speak to him. At first the king was angry, but the message was repeated, and Svasi proved to be the Laplander whom Harald had known long before. He reminded the king how, when in old days they had travelled together, he had promised to visit his home; and now it, he said, stood only just beyond the nearest ridge of mountains. The king complied; and when he got to the hut of Svasi, there stood a beautiful maiden, Snæfrid, who held out a cup of mead to the king. No sooner had he drunk it than, says the saga, it was as if a fire ran through his whole body; he fell so passionately in love with the maiden that he determined, low-born as she was, to make her his wife at once. Eventually Snæfrid died. But her corpse never changed, and remained as fresh and rosy as when she was alive. The king constantly sat by her, and thought that she would come to life again. At length, as he was seen to neglect all affairs of state, one of the courtiers, by a device, induced Harald to raise up the body, and then it was found to be full of all sorts of corruption, and worms and toads and all manner of reptiles came out of it.

The Norse tradition of Gunhild is that she was by birth a Norse girl, who went away to a Lapland hut to be instructed in Lapland magic. And the Saga gives a curious picture of her, watched over by two Lapp brothers, who were so jealous of each other that she was safe with them. There she was discovered by some followers of Erik, Harald's son. She assisted them to kill the brothers; then they brought her away to their master. Erik, as his father with Snæfrid, fell in love with her at once, and determined to marry her out of hand. This is the story. In reality it is more likely that Gunhild was a Danish princess. She is said to have been very beautiful and very clever, but of an evil disposition. After the death of her husband she took a part in all the schemes for restoring his family to the throne of Norway.

Meanwhile Hakon, the Norse king, had begun to forfeit some of the popularity which had accompanied his first return to Norway, through his efforts to introduce Christianity into the country. He began by destroying several temples; until at the last, at the Frosta Thing, the Throndhjem people came armed to resist these encroachments upon their ancient beliefs and customs. They put up one of their number as a spokesman, and he roundly declared that they, the Throndhjem bonders, who had been the means of raising Hakon to the throne, would turn against him and depose him unless he conformed to their ancient customs. Earl Sigurd came forward as a mediator; and he did his best to persuade Hakon to go through the rites of sacrifice; but the king performed his part very unwillingly. Both sides left the feast in bad humour; and Hakon swore that he would collect an army and punish the Throndhjem people for their insolence.

Gunhild and her sons had already begun to bestir themselves to win back the crown of Norway. Their first movement was to seek aid from the King of Denmark, Harald Bluetooth (Blåtand), the son of Gorm the Old, the first sole king of the country. It is possible that Gunhild was a sister of this monarch, whom Hakon had offended, by plundering his dominions. Harald received the Norse princes kindly, and adopted as his foster-son one of their number, a namesake of his own. But he could do nothing immediately to help to restore Gunhild's sons to what they deemed their rights. There was at present no career open to them, but that which for nearly two centuries had been the career of all dispossessed men of noble or peasant blood—the career of Vikings. And they spent many years in this pursuit, plundering the coasts of Norway, or of other Baltic lands farther east.

About the time of the disputes, whereof we have just spoken, between Hakon and his subjects—the news of which was no doubt wafted to the ears of Gunhild and her sons—these last made their first great stroke for the recovery of the Norwegian crown. Hakon had returned in a sullen fit to Möre (the country lying between Throndhjem and Romsdal), when news reached him that the sons of Erik had come to the south, and had driven out the under-king of the Vik country; and that many of the people had submitted to them. Hakon reconciled himself with his Throndhjem subjects, collected a large fleet and army, and sailed southward. Meantime the brothers, the Erikssons, had sailed round to the west coast, and the rival fleets met near the island of Karmö. Karmö lies just on the north side of the Bukken Fjord, and thus nearly opposite Stavanger; steamers, as we have said, pass just inside of it on their way from Stavanger to Bergen. Here there was a hard-fought battle. But Hakon gained the victory, and with his own hand slew one of the sons of Erik, Guthorm by name. The others took to flight, sailed out to sea, and returned to Jutland.

Gunhild's sons continued to make predatory expeditions, now against one part of the country and now against another. Sometimes they came in force sufficient to venture upon an attack on the fleet commanded by the king. We have already pointed out how the formation of the coasts and islands of Norway lend themselves to this sort of desultory warfare by sea, as the formation of the ridges and valleys of the kingdom lend themselves to the same kind of desultory warfare by land; and how difficult it is for the ruler of the country to force an inferior enemy to a decisive engagement. Hakon, however, held his own during a reign of six-and-twenty years. His nephews never abandoned their hopes and schemes. The unappeasable Gunhild took good heed that they should not do so.

There is, as we have said, some reason to believe that Gunhild, whom Norse traditions represent as a sorceress, brought up by the Finns, was really the sister of King Harald of Denmark, and that this accounts for the fact that Harald became foster-father to her son Harald. He generally assisted Gunhild's sons with troops and ships when they made their attacks upon Norway. And it would seem that when they finally attained the crown of Norway they ruled in a certain degree as vassals of the Danish king.

The second serious attempt was made in the twenty-first year of Hakon's reign. The king was then staying on the island of Frædö, near the more modern Christiansund, and had with him only his personal bodyguard and some of the neighbouring bonders, whom he had bidden to the house. News was brought that Erik's sons lay with a fleet just to the south of Stad, the most westerly point of the Norse mainland. Hakon sent round the war-token (a split arrow), and hastily collected a small force and fleet; then he set sail to meet the fleet of Erik's sons. The two fleets approached, and landed their men at two opposite sides of the promontory of Frædarberg, which lies at the entrance of the Sundal Fjord. Hakon had but nine ships' crews and Erik's sons had twenty. But the battle was won for the reigning king by a device of the Nestor of his army, a certain old soldier Egil, who had fought under Harald Fairhair. The device was one which any one familiar with the uneven character of the Norwegian ground will best appreciate. In the thickest of the fight the army of Erik's sons, turning round, saw advancing to near the crest of a low hill twelve standards which, from their spacing and alignment, clearly betokened the advance of another troop of the royalists. But in the direction of their advance they threatened to cut off the communication between the pretenders' troops and their ships. The nerves of these began to give way at the sight. They thought, at any rate, of the desirability of securing their base. But as they began to retire, Hakon's men pressed on more eagerly in front, and at last the retreat of the Erikssons' army became a flight. Too late one of the brothers now observed that, after all, those twelve standards never advanced above the ridge of the hill, and surmised the truth that had they done so, they would have displayed the fact that they were held by twelve men with due intervals between them: but that there was no other body of troops but these twelve men advancing to attack the sons of Erik.

In this engagement another of Erik's and Gunhild's sons fell. His name was Gamle Eriksson. The other brothers retired again to wait for a better chance.

At last came the opportunity, which always comes to those who can wait for it. The story of this final and successful effort of theirs and of Hakon's last battle is so well narrated by the Saga writer, that it is worth while to re-tell it—only abridging a little. Norway had been so much troubled by the continual raids of the pretenders, that Hakon had divided the whole country up into ship-districts, for the support of an adequate fleet and other things necessary for what we should call a system of national defence. He likewise caused beacons to be erected to flame out from headland to headland their alarm to the neighbourhood; and thus at last to all the country. The traveller in Norway may himself, on Midsummer Eve, or some other festival, have the opportunity of seeing the beacons which to-day are lit up on the 'Nesses' of the fjords; and this may give him some picture of Hakon's beacons flaring out their warning fires over the waters. But the worst of precautions of this kind is, that they are often abused. Many a time the petty raid of some obscure Viking was converted by terror into the advent of Erik's sons and their fleet, and the beacons were set on fire without due cause; so that Hakon had to enact severe penalties for the wanton lighting of the fires. The result was what might have been expected: 'wolf' had been cried too often; and when the real danger came there was no alarm.

Hakon was on the island called Stordö at the mouth of the Hardanger Fjord. The steamers from Stavanger to Bergen pass this island, as do those which sail from Bergen into the Hardanger. With its rounded shape and green niches the island is not distinguishable in character from its neighbours, but the traveller may well note it as he passes for the sake of this picture which comes to us from nine hundred years ago. King Hakon was staying at the house of a bonder, and had with him only the soldiers of his household—housecarles, as they were called—and the bonders from the neighbourhood. Just as the king sat down to table, the look-outs on the island observed what they took for a considerable fleet making for the spot; but the king had been so severe upon all who had given false alarms, that they were afraid to light the beacon, or even to warn the king. At last they sent for one of the king's men, who was likewise a famous skald and a favourite at Court; and he, seeing the seriousness of the danger, went to the house and roused his master.

'Thou art too brave a fellow, Eyvind,' said the king, 'to bring me false alarms.'

The king then left the hall, and went out to survey the approaching fleet. It was now too late to raise the country side; but there might yet be means of escape. Hakon held a council of war to decide whether this was the course which should be adopted.

'For it is easy to see that we must now fight against a much greater force than we have ever had arrayed against us before; though we thought the same the last time we fought against Gunhild's sons.'

While others hesitated to answer, Eyvind spoke a verse, advising that they should give battle and with no thought of the odds against them.

Hakon answered, 'Thy counsel is manly, Eyvind, and after my own heart; but I will wait to hear the opinion of others upon the matter.'

Then, as our saga-writer slily adds, 'as the king's men thought they saw in what direction the king leant, they replied that they would rather fight and fall like men than fly before the Danes, and that they had often gained a victory against greater odds than these.' So the king put on his armour, and girt at his side his famous sword—a present from the English King Athelstan—which was called 'quern-biter' because it would cut (if you like to believe it) to the heart of a mill-stone; and he drew up his men, house-carles and bonders and bonders' men, in a body, and set up his standard.

Erik's sons had a force six times as strong as that of Hakon. But the prowess of the king and of some of the men of his chosen bodyguard counted for much.

On both sides they fought bravely, and much blood was shed. The king had on a golden helmet which gleamed in the sunlight, and attracted many hostile darts. But it was said that he had thrown off his armour before the battle began. His henchman, Eyvind, put a cap over the golden helmet. Then one of the champions from the other side called out, 'Does the King of the Norsemen hide himself?' Hakon shouted back, 'Come on as ye are coming, and ye will find the King of the Norsemen;' and before long the man who had thus spoken fell before a blow from the king.

And now the Norse king went forward, cutting down all who stood before him. Then there flew an arrow, a three-edged dart, and entered the king's arm. He had gained the victory, and Erik's sons were in flight. But when the day was over, and Hakon bethought him of having his wound bound up, the blood flowed from it so fast, that it could not be stopped, and it soon appeared that the king's life was ebbing away. He commanded that they should place him in his boat and row him northward; for he hoped that he might reach a property of his which lay very near to the present town of Bergen. In these last hours, Hakon began to repent him that he had not been more zealous in spreading Christianity in Norway.

'If fate,' he said, 'should prolong my life, I intend, in any case, to leave the country and go to some Christian land, and do penance for my sins against God. But if I die in a heathen land, let them bury me as they think fit.'

Having no children of his own, Hakon left the succession to those life-long rivals of his, the sons of Erik.

But he never reached his homestead. When the rowers had reached the island of Askö (it lies just to the north of Bergen, and many people visit it by about one hour's steam from that town, for the sake of the fine view which may be had from its upper ridge of the islands and the fjords round about), the rowers put into the mainland, for the king was almost lifeless. Strange to say, they had reached a spot to which some forty, or two-and-forty, years before a girl, who had been a sort of servant of Harald Fairhair, and was with child by him, had been carried on her way to seek the father of her coming child in a farm where Harald was staying. Like Hakon now, this girl—Thora by name—was sailing northward; taken suddenly by the pangs of childbirth, she had been carried ashore to the very place to which Hakon was now carried. There, lifted from her boat, but lying only on the bare rock by the sea, she had given birth to her child, none other than this very Hakon, who had now come to suffer on the same spot, a death as untimely as his birth had been. (*Circ.* A.D. 961.)

Thus ended the long and prosperous reign of this king, whose name was preserved in tradition as Hakon the Good. 'During his reign,' says the Saga, 'the country had nearly always good harvests.'

It went very differently with Norway during the reigns of Hakon's successors, the children of the witch Gunhild. Not but that in many ways they seemed likely men enough. Many of the brothers had been slain during the years of contest with Hakon; and the eldest of them now, the ensuing king of Norway, was that Harald, who had been adopted as his foster-son by

Harald, the son of Gorm, king of Denmark. This Harald reigned as the chief among the brothers; but all had their share in the kingdom.

Norway only half submitted to their rule. They were not popular in either of the districts of Throndhjem or Vik; in consequence they generally made their home in the fjord district. They probably had relations with the Norsemen in the west, and hoped, in case of need, for support from the men of the Orkneys or the Shetlands. Soon Gunhild began to display those arts of a Brunehault or a Fredegonde, for which her name is handed down in Northern history. By her advice and assistance Harald compassed the removal of his more dangerous rivals. There were other descendants of Harald Fairhair down in the south. Harald and his brothers contrived the death of one of them after another. The most important of these minor kings in Viken district was one Tryggvi Olafsson, a grandson on the mother's side, of Harald Fairhair, second cousin, therefore, of Gunhild's sons. Gunhild contrived his death, and his widow, carrying the hope of Norway in her womb, had to flee away through unheard-of perils and sufferings till she reached Sweden. This, at least, is the legend, which we shall presently relate.

In the north, in Throndhjem district, the real power lay in the hands of Earl Sigurd of Lade, who had been a close friend of the late king, and was not, therefore, likely to be a *persona grata* to his successors. Gunhild's sons excited the jealousy of Sigurd's brother, Griotgaard, and engaged him in a plot against the life of the earl. Griotgaard sent word to the sons of Gunhild that his brother had gone very slenderly attended to a farm of his at Stordal, south of Molde. King Harald and his brother Erling came by night—by starlight, as the author tells us—and surrounded the house, and set fire to it, burning Earl Sigurd and all his men inside. This act of treachery was of no avail to Griotgaard, nor to the sons of Gunhild. For all the Throndhjem people rose to defend the rights of Sigurd's son, Hakon, a man, moreover, well able to defend himself; and after many years of struggle, Harald had to acknowledge him as the Earl of Lade, with all the powers which his father had possessed.

Harald, Erik's and Gunhild's son, is represented—despite his many acts of infamous treachery—as a proper man enough in himself, of a good presence, and a brave man of war. He had a good sense of humour too, and he got the nickname of Gráfeld, grey-skin, by which he is known in history in the following wise:—

While he was lying in one of the fjords there came there a trading ship from Iceland full of skins. Many people visited the vessel, but no one bought the skins. Harald was among the number of visitors, and the merchant complained to him that he could do no trade. 'Well,' said the king, 'will you give me one of your skins?' 'Willingly,' replied the other, 'as many as you please.' So the king chose out a grey skin, put it on immediately, and went in this guise from the ship. Before nightfall, everybody who had the money had bought a skin as much like the king's as could be, and the merchant sailed away next day well content.

Howbeit, an evil time for Norway followed the accession of Gunhild's sons. Earl Hakon, of the

Throndhjem district, though he had nominally made peace with the murderers of his father, knew that he could never consider himself secure, and eventually he escaped to the court of Harald, king of Denmark. All the causes of division, which made the weakness of the Scandinavian nations, had now begun to operate. In the previous century the Viking hordes, who came swarming over Europe, had seemed like different parts of one vast army of heathenism which was bent on the conquest of Christendom. Since then, the Scandinavian nationalities had united into three or four large states; but there was less unity between these separate states than there had been among different bands of Viking freebooters. Denmark was at war with Norway; Norway turned its arms against Sweden, against the Orkneys, or against Iceland. Wherefore, every discontented subject could find a refuge in one of the neighbouring states. About the same time, two of the subjects of Gunhild's sons sought in different guise protection at two of the Scandinavian courts. Earl Hakon came with a powerful fleet to Denmark, and was well received there. Astrid, the widow of King Tryggvi (so at least the story goes), with hardly a companion, but carrying her infant son, Olaf, known in history as Olaf Tryggvason, sought asylum in Sweden.

Earl Hakon was a man of cunning as well as of courage. His morality was the untinged heathen morality of an age that was passing away. He contrived, first of all, the treacherous slaughter of Harald Grey-fell by a Danish Harald, called Gold Harald, the half-brother of Harald, the king of Denmark, and directly after that, the no less treacherous slaughter of this Gold Harald by himself, with consent of the Danish king. The latter now proclaimed himself King of Norway as well as of Denmark. But he placed Earl Hakon under him, titularly as viceroy, but in reality as an almost independent regent of the country. Hakon was expected to pay 'scat' (scot—tribute) to Denmark. As a matter of fact he rarely fulfilled the obligation; but still, during his life, Norway could hardly consider itself more than an earldom tributary to the Danish crown.

CHAPTER VIII

HISTORY

Olaf Tryggvason (A.D. 995-1000)

'At the time that Gunhild's sons came to the kingship in Norway there ruled in Gardariki (Russian Sweden) a king called Valdemar,[1] whose wife was called Allogia. She was wise and beneficent, though still a heathen. King Valdemar had a mother who was so old and infirm that she lay always a-bed. But she was well skilled in spæ-dom. And it was always the custom that at Yule-time, when the guests assembled in the hall of the king, the king's mother was borne in thither and placed in the king's high seat. There she prophesied touching any danger overhanging the country or similar thing, according to the questions which were put to her.

'Now it happened one winter that when the king's mother had been borne in after this fashion, King Valdemar asked her whether any foreign prince or warrior would turn his arms against, or come to, his kingdom the following year. "I discern no token of any disastrous war, or other misfortune," she answered; "but one wonderful event I see. In the land of Norway there has been lately born a child who will be bred up here in Russia until he grows to be a famous

[1] Vladomir.

prince. He will do no hurt to this kingdom; on the contrary, he will in every way increase thy fame. He will return to his native land while he is still in the flower of his age, and will reign with great glory in this northern portion of the world; but not for long. Now carry me away."'

This passage brings before us the romantic personality of Olaf Tryggvason, about whom so many stories and myths lingered in the north. The passage comes from what is called the Longer Olafs-Saga, and is not to be found in the Heimskringla. But the longer and shorter Sagas alike tell the history of the flight of Astrid, Olaf's mother, across the border to Sweden, and of her attempt to make her way to the Greater Sweden (Gardariki), where she had a brother, Sigurd, in the service of its king, King Valdemar.[1]

But on the way they were captured by pirates; and the mother was separated from her son. Both were sold into slavery. Olaf, his foster-father Thorolf, and Thorgils, Thorolf's son, made one 'lot.' The purchaser, a farmer of Esthonia named Klærkon, thought that Thorolf was not worth his keep, so he killed him. The two boys he subsequently sold again to a man named Klærk; and Klærk sold Olaf to one named Reas, who gave a good cape in exchange for the Hope of Norway.

Olaf was six winters with Reas in Esthonia. One day there came a great man from the court of Novgorod to collect the king's dues from this part of the country. He saw a very handsome boy standing in the market-

---

[1] Valdemar's (Vladomir's) reign is given A.D. 970 to 977. He became a convert to Christianity, and is spoken of as the first Christian king of Novgorod. His successor was Jarisleif (Yaroslav), called the Legislator.

place, and asked him his name and parentage. The boy was Olaf, and the king's agent was Olaf's Uncle Sigurd. As soon as he learnt Olaf's parentage he bought him and carried him away, but did not tell Olaf that he was his uncle. Not long after this the young Olaf, who could not have been more than seven or eight, saw in the market-place of Novgorod his first owner, Klærkon, the same who had killed his foster-father Thorolf. Olaf went up to Klærkon, and, having a small child's axe in his hand, struck Klærkon with it such a blow that the iron entered into his brain and he fell down dead. Sigurd, in order to save the boy from the penalty for his act, carried him off to the Queen Allogia; and she readily promised her protection to the handsome child.

About this time Olaf was again the subject of prophecy among the wise men in Russia.

'At the time when Olaf came to Gardariki there were in Holmgard[1] many people who could foretell the future. Their second sight told them that there had come to the country the "genius"[2] of an outland man,[3] one so highly gifted that there had never before been seen such a noble Fylgja. They had no idea where the man was; though they declared that the light which shone from him sent a reflex over all Gardariki, and round about over the eastern side of the earth. Queen Allogia herself, who was in some sort a

[1] Novgorod.
[2] Fylgja, a sort of double, which at the same time had, so to say, a more direct communication than the ordinary body with the spiritual world, and passed on its knowledge to the man himself. It might be likened to the Astral Body of the Theosophists. It is not accurate to speak of the Fylgjar as guardian angels; though under the influence of Christian ideas they came to be regarded as much the same thing.
[3] Foreigner.

spæ-woman, perceived the very first time she saw Olaf that the boy was destined to the highest fortunes, and that he would be a glory to that country. This was the reason why the boy was held in such high esteem by both the king and queen.'

The Saga here goes on, quite opposed to historic truth, to represent Olaf as already a Christian, and refusing to accompany the king into the heathen temples. 'I pray you,' says King Valdemar, 'to do all in your power to show honour to the gods and to pacify them; otherwise I fear they will make you feel their might.' 'I shall never fear the gods whom you serve,' said Olaf. 'For there is no saying that they have either sight or hearing, understanding, or anything else. And of what nature they are, I can best judge by this, that you, my king and foster-father, at all other times have been in my eyes a mild and beaming (supernaturally shining) countenance, save only when you have been to sacrifice in the temples. Then, when you come out, you have ever a dark and forbidding aspect.'

Such are some of the myths which gathered about this famous name.

The era upon which we have now entered is the most heroic age in the history of Norway; nay, in many respects, the most heroic in the history of the whole Scandinavian world. For Norway it includes the reigns of Olaf Tryggvason and of Olaf the Saint; but, unfortunately, likewise a humiliating interval during which this country was only a fief of Denmark. For Denmark it includes the great reigns of Svend (Sweyn) and Cnut (Canute), and, as the reader does not need to be reminded, the complete subjugation of our country by Denmark, the greatest achievement which lies to the credit of any Scandinavian power. For Sweden it includes the reign of a victorious King Erik, but also that of Olaf, known as *Skatt-Konung*, or Olaf the Tribute King: the only king of Sweden who as yet had been tributary to the Danes. To the same era belonged in Greater Suithiod or Gardariki (Scandinavian Russia) the reign of the first Christian king, Valdemar (Vladomir), and of Jarisleif (Yaroslav), his successor, the lawgiver. In the Orkney Islands, too, it nearly corresponds to a very great period, the reigns of the two celebrated earls, at first joint rulers, afterwards rivals, Rögnvald and Thorfinn. It is the era of the conversion of Iceland and of the Orkneys, so that the two extremities, Russia and Iceland, were, like the intermediate country Norway, converted during this period. For Iceland it is the end of what we may call the period of settlement, the beginning of the Saga Age.

We may say, indeed, that the chief growth of Norse literature belongs to this age. It is just to about the end of the tenth and the beginning of the eleventh century that we may refer the development of the Edda poetry in Celtic Scandinavia, as we may call it; and parallel with that, or a little later, the growth of the Saga prose in Iceland.

But this is likewise the age in which the mutual jealousies and mutual hostilities of the different Scandinavian nations begin to be most accentuated. The ambition of Denmark for the conquest of Norway and of Sweden; the attempts of Norway to dictate to the people of Iceland, and to obtain possession of the Orkneys by taking the part of one earl against his rival;

the efforts of the Orkney earls to extend their sway over the Hebrides, and Man, and Dublin.

In the account which the Saga gives us of the accession of Svend (Sweyn), king of Denmark, the father of our Canute, we have a curious picture of the way in which the different Scandinavian states of Greater Scandinavia were connected by ties both of friendship and hostility. King Sweyn bade to his succession-feast (*arvöl*, heirship-ale, is the technical name for such a feast), not only the chiefs of his own dominions, but some of the leaders of the republic of the Joms Vikings, who had their seat in Mecklenburg, somewhere near the modern Stettin. At these feasts, when men had well drunk, they had the custom of pledging each other in what was called a Bragi-cup, and over this cup they took oaths of what they would accomplish afterwards. It need not be said that they often regretted their rash vows[1] when next morning brought reflection. On this occasion Svend, over the Bragi-cup, swore that he would hunt King Æthelred out of England; a threat which, as we know, he fulfilled. Earl Sigvald, the chief of the Jomsburgers, swore for his part that before three years were over he would either kill Earl Hakon of Norway or chase him out of the country.

Olaf Tryggvason, on his side, had been in company with Svend, and was harrying round the English coast. He allied himself, moreover, with some of the chief Scandinavian settlers in the British Isles. He is said to have

---

[1] This Bragi-cup is a relic of the old custom which Tacitus notes among the Germans of his day (*Germ.* 22), of deciding on matters when drunk, but reserving the details of carrying out the decision till they were sober. The same custom prevailed among the ancient Persians.

married at this time Gyda, the sister of the Norse king of Dublin, Olaf Quaran. At first Olaf Tryggvason plundered wherever he could the territory of the Christians, and passed south to the Scillies; and at this time a curious circumstance led to his conversion to Christianity.

News was brought to him of a certain hermit, a Christian, who had wonderful knowledge of the future. Olaf, to try him, dressed up one of his men, the handsomest and stoutest among his bodyguard, and told him to go to the hermit and represent himself as King Olaf, for, says the Saga-writer, King Olaf was known in all countries as handsomer, stronger, and braver than other men. But the holy man was not deceived. 'Thou art not the king,' he said, 'but I advise thee to remain faithful to thy king.' After this proof of the seer's knowledge, Olaf himself consulted him; and the hermit admonished the Norse king to abandon his heathen faith, at the same time giving a further proof of his inspiration by foretelling an event which happened a few days later.

The same story is told of Totila, the Goth, who visited St. Benedict on Monte Cassino; therefore it may be apocryphal here. But what is certain is that Olaf Tryggvason became a much more zealous Christian than any of the preceding rulers in Norway. Hakon the Good had been a Christian, and had made some attempt at the conversion of Norway. The sons of Gunhild even were nominally Christians, though their faith was of a very lukewarm sort. Olaf's was of a very different description. His proceedings, if the accounts in the Saga are to be believed, were sometimes as high-handed as Charlemagne's in the conversion of the heathen Germans.

At the present moment Norway had a ruler who was more genuinely attached to Odin-worship than any which the country had possessed for some time. Earl Hakon, as we saw, had got his rule (his kingdom as it really was) by bringing about the slaughter of Harold Greyfell at the hands of the brother of the King of Denmark, and then, by previous connivance with that king, falling upon and slaying the victor. From this time Hakon was the virtual ruler of all Norway. But he was at the same time the nominal tributary of the king of Denmark, Harald Blátand. In the year 965 Otto the First, the German Emperor, made an attack upon Denmark, and, having defeated Harald, the king compelled him to accept baptism. Oddly enough King Harald seems to have become at once a zealous convert to the new faith. Or else he felt like the fox in the fable who had lost his tail, and could not bear, since he had been compelled to undergo baptism, that his vassal, Hakon, should escape the same indignity. For he summoned Hakon to him, while he held his court in Zealand, and tried all he could to make the earl change his creed. The Norseman absolutely refused to do this, and went the length of shaking off all allegiance to Harald. He carried his fleet away, and set to work to plunder the dominions of his former lord. King Harald of Denmark retaliated by bringing a fleet to the Sulen Isles, at the mouth of Sogne Fjord. Thence he went right into the fjord. Only five houses, says the Saga, were left standing in Lærdal. The people fled far inland up that beautiful valley past Husum and Borgund to hide themselves among the hills.

The Vik part—the southern part—of Norway seems to have adhered to its allegiance to the Danish crown; so that Hakon henceforward ruled only over the country of the east coast—that is to say, over his ancient earldom of Throndhjem, and all the coast downwards to the southernmost angle of the kingdom, the entrance to the Skagerrak; sixteen districts in all. Other small kings reigned in the Vik country, and in the country immediately behind it; they reigned as vassals of the Danish king. Hakon's portion of Norway became once more totally independent, and Hakon, in fact, though not in name, a king.

This change had taken place some time ago, for, as we have seen, Harald had died, and Sweyn, his son, succeeded to the crown of Denmark. Now there hung over Hakon—though as yet he knew nothing of it—that threatened attack of the Joms-vikings. The day after the feast Sigvald and his comrades—though, as our Saga-writer says, they thought that they had spoken more than enough the night before—set to work at once on the preparations for their expedition. The first news of these preparations came to Earl Erik, Hakon's son. He at once set to work to collect as many troops as possible in the inner districts, and then marched north to join his father at Throndhjem. Hakon and Erik sent along all the coast districts the famous wartoken, the split arrow; they collected all the ships they could from the Throndhjem Fjord; then they rowed out, going round the coast from fjord to fjord, beating up troops, and adding to their fleet. Meanwhile the Joms-

M

vikings were sailing northward along the same western coast, plundering and burning wherever they came.

Those who are familiar with the Norwegian coast, and know how all along it headlands and rocky islands succeed each other in bewildering confusion, will appreciate this picture of the two fleets approaching each other, and yet each having no idea of the other's whereabouts. The place where they did at last meet, the scene of the battle which the Saga describes so vividly, is the Jörund Fjord, in South Möre, perhaps the finest of the Norwegian fjords. The steamers from Hellesylt to Aalesund pass the mouth of it.

As might be imagined, the Norse leaders were best served by their spies and look-outs. One man came in a swift-rowing vessel north to the earls, and told them of the approaching danger, showing the stump where his hand had been cut off as a proof that he had met the Jomsburgers. The Norse peasants, on the other hand, would give no information to the Vikings. At last one old man, seeing them driving down cattle and captives, asked Sigvald and his comrades why they attacked cattle instead of surprising the bear himself in his lair, assuring them that Hakon was close to with only a few ships. In reality Hakon and Erik were hard by, with a hundred and eighty ships in all.

The Joms-vikings had just one-third that number, but when the battle was joined they fought with desperate courage. There are some strange and picturesque details of this battle and its sequel given us in the Saga. One of the Joms chiefs, Bui by name, who had fought all day, and cleared more than one ship of the Norsemen, found himself at last overpowered.

So he seized two chests of gold which lay in his ship, and shouting, 'overboard all Bui's men,' plunged into the water, and, of course, instantly sank to the bottom with his treasure. Most of his men followed his example, and plunged in after the Joms-vikings' leader. Earl Sigvald, however, fled with rather more than half the fleet. The crews of all the rest were killed or taken captive.

Then we have a picture of a number of the prisoners sitting in a row upon a fallen tree, all bound together as to the feet, but with their hands free; and a certain Thorkel Leire, who had a special motive for revenge against these heroes of the Bragi-cup, going along the row smiting off one head after another. One of them said, 'I will stick this fish-bone that I have in my hand into the earth, if it be so that I know anything after my head is cut off.' His head was cut off, but the fish-bone fell from his hand. Another man, Sigurd, the son of Bui, the hero of the gold chests, who was remarkable for his long and beautiful hair, called out, 'I fear not death; but let no slave touch my hair nor let blood defile it.' So one of the Norse men-at-arms stepped forward to hold up his hair while he was being beheaded. But Sigurd contrived by a sudden twist to bring the man's hands in the way of the axe, so that they, and not his head, were cut off. This trick so delighted Earl Erik, the son of Hakon, that he ordered Sigurd's release, and eventually that of the Jomsburgers who remained alive; and he took them all into his service. His father, Hakon, was, however, much displeased at this proceeding.

News came to Hakon of the doings of that

distinguished man who had gone out to the west, and who at present went among men's mouths by the name of Ole simply. Hakon suspected the truth, that Ole was no other than Olaf Tryggvason; so he sent one of his henchmen to Dublin, where Olaf was then living, to entice the stranger over to Norway. The man fulfilled his mission; but when Olaf Tryggvason did arrive in his native land he found that Hakon had been hunted from the throne by his enraged subjects. For he had, during these later years, given the rein to his unbridled passions. The bonders of Throndhjem, exasperated by a wanton outrage done to one of their number, rose in a mass; and the earl, to escape their fury, had to hide himself in a pit dug beneath a pig-sty, along with a single companion, a thrall named Kark, who he thought was devoted to him; for this Kark had been born on the same day as Hakon, and had been his thrall almost from birth. But Hakon began to suspect Kark, and for a night or two Hakon and the man kept watch upon each other, neither daring to go to sleep. At last Hakon slept, but he dreamed so ill that he drew his legs under him, and raised his head in his sleep, and screamed violently, so that Kark, in terror lest they should be discovered, took out his knife and cut his master's throat. Afterwards he severed the head and bore it to Olaf Tryggvason, the new King of Norway, hoping for a reward. Olaf had him executed.

Thus comes on the theatre of authentic history the great hero of Norwegian history, Olaf Tryggvason, of whose early adventures (fabulous for the most part) we have already spoken. Of Olaf Tryggvason's early years we actually know little more than that he was a Norseman who, for a long time, had a close connection with the Western Islands. There were several Olafs kings of Ireland. One of them, Olaf Quaran by name, was said to have been the brother-in-law of our Olaf. Christianity had taken a pretty firm hold upon the Norsemen of the west by this time. The first Christian Scandinavian king in England had been the Guthorm, of the baptism at Wedmore, the rival of Alfred, who had been converted 130 years earlier.

There had been a Christian king in Northumbria before the end of the ninth century. We know that though the Orkney earls had not yet become Christians, Erik's sons had taken up the new faith while in the West. There was nothing strange, therefore, in this Olaf from the West being a Christian of a sort. But Olaf Tryggvason is distinguished from his contemporaries by the zeal with which he adhered to the new faith.

He is a romantic figure. Tall, strong, and handsome beyond all Norsemen of his day, with the kingly attribute of beautiful fair hair, which was supposed to prove him to be of the genuine Yngling race; he became celebrated among the Scandinavian nations long before he was called to become a candidate for the Norwegian throne. Not only was he a mighty and approved man of war, but he was superior to all men in those athletic exercises—swimming, climbing, running, skating, or 'ske-ing,'—running on snow-shoes—and spear-throwing, in which the Norsemen took such delight. He is said to have scaled the precipitous Hornelen, and placed his shield upon the summit.

Olaf came into Norway with the fixed determination

to convert the country, definitely and finally, from the old faith—from what we may call the discredited Odin-worship of its old days. The licentious character of the last earl and his miserable end might serve as warnings against adherence to Odin-worship. 'No other name,' says the Saga, 'was allowed to Earl Hakon but Hakon the Bad;' 'and yet,' adds the liberal Snorri, 'he was in many ways fitted to be a leader: first, because he was born of a good stock; next, because he had the wisdom and understanding to govern; and he was a brave man of war, and very fortunate in killing his enemies.' But the same writer goes on to say: 'The misfortunes of his later days came upon him because the Odin religion was doomed.' People could no longer tolerate the licence which an old heathen like Hakon allowed himself.

We find all through in reading these Sagas how entirely conversion to a new creed takes its analogy from the act of taking service with a new commander. Once the king or the subject has allowed himself to be baptized, he has practically taken an oath of fealty to Christ, and he is bound to take part against the enemies of his new creed. We saw how Harald of Denmark, though he only accepted baptism under compulsion in the first instance, became zealous to put the yoke of the new faith on others.

Olaf, therefore, knew that he might proceed with the conversion of large batches of men. Let him persuade the chiefs and their followers of one district, or the people thereof assembled in the Thing, to follow him in his change of faith, and he at once obtained zealous adherents thereto, not indifferent converts only; and if he should proceed to the same ends by force (as the Emperor Otto had done with Harald Bluetooth), he would still swell the army of believers.

He began by calling into council his own relations. He would carry it so far, he told them, that all Norway should become Christian, or he would die in the attempt. And he promised to make these relatives of his, who were great men in the Viken country, the foremost in the promotion of the work, and great and mighty men in Norway if they would aid him. This they consented to do, and the result was that Viken—which we have said may have already received some seeds of Christianity, while it alone of Norway acknowledged the suzerainty of Harald of Denmark—accepted the new creed, as it had accepted the new ruler, without demur.

But it did not always go so smoothly for Olaf. It was not so easy to persuade the peasants of other districts assembled at their Things. The first meeting at which Olaf sought to propagate his views took place at a Thing held in Rogaland (in what is now Stavangeramt). The king spoke first, and, as the Saga says, good-humouredly to the people. For all that he let them see plainly enough before he had done that he was bent on their accepting Christianity, and that whoever refused to do so might expect his heavy displeasure.

Now, before the Thing assembled, the bonders had selected three of the best speakers of their number, who were charged to answer whatever the king might say. Olaf Tryggvason was as well known for a ready and clever speaker as for a famous wielder of arms; and the bonders were anxious to find spokesmen who should state their case to the best advantage. But when the first of the three spokesmen got up he was seized with such a cough and such a difficulty of breathing that he could not bring out a word. The second one got up; but he became so confused that he could not find a word to say, and had to sit down again. Then the third tried; but he again was so hoarse that though he spoke no one could hear what he said. And as after that no one could be found to take up their case, the bonders could make no further objection, but received baptism as King Olaf desired. Such is the story which the saga tells, a story handed down probably by some of the Christian priests.

This was but a beginning. Of far more importance was it to get the assent of the Gula Thing, the great Thing for the fjord district. At that Olaf was met by a curious counter-proposal from some of the chief men of the country: If the king would promote one of their number, a certain Hersi Erling, by marrying him to Olaf's sister Astrid, they would do what he wished in the matter of a change of faith; and this arrangement was carried out. This Erling Skjalgsson became one of the most powerful men in Norway during the reign of Olaf Tryggvason, during the interregnum which followed it, and during a great portion of the reign of Olaf the Saint.

At the Thing held in the Throndhjem country the bonders were more difficult to persuade. They remembered how Hakon the Good had tried to convert their forefathers, but had ended by being obliged himself to assist at the sacrifices to Thor and Odin. And they summoned Olaf to meet them at Mæra and do the same thing there. This Mæra lay up the Throndhjem Fjord very near to the present village of that name. Times were, however, changed since the days of Hakon. The heathen party was not so strong as it fancied itself, and it had a stronger and a most cunning antagonist. Olaf made a great feast at Lade (a place of which we have often had to speak[1]), and invited all the *hersar* and principal bonders thereto. They ate and drank well. But Olaf had stationed a sufficient bodyguard of his trusty men-at-arms about the house. The next morning the Thing was summoned. Olaf spoke to the people and reminded them how he on his side had invited them to come and be baptized; while they for their part had bade him meet them and make sacrifice to their gods. 'Now if I,' said Olaf, 'with you will turn again to making sacrifices, then will I make the greatest of sacrifices that are in use; I will sacrifice men. But I will not select slaves nor malefactors for this, but I will take the greatest men only to offer to the gods. And for this I select Orm Lygra of Medalhouse, Styrcar of Gimsum, Kaar of Gryting, Asbjörn Thorgbergsson of Varness, Orm of Lyxa, Haldor of Skirdingstead, and five more of the principal men beside.' It need not be said that the chiefs who were in Olaf's power showed no willingness to press him to carry out the sacrifice, but on the contrary, accepted baptism; and a peace was made.

These stories show us the various means which the king adopted for the conversion of his subjects. The heathen powers earthly and spiritual did what they could. We have one account how Olaf was bewitched

---

[1] Lade is the first station on the Throndhjem-Storlien railway into Sweden.

in the Salten Fjord in Halogaland (Nordland)—it lies about opposite the southern end of the Lofotens—when he sought to carry the new faith into those far northern countries. There are, on the other hand, accounts of excessive cruelties practised by Olaf upon individuals who resisted all gentler persuasion. But we may believe that these stories are not authentic.

It is certain, however, that Olaf proceeded in a sufficiently high-handed fashion. Not content with the conversion of Norway, he accomplished that of the Orkneys and Shetlands and of the Faroes. Finally, he looked to Iceland, and sent thither a strange sort of missionary, one Thangbrand, a Saxon priest, 'a passionate, headstrong man, and a great man-slayer.' Thangbrand came to Iceland, and obtained the countenance and assistance of one of the leading men of the country called Hall of Side. Njal, too, the hero of the Njals Saga, accepted baptism, as did many others. There is a curious account of the proceedings of Thangbrand and his companion Gudleif in the Njals Saga. The two missionaries seem to have challenged every man who would not accept the new faith; and the slaying of one of the great chiefs of the country was taken very ill by his kin at the Thing assembled. Hall, however, and Njal stood by Thangbrand. If it was a woman whom he encountered, a 'sorceress,' *i.e.* a spaewife of the old heathen kind, Thangbrand tried with her a battle of words.

'Hast thou heard,' said one of these, 'how Thor challenged Christ to single combat, and how he did not dare to fight with Thor?'

'I have heard tell,' said Thangbrand, 'that Thor was

nought but dust and ashes, if God had not willed that he should live.'

It was, however, Olaf's fascinating personality which did more than anything else for the spread of his opinions. Of his feats of strength and daring the Saga is full. We have already referred to the story of his ascent of the inaccessible Hornélen on Bremanger Island, at the entrance to the Nord Fjord, which travellers are always bidden to look out for on the route by steamer from Bergen to Molde. Of the way that Olaf dealt with men we have charming examples in the two following anecdotes.

Kjartan Olafsson, a son's son of Höskuld, and a daughter's son of Egil Skalagrimsson, came one autumn from Iceland to Nidaros (Throndhjem). He was considered to be the most agreeable and hopeful man of any born in Iceland. There was also Haldor, a son of Gudmund of Mödrovald, and Kolbein, a son of Thord, Frey's-priest, and a brother's son of Brennuflosi, together with Swerting, a son of the Brennuflosi Runolf. All these were heathens; and besides them there were many more,—some men of power, others common men of no property. There came also from Iceland considerable people, who, by Thangbrand's help, had been made Christians; namely, Gissur White, a son of Teit Ketilbjörnsson; and his mother was Alof, daughter of Hersi Bödvar who was the Viking Kare's son. Bödvar's brother was Sigurd, father of Eric Bjódaskalli, whose daughter, Astrid, was King Olaf's mother. Hjalti Skeggjason was the name of another Iceland man, who was married to Vilborga, Gissur White's daughter. Hjalti was also a Christian; and King Olaf was very friendly to his relations Gissur and Hjalti, who lived with him. But the Iceland men who directed the ships, and were heathens, tried to sail away as soon as the king came to the town of Nidaros, for they were told the king forced all men to become Christians; but the wind came stiff against them, and drove them back to Nidarholm. They who directed the ships were Thorarin Nefjulsson, the skald Halfred Ottarsson, Brand the Generous, and Thorleik, Brand's son. It was told the king that there were Icelanders with ships there, and all were heathens, and wanted to fly from a meeting with the king. Then the king sent them a message forbidding them to sail, and ordering them to bring their ships up to the town, which they did, but without discharging the cargoes. They carried on their dealings, and held a market at the king's pier. It happened one fine day that many set out to swim for amusement, and among them was a man who distinguished himself above the others in all bodily exercises. Kjartan challenged Halfred Ottarsson to try himself in swimming against this man, but he declined it.

'Then will I make a trial,' said Kjartan, casting off his clothes, and springing into the water. Then he sets after the man, seizes hold of his foot, and dives with him under water. They come up again, and without speaking a word dive again, and are much longer under water than the first time. They come up again, and without a saying a word dive a third time; until Kjartan thought it was time to come up again, which, however, he could in no way accomplish, which showed sufficiently the difference in their strength. They were under water so long that Kjartan was almost drowned.

They then came up, and swam to land. This Norseman asked what the Icelander's name was. Kjartan tells his name.

He says: 'Thou art a good swimmer; but art thou expert also in other exercises?'

Kjartan replied that such expertness was of no great value.

The Norseman asks: 'Why dost thou not inquire of me such things as I have asked thee about?'

Kjartan replies: 'It is all one to me who thou art, or what thy name is.'

'Then will I,' says he, 'tell thee: I am Olaf Tryggvason.'

He asked Kjartan much about Iceland, which he answered generally, and wanted to withdraw as hastily as he could; but the king said: 'Here is a cloak which I will give thee, Kjartan,' and Kjartan took the cloak with many thanks.

When Michaelmas came the king had high mass sung with great splendour. The Icelanders went there, and listened to the fine singing and the sound of the bells; and when they came back to their ships every man told his opinion of the Christian men's worship. Kjartan expressed his pleasure at it, but most of the others scoffed at it; and it went according to the proverb, 'the king has many ears,' for this was told to the king. He sent immediately—that very day—a message to Kjartan to come to him. Kjartan went to the king with some men, and the king received him kindly. Kjartan was a very stout and handsome man, and of ready and agreeable speech. After the king and Kjartan had conversed a little, the king asked him to adopt Christianity. Kjartan replies that he would not say no to that if he thereby obtained the king's friendship; and as the king promised him the fullest friendship, they were soon agreed. The next day Kjartan was baptized, together with his relation Bolli Thorlaksson, and all their fellow-travellers. Kjartan and Bolli were the king's guests as long as they were in their white baptismal clothes, and the king had much kindness for them. Wherever they came they were looked upon as people of distinction.

As King Olaf one day was walking in the street some men met him, and he who went the foremost saluted the king. The king asked the man his name, and he called himself Halfred (Ottarsson).

'Art thou the skald?' said the king.

'I can compose poetry,' replied he.

'Wilt thou then adopt Christianity, and come into my service?' asked the king.

'If I am baptized,' replies he, 'it must be on one condition: that thou thyself stand my godfather; for no other will I have.'

The king replies: 'That I will do;' and Halfred was baptized, the king holding him during the baptism.

Afterwards the king said: 'Wilt thou enter into my service?'

Halfred replied: 'I was formerly at Earl Hakon's court; but now I will neither enter into thine nor into any other service, unless thou promise me it shall never be my lot to be driven away from thee.'

'It has been reported to me,' said the king, 'that thou art neither so prudent nor so obedient as to fulfil my commands.'

'In that case,' replied Halfred, 'put me to death.'

'Thou art a skald who makes difficulties,' says the king; 'but into my service, Halfred, thou shalt be received.'

Halfred says: 'If I am to be named the maker of difficulties,[1] what dost thou give me, king, on my name-day?'

The king gave him a sword without a scabbard, and said: 'Now, compose me a song upon this sword, and let the word sword be in every (half-) line of the verses.'

Halfred sang thus :—

> One sword of swords is there that sword-rich maketh me;
> Among swift sword-bearers there shall now be sword-bounty.
> No lack of swords now; of three swords am I worthy;
> Well were it were there likewise a sword-sheath to my sword.

Then the king gave him the scabbard, observing that the word sword was wanting in one (half-) line of his strophe. 'But there are three swords at least in one line,' says Halfred. 'So it is,' replies the King. 'Out of Halfred's lay,' says the narrator, 'we have taken the most of the true and faithful accounts that are here related about Olaf Tryggvason.'

This introduction of Christianity into Norway ends the first and most prosperous half of Olaf's reign. Along with this change of faith came other changes, which in the history of Europe generally so often accompanied it. Norway takes steps towards the increase of its foreign trade. We have already said that the Norse Vikings of the previous century were great trading men as well as warriors; so were their descendants, the colonisers of Iceland. Norway may

---

[1] Vandrædaskald—'The troublesome poet.'

have remained less active and adventurous in the century which followed, having too much to occupy her in internal affairs. But now Olaf, who we say had come from the west, the country not only of Christian Scandinavians, but of Scandinavian merchants, set to work to found a 'merchant's town' in his own kingdom. This was the origin of Throndhjem, almost the earliest of the towns in Norway. The name of the town which Olaf built and its name for long afterwards was not Throndhjem but Nidaros Nidar-mouth, as it lay at the mouth of the Nidar. It was, too, very generally called 'the merchants' town'—Kaupstad or Kaupmannaborg, a name almost equivalent to Copenhagen (Kjöbenhavn).

Another of Olaf's activities was in the building of ships of war, of which he possessed the finest that were known in those days. One called the *Serpent* was considered the chief of all ships of war, until Olaf built a finer vessel still, which he called the *Long Serpent*, so that the old *Serpent* became the *Short Serpent*. The *Long Serpent* was built on the Throndhjem Fjord at Ladehammer.

Hakon had left a strenuous son, Erik, behind him, who was not likely to submit for ever to being dispossessed of his father's rule. Erik went first to Sweden. He spent a year in Viking cruises in the Baltic. After that he went to Denmark, and married the daughter of the king, Svend, the father of our Cnut. Almost at the same time King Svend, whose first wife had just died, married the Swedish queen-mother, Sigrid, called 'the haughty.' Now, it happens that a few years before Olaf Tryggvason had been a suitor for this queen's hand. She was not young; but an alliance with her might have ended in a union of Sweden and Norway: then Olaf would have been strong enough to defy the power of Denmark. But Queen Sigrid refused to accept Olaf's new religion; and Olaf, who, as we have seen, was something of a fanatic, was so enraged with her for her obstinacy that he raised his hand and struck her in the face with his glove, saying: 'Why should I marry thee, a heathen jade?' The Queen answered: 'This blow may some day be thy death.' And the truth of her words was now about to be proved.

There soon arose an occasion of enmity between the kings of Denmark and Norway. Svend had disposed of his sister Thyri to a Slav king of Vendland (*i.e.* somewhere about Mecklenburg or Pomerania); Burislaf was his name, and he was a heathen. Thyri was so grieved at being sent among heathens that she would neither eat nor drink among them. After seven days, by the aid of her foster-father, she stole away, hid herself in a wood, and eventually effected her flight out of the country. She took ship and came to Norway, to Nidaros, where King Olaf was. Eventually a marriage was brought about between Olaf and Thyri.

There was now a queen at either court bent on stirring up strife between the two kings. Thyri claimed all the dower which Svend had paid over to Burislaf. She taunted Olaf that he dared not go to the Danish dominions for fear of Svend. Olaf replied with a loud oath: 'Never did I fear thy brother Svend, and if we meet he shall give way before me.' Sigrid, too, was busy in trying to excite the enmity of her husband against Olaf. However, in the matter of Thyri's portion,

Olaf's business was rather with Burislaf, the Wend, Thyri's late husband, than with her brother; for to the former the queen's dowry had been paid. In the summer of the year 1000—a memorable year in Norse history—Olaf Tryggvason set sail for Burislaf's dominions, which, as we have said, lay about the mouth of the Oder. The negotiations were conducted in a most friendly manner. Olaf was too great and too fascinating a personality not to excite the admiration of any generous mind, unless warped by some personal enmity or interest.

But still his greatness was a menace to lesser men, to the rulers, or would-be rulers, of the other Scandinavian communities of the Baltic. Of the men in this position there were four, and they had by this time entered into a league against the Norse king. At the head of the league stood the King of Denmark, the Svend of whom we have often spoken. With him went Olaf, king of Sweden, a man of small worth, and Earl Erik, the strenuous son of Hakon, bound not only by his ambition to recover the territory of his forefathers, the Earls of Lade, but by his blood to avenge the death of his father, on whose head Olaf had set a price.

Joined with these three—joined by common interest to resist the over-mastering greatness of the King of Norway—was one whom Olaf had no reason to distrust: Earl Sigvald, the head of the Joms-vikings. The Joms-vikings had preserved the same dauntless valour which they showed when they fought against Earl Hakon, and when Bui and his men jumped overboard to escape capture. Olaf held Sigvald in high respect, and he had no reason to believe but that the other felt as cordially towards him. In reality, however, the earl was in the secrets of the three leaguers, and had been deputed by them to worm himself into the confidence of the Norse king, in order to lead him to his destruction. Jomsborg, the seat of that little republic of Scandinavians on the German coast, of which Sigvald may be called the president, lay almost within the territory of Burislaf. Sigvald was the brother-in-law of this king; and when Olaf sailed to the mouth of the Oder the Viking chief met him there and accompanied him to the court of Burislaf.

Meantime Svend had been doing his best to collect the fleets of his allies; and it was Sigvald's business to detain Olaf as long as possible in order that they might be more ready to strike at him as he sailed homewards. The crew of the Norse fleet could not understand the delay, as they waited with their ships bound for the voyage, and ready for the first favourable gales; but still the order to sail never came. At length Sigvald got news that the leaguers were ready and waiting in a harbour in the Isle of Rügen. Then he made no further difficulties. He offered to accompany King Olaf on his homeward voyage; and it was reckoned in those days no small thing to secure the consort of a Jomsviking fleet.

Olaf had sixty sail and Sigvald eleven; and it may safely be said that this fleet of seventy-one sail, comprising as it did ships like the *Long Serpent*, the *Short Serpent*, and the *Crane*, and several others, of a size and weight quite unusual for those days, would, unless there had been treachery at work, have been a match for any fleet which could have been brought against it.

But Sigvald's treachery decided the fate of the Norse king.

The exact details of the famous battle which now took place are rather difficult to recover. We may believe that the fleet of the allies had stationed itself on the western side of the island of Rügen, where it would be well concealed from any wanderers of Olaf's fleet which had come to the Oder, no doubt by the east of the island. The Kubitzerbodden would be a suitable place for them to lie in. But it is possible that they were in a harbour of the mainland, say the Prohner Wick. Olaf, on his side, directed his course along the narrow channel between Rügen and the mainland which is called Der straler Sund (from which Stralsund gets its name). Sigvald pretended that as Olaf's ships were of unusual size they were in danger of running aground, and that it would be best for him who knew the channel well to go first with his fleet. They navigated the channel safely enough; although a race sometimes runs through this part which is called the Vierendehler Strom, and which the Norsemen of this expedition knew by the name of Svold.

To the surprise of the foremost ships of the Norse fleet, as soon as Sigvald's vessels passed a certain point of land they turned round into the bay instead of continuing their course. The Norsemen followed; but they called out to Sigvald to ask why he sailed that way. The earl answered that he was waiting for King Olaf, as he feared there were enemies in the way. All lay upon their oars; and presently were seen the three great ships of Olaf's fleet, first the *Crane*, then the *Short Serpent*, with Thorkel Nefia at the helm, and finally

the *Long Serpent*, which Olaf steered. The fleet of the
allies was lying within the bay, just out of sight; and
Earl Erik and the two kings had mounted the hill
behind, where they could watch unseen the vessels
sailing up the sound. We can see with their eyes the
imposing spectacle of this fleet of seventy-one sail
passing, one vessel after another, along the channel.
Presently they saw an unusually large ship, brilliantly
painted, and the two kings said: 'That is a very large
and beautiful vessel; that will be the *Long Serpent*.'
Earl Erik replied: 'That is not the *Long Serpent*,' and
he was right, for it was a ship of Eindridi's of Grimsar.

Soon after they saw another vessel come sailing
along much larger than the first; but it had not the
dragon head, the famous figure-head of the *Long Serpent*.
Then says King Svend: 'Olaf Tryggvason must be
afraid; for he does not venture to sail with the figure-
head of the dragon on his ship.'

Says Earl Erik: 'That is not the king's ship yet; for
I know that ship by the coloured strips of cloth in her
sail. That is Erling Skalgsson's.'

Presently they saw three ships coming along under
sail, and one of them very large. King Svend ordered
his men to go to their ships, 'For there comes the *Long
Serpent*.'

Earl Erik says: 'Many other great and stately vessels
have they besides the *Long Serpent*. Let us wait a
little.'

Then said many, 'Earl Erik will not fight and avenge
his father. And it is a great shame that it should be
told that we lay here with so great a force, and allowed
Olaf to sail out to sea before our eyes.' But when they

had spoken thus for a short time, they saw four ships coming sailing along, of which one had a large dragon head richly gilt. Then King Svend stood up, and said: 'That ship shall carry me this evening high, for I shall steer it.'

The Danish fleet then, we may suppose, put at once to sea, in time to cut off Olaf from a large portion of his fleet; though precisely how this manœuvre was effected is not very clear to us. For while one account represents Sigvald as piloting the fleet through the Sound, another account implies that his vessels came between Olaf and the vanguard of his fleet. Even now the Norse king might have escaped by holding on his course; and when it appeared how large a fleet was sailing out to intercept him, some of his men urged Olaf to do this. But the king cried out from the quarter-deck: 'Strike the sails; never shall men of mine think of flight. I never fled from a battle. Let God dispose of my life, but flight I will never take.' In truth, he could only have saved himself by sacrificing his rear-guard.

When a fleet got ready for fight, it was usual to fasten the vessels together by chains, in order that they might be kept in line. Enough space must, of course, have been left between the vessels for the use of the oars.

King Olaf ordered the war-horns to sound for all his ships to close up to each other. The king's ship lay in the middle of the line, and on one side lay the *Little Serpent*, and on the other the *Crane*; and as they made fast the stems together, the *Long Serpent* and the *Short Serpent* were fastened together at their stems. But when the king saw it, he called out to his men, and ordered them to lay the larger ship more in advance, so that its stern should not lie so far behind in the fleet.

Then said Ulf the Red: 'If the *Long Serpent* is to lie as much more ahead of the other ships as she is longer than them, we shall have hard work of it here on the forecastle.'

The king replies: 'I did not think I had a forecastle-man who was afraid.'

Says Ulf: 'Defend thou the quarter-deck, as I shall the forecastle.' The king had a bow in his hands, and laid an arrow on the string, and aimed at Ulf.

Ulf said: 'Shoot another way, king, where it is more needful: my work is thy gain.'

King Olaf stood on the *Serpent's* quarter-deck, high over the others. He had a gilt shield, and a helmet inlaid with gold; over his armour he had a short red coat, and was easy to be distinguished from other men. When King Olaf saw that the scattered forces of the enemy gathered themselves together under the banners of their ships, he asked: 'Who is the chief of the force right opposite to us?'

He was answered that it was King Svend with the Danish army.

The king replies: 'We are not afraid of these soft Danes, for there is no bravery in them; but who are the troops on the right of the Danes?'

He was answered that it was King Olaf with the Swedish forces.

'Better it were,' says King Olaf, 'for these Swedes to be sitting at home killing their sacrifices, than to be venturing under our weapons from the *Long Serpent*.

But who owns the large ships on the larboard side of the Danes?'

'That is Earl Erik Hakonson,' say they.

The king replies: 'He, methinks, has good reason for meeting us; and we may expect the sharpest conflict with these men, for they are Norsemen like ourselves.'

The kings now laid out their oars, and prepared to attack. King Svend laid his ship against the *Long Serpent*. Outside of him Olaf, the Swede, laid himself, and set his ship's stern against the outermost ship of King Olaf's line; and on the other side lay Earl Erik. Then a hard combat began. Earl Sigvald held back with the oars on his ships, and did not join the fray.

This battle was one of the severest told of, and many were the people slain. The forecastle men of the *Long Serpent*, the *Little Serpent*, and the *Crane* threw grapplings and stern chains on to King Svend's ship, and used their weapons well against the people standing below them, for they cleared the decks of all the ships they could lay fast hold of; and King Svend, and all the men who escaped, fled to other vessels, and laid themselves out of bow-shot. It went with this force just as King Olaf Tryggvason had foreseen. Then King Olaf, the Swede, laid himself in their place; but when he came near the great ships it went with him as with them, for he lost many men and some ships, and was obliged to get away. But Earl Erik laid the *Iron Beard* side by side with the outermost of King Olaf's ships, thinned it of men, cut the cables, and let it drive. Then he laid alongside of the next, and fought until he had cleared it of men also. Now all the people who were in the smaller ships began to run into the larger, and the earl cut them loose as fast as he cleared them of men. The Danes and Swedes laid themselves now out of shooting distance all around Olaf's ship; but Earl Erik lay always close alongside of the ships, and used his swords and battle-axes, and as fast as people fell in his vessel, others, Danes and Swedes, came in their place.

Then the fight became most severe, and many people fell. But at last it came to this, that all King Olaf Tryggvason's ships were cleared of men, except the *Long Serpent*, on board of which all who could still carry their arms were gathered. Then Erik laid his ship *Iron Beard* alongside the *Serpent*, and the fight went on with battle-axe and sword.

Earl Erik was in the forehold of his ship, where a 'shield-burg' had been set up. In the fight, both hewing weapons, sword, and axe, and the thrust of spears had been used; and all that could be used as weapons for casting were cast. Some used bows, some threw spears with the hand. So many weapons were cast into the *Serpent*, and so thick flew spears and arrows, that the shields could scarcely receive them; for on all sides the *Serpent* was surrounded by warships. Then King Olaf's men became so mad with rage, that they ran on board of the enemies' ships, to get at the people with stroke of sword and kill them; but many did not lay themselves so near the *Serpent*, in order to escape the close encounter with battle-axe or sword; and thus the most of Olaf's men went overboard and sank under their weapons, thinking they were fighting on plain ground.

Einar Tambarskelfir, one of the keenest of bowmen, stood by the mast and shot with his bow. Einar shot an arrow at Earl Erik, which hit the tiller-end just above the earl's head so hard that it entered the wood up to the arrow shaft. The earl looked that way, and asked if they knew who had shot; and at the same moment another arrow flew between his hand and his side and into the stuffing of the leader's stool, so that the barb stood far out on the other side. Then said the earl to a man called Fin—but some say he was of Finn (Laplander) race, and was a superior archer: 'Shoot that tall man by the mast.' Fin shot, and the arrow hit the middle of Einar's bow just at the moment that Einar was drawing it, and the bow was split in two parts.

'What is that,' cried King Olaf, 'that broke with such a noise?'

'Norway, king, from thy hands,' cried Einar.

'No! not quite so much as that,' says the king; 'take my bow and shoot,' flinging the bow to him.

Einar took the bow, and drew it over the head of the arrow. 'Too weak, too weak,' said he, 'for the bow of a mighty king!' and throwing the bow aside, he took sword and shield and fought valiantly.

The king stood on the gangway of the *Long Serpent* and shot the greater part of the day; sometimes with the bow, sometimes with the spear, and always throwing two spears at once. He looked down over the ship's side, and saw that his men struck briskly with their swords and yet wounded but seldom. Then he called aloud: 'Why do ye strike so gently that ye seldom cut?' One among the people answered: 'The swords are blunt and full of notches.' Then the king went down into the forehold, opened the chest under the throne, and took out many sharp swords, which he handed to his men; but as he stretched down his right hand with them, some observed that blood was running down under his steel glove, but no one knew where he was wounded.

Desperate was the defence in the *Serpent*, and there was the heaviest destruction of men done by the forecastle crew and those of the forehold, for in both places the men were chosen men, and the ship was highest; but in the middle of the ship the people were thinned. Now, when Earl Erik saw there were but few people remaining beside the ship's mast, he determined to board, and he entered the *Serpent* with four others. Then came Hyrning, the king's brother-in-law, and some others against him, and there was the most severe combat, and at last the earl was forced to leap back on board the *Iron Beard* again, and some who had accompanied him were killed, and others wounded.

Now the fight became hot indeed, and many men fell on board the *Serpent*; and the men on board of her began to be thinned off, and the defence to be weaker. The earl resolved to board the *Serpent* again, and again he met with a warm reception. When the forecastle men of the *Serpent* saw what he was doing, they went aft, and made a desperate fight; but so many men of the *Serpent* had fallen that the ship's sides were in many places quite bare of defenders, and the earl's men poured in all around into the vessel, and all the men who were still able to defend the ship crowded aft to the king, and arrayed themselves for his defence.

Kolbjörn, the marshal, who had on clothes and

arms like the king's, and was a remarkably stout and handsome man, went up to the king on the quarter-deck. The battle was still going on fiercely, even in the forehold. But as many of the earl's men had now got into the *Serpent* as could find room, and his ships lay all round her, and few were the people left in the *Serpent* for defence against so great a force; and in a short time most of the *Serpent's* men fell, brave and stout though they were. King Olaf and Kolbjörn, the marshal, both sprang overboard, each on his own side of the ship; but the earl's men had laid out boats around the *Serpent*, and killed those who leaped overboard. Now, when the king had sprung overboard, they tried to seize him with their hands and bring him to Earl Erik, but King Olaf threw his shield over his head, and sank beneath the waters.

Such is the vivid account which the Saga gives of the famous battle called the Battle of Svold, and of the death of the greatest hero of Norse history.

CHAPTER IX

HISTORY

St. Olaf (A.D. 1015-1030).

The Sagas from which Snorri compiled are very partial in the attention which they bestow upon the different rulers of Norway. Of those whom they can treat as independent sovereigns, the true heirs of Harald Fairhair, they have much to tell us; but when we come to the family of the Earls of Lade, who reigned as kings, but yet either as vassals of the King of Denmark, or else over a portion only of Norway, their epochs the Saga writers pass over with a few words, as if they were short and slight interruptions in the independent history of Norway. These intervals are in reality often longer than the reigns which the Sagas record at length.

Thus it is with the history which follows Svold. The league of the two kings and Earl Erik had been founded upon a compact, disgraceful enough for the latter, for the partitioning Norway among the allies. Svend, the Danish king, was to get Viken, the richest province of Norway; the king of Sweden, Olaf, was to have a portion of the Throndhjem country, as well as Möre and Romsdal; and Erik the Earl got the rest of Norway.

For fifteen years this Earl Erik carried on his government unchallenged. In the meanwhile Svend died, and Cnut—our Cnut—succeeded to the throne of Denmark, and to his father's claims on England. Svend died in A.D. 1014. Æthelred, we know, had been expelled and now returned. Cnut set on foot a great expedition for the invasion of England, and invited, says the Saga, or, it may be, bade Earl Erik to accompany him in it. Earl Erik was Cnut's brother-in-law, having married the daughter of Svend. The earl, the Saga says, was celebrated for his luck in campaigning, for he had been victorious in the two hardest fought engagements which had taken place in the north. The one was that in which the Earls Hakon and Erik had encountered the Joms-vikings; the other was that in which Earl Erik with his allies fought against Olaf Tryggvason at Svold.

The earl set sail for England. He was present with Cnut when he took the 'Castle of London,' and likewise in a battle westward of London, where he killed Ulfkel Snelling; but the next year he died.

Meantime, during the fifteen years that Erik had ruled peacefully in Norway, another claimant of the throne had been growing to manhood. This was a second Olaf, a son of Harald, one of the petty kings of southern Norway, who claimed descent from Harald Fairhair. Harald was king of the district called Grænland (it is the country immediately south of Thelemarken), whence he goes in the Sagas by the name of Harald Grænske. He himself was a man of little mark or likelihood; but his wife, Aasta, the mother of Olaf, was a woman of spirit and character. Harald met his death on a journey to Sweden; and his widow married another petty king, Sigröd or Sigurd, by whom she had a second family, of which one of the children was Harald, afterwards known as Harald Hardradi, whom we shall hear of again.

Olaf Haraldsson was brought up at the house of his step-father. But at twelve years of age—the Norse youth was supposed to reach maturity at twelve years of age—he was sent out upon Viking expeditions under the tutorship of his foster-father, Rani, who was called Rani the Far-travelled. In this Viking life Olaf spent many years of his early manhood. He went eastward into the Baltic lands and plundered in Sweden and right up the Gulf of Bothnia, among the magic-dealing Finns. He next met the leader of the Joms-vikings near Denmark, and went into partnership with him. They sailed together, plundering down the west coast of Jutland, and on to Friesland or Holland. From thence Olaf sailed to England, and took service on the side of Æthelred II. against Svend, and lent a hand towards the restoration of Æthelred after Svend's death.

Olaf had returned again for a while to his Viking life. He intended, the Saga tells us, to sail into the Mediterranean, and by that way on to Jerusalem. But he was warned by a dream against this course, and was told that a greater future lay before him in his own land.

An opportunity was made for him by the ambitious schemes of Cnut, who, as we have seen, had collected all his forces for the invasion of England, and had carried Earl Erik with him. At the beginning of the war Olaf, mindful of his old alliance, lent a hand to the sons of Æthelred and Emma against the Dane. He had met them at the Norman court at Rouen, and he joined his fleet with theirs when, after the death of their brother, Edmund Ironside, they attempted to drive Cnut from this country. But when their attempts proved quite abortive, and they were obliged to return again to Normandy, Olaf parted company with them, and after plundering a while on the English coast he set sail, with only two ships, for Norway. The spot at which he first landed was Sælö, close to Cape Stad.

Earl Erik's son, Hakon, and his brother, Svein, had succeeded to his rule. Almost immediately on his arrival Olaf had the good fortune to surprise the former of these two earls as he came, ignorant of danger, sailing up the Saudungssund (opposite the Dal Fjord, and just north of Sogne Fjord), with only a single ship, and to take him prisoner. He exacted from Hakon, as the price of his life, an oath renouncing all his claims in Norway, and engaging to leave the country for ever.

After this Olaf proceeded to the south country, and made his way to the Uplands, where lay the territory ruled over by his step-father, Sigröd Syr. This peaceful farmer-king was at first little disposed to aid Aasta's son in his daring projects. But Olaf's courage and address, and the influence of his mother, soon formed for the pretender a party in the south of Norway. The petty kings or chiefs in Gudbransdal, Hedemark, Raumariki, Valders, Hadaland, Thoten (all the country which lies about Lake Mjösen, and as far north as the Dovrefjeld), and the Thing for these districts acknowledged the new comer as their sovereign. Olaf's difficulty lay in the Throndhjem country, where the family of the Earls of Lade had been great landowners and great chiefs as long as any of the race of Harald Fair-hair had held the crown in Norway. Since the battle of Svold, moreover, and the partition treaty of the three leaders, who had united to destroy Olaf Tryggvason, the Swedish borders had been advanced; so that many of the bonders of the upper country who once paid taxes to the Norse king now paid them to the Swede. The King of Sweden at this time was the same who had taken part at Svold, another Olaf called Olaf the Swede by the Sagas, and also Olaf Skattkonung, Olaf the Tribute-king.

Though Hakon had been disposed of, Earl Svein, his uncle, still remained. Svein, so soon as he heard what this new-comer was doing in the south, collected an army and a fleet, and sailed round towards the southern fjords to look for him. It is strange to find in the party opposed to Olaf Haraldsson some of the men who had been the most famous of the adherents of Olaf the son of Tryggvi, men such as Einar Tambarskelfir, who had drawn the bow so well at Svold, and Erling Skjalgsson, Olaf Tryggvason's brother-in-law, who was reckoned the strongest and bravest man in Norway. But so it is. And it must have added not a little to the difficulties of the new aspirant to the throne to discover that such famous warriors had reconciled themselves to the party of the earls.

At first there was some manœuvring between the rival hosts. When Svein approached from the sea, Olaf passed into the Uplands: neither party seemed ready to risk an engagement. But at length, on Palm

Sunday A.D. 1015, almost a year and a half after Olaf had returned to Norway, the rival fleets met off a place which the Saga calls Nessjar, and which is apparently the promontory of Laurvik, just at the entrance to the Christiania Fjord. There Olaf gained a complete victory. That to which most of all he owed his success was the band of hardy adventurers, that, in bygone years, had accompanied him in his voyages, and in his attacks on the coasts of England and of France; a wild but faithful corps of buccaneers, who knew no law but that of fidelity to their chief, and had, maybe, a touch of the fanatical adherence to Christianity, which was beginning to be found in many of the Northmen. They were a well-armed, well-disciplined band. They bore white shields, with a gilt cross upon them. For Olaf came as the determined champion of the Christian creed. When Svein found that the battle was going against him, he sought to cut himself from the boats which (as was the common custom in naval battles) were bound to his vessel by cords or chains. Olaf's men on their side, who, having destroyed half Svein's crew, were preparing to board, sought by throwing out their grappling-irons to keep hold of Svein's ship. At last the earl got away, and Einar Tambarskelfir with him; and one by one, as they got the opportunity, the rest of the fleet followed suit.

In this wise did the young adventurer Olaf, thanks to his own daring and address, to his royal descent, and to a name which recalled the popular hero Olaf Tryggvason, make himself King of Norway, and begin a reign which was to leave the deepest traces in Norwegian history. Olaf Haraldsson had not the same claims to popularity which his namesake and predecessor possessed. He was not, like Olaf Tryggvason, the tallest, handsomest, and strongest man in Norway. His middle-sized, thick-set figure gained this Olaf the name of Digri, or 'the stout.' He was brave enough, and had proved in the thirteen battles fought in foreign lands [1] of what metal he was. But there are no wonderful feats of daring and strength recorded of him. All the more to Olaf's credit, therefore, is it that he accomplished so much, and that he left behind him a reputation great enough to overshadow even that of his great predecessor. He was, our Saga tells us, very gentle in manner and chary of speech. That which gained him his reputation in later centuries was the part which he took in the spread of Christianity, or say, in the confirmation of it throughout his dominions. Norway had been nominally Christian since the days of Olaf Tryggvason. So had Iceland; so had the Orkneys—the subject colonies of Norway. But nowhere since the first Olaf died had any great efforts been made to root out heathenism and its customs. Most of the coastmen had been baptized in Olaf Tryggvason's days: that was about all. The inland men were often not even nominally Christians. Olaf Digri caused 'Christian law' to be proclaimed everywhere, first in the Viken country, afterwards in the north. By 'Christian law' is meant the canon law for the due observance of Christian festivals, prohibiting customs which partook of heathenism, especially the eating of horse-flesh; laws, again, forbidding the exposure of infants, and regulating the use of slaves.

[1] Whereof Olaf's court poet, Sighvat, has left the record.

The new king caused, we are told, inquiry to be made into the condition of Iceland (from a 'believer's' point of view) and of the Orkneys; and was little satisfied by what he heard.

The early years of Olaf's reign were largely occupied by his disputes and negotiations with his namesake, the King of Sweden. Olaf Skattkonung had, we know, taken part in the battle of Svold. Ever since then the Swedish boundaries had been advanced at the expense of Norway. Olaf Haraldsson determined to readjust the boundaries of his kingdom as in the days of Harald Fairhair. The result was constant disputes between the two kings; until the Swede became furiously incensed against the Norseman, and swore that he would make a complete levy of his subjects, and would burn and harry in Norway from south to north. The Norse king, on his side, was constantly attacking the Swedes who dwelt just over his southern boundary, which, in those days, was the Göta river; and the west Gothlanders, who suffered most from these attacks, were earnestly desirous of a peace between the two countries. Before long the Norse Olaf made friends with Rögnvald, the Earl of West Gothland, whose wife was a descendant of Harald Fairhair. The earl was anxious, both for the sake of his subjects and of his friendship for the King of Norway, to further a peace between the two countries. Olaf Haraldsson was, on his side, ready enough to open negotiations; but it was said that the Swedish king was so incensed with his rival, 'that fat fellow,' as he called him, that he would not even hear his name spoken.

Howbeit Olaf the Thick appointed an embassy to

the court at Upsala, which was to make offers of peace on what would, in modern diplomacy, be called terms of the *status quo*—the boundaries of the two kingdoms to be once more what they were in the time of Olaf Tryggvason. Björn was the nobleman deputed to head this embassy; and with him went a certain Hjalti, an Icelandic bard, who had been staying at the Norwegian court.

The part which the Icelandic skalds, such as this Hjalti, take in the history of those days is a peculiar and fascinating one. Iceland may be described as a genuine 'Republic of Letters' among the states of the north. Except for certain dues, not often paid to the crown of Norway, it was an independent republic, and it was the literary state *par excellence* amongst the Scandinavian group. From it came bards to every court. The skalds of two rival kings might often be friends who had known each other at home; and so they served as connecting links between one country and another. Sometimes, of course, they might be enemies who had left Iceland with a blood-feud between them; and then their royal patrons were often led to espouse their private quarrel. In the present case, after Björn and his suite had been entertained a while by Earl Rögnvald, it was agreed that Hjalti, the foreigner, should go first to the Swedish court, where there were already living two fellow-countrymen of his, skalds likewise, whose names were Gissur the Black, and Ottar the Black. Hjalti was well entertained by his countrymen and by their patron. But the only time that he ventured to breathe to the Swedish Olaf a hint of the desirability of peace between his country and Norway, he was warned never to broach the subject again. 'For this time I will not take it amiss of thee,' said Olaf the Swede, 'as thou dost not know what people have to avoid here. That fat fellow shall never receive the name of king in my court.' Hjalti, however, made good use of his time in singing the praises of the Norse king to Ingegerd, the daughter of Olaf, and eventually got so far as to ask her, 'What would be thy answer if the Norway king, Olaf, sent messengers to thee, with the errand to propose marriage to thee?'

She blushed, and answered slowly but gently, 'I have not made up my mind to answer to that; but if Olaf be in all respects so perfect as thou makest him out to be, I would not wish a better husband; unless thou hast gilded him overmuch with thy praise.'

Olaf, the Swede, held firm to his refusal. But his subjects were of a different mind, and were growing more and more incensed at their king's obstinacy. We have a vivid description of the holding of the great Thing at Upsala, whereat Olaf was compelled to listen to the proposals of peace. This took place after the return of Hjalti, when it was decided that Björn must go to the Swedish court, a journey in which Earl Rögnvald agreed to accompany him. On their way they paused at a house of a certain old bonder called Thorgnyr, who was the *Lag-man* or lawgiver of the Upsala Thing. This man is a characteristic figure for those days. 'In the high seat sat an old man; and never had Björn and his companions seen a man so stout. His beard was so long that it lay upon his knee, and was spread over his whole breast; and the man, moreover, was gay and lively. . . . They remained there some days before the earl disclosed his errand. . . . When the earl had done speaking, Thorgnyr sat silent for a while, and then took up the word. "Ye have curious dispositions, who are so ambitious of honour and renown, and have no prudence or counsel in you when ye get into any mischief. Why did you not consider, before you gave your promise to this adventure, that you had no power to stand against King Olaf? In my opinion it is not a less honourable position to be in the number of bonders, and have one's words free, and be able to say what one will, even if the king be present. But I must go to the Upsal Thing, and give thee such help that, without fear, thou canst speak before the king what thou findest good."'

And when the Thing was opened Thorgnyr showed how aptly this description fitted his case.

There was a great assemblage of people at the Thing, and Olaf was there with his court. The king took his seat upon one chair, and his court stood round him; and on the opposite seat sat together Earl Rögnvald and Thorgnyr on one seat. And first rose Björn, setting forth how he had been sent there by his own king, the Norse Olaf, who offered to the Swedish king peace, and 'the frontiers which, in old time, were fixed between Norway and Sweden.' Earl Rögnvald supported the proposal of peace; but when he had spoken, King Olaf the Swede rose up and spoke violently against any thought of reconciliation, reproaching the earl bitterly for making friendship with Olaf the Thick, which he deemed treason against himself. The king spoke long and bitterly. 'When he sat down not a sound was to be heard at first. Then Thorgnyr stood up; and when he arose all the bonders stood up, who before had been sitting, and rushed together from all parts to listen to what lagman Thorgnyr would say. At first there was a great din of peoples and weapons, but when the noise was settled into silent listening Thorgnyr made his speech '—which it would be pleasant to give, as a fine specimen of the independent speaking of those times. It ended by the open threat: 'If thou wilt not do as we desire, make peace with the king of Norway, we will now attack thee and put thee to death, for we will no longer suffer law and peace to be disturbed.' Thereupon the whole public approved, with clash of arms and loud shouts, the lagman's speech.

Olaf Skattkonung had to give way. His daughter, Ingegerd, was betrothed to Olaf of Norway. But her father continued to postpone the marriage, and finally gave her hand to the Russian king—king, that is, of Greater Suithiod—Jarisleif. The Norse Olaf, by the help of Earl Rögnvald, and without asking the consent of her father, got for his wife Astrid, Olaf's illegitimate daughter, 'but,' as the Saga says, 'a very lovely girl: her words came well in her talk; she was merry, but modest and very generous.'

Not long after this the Swedes deposed their king, and raised his twelve-year-old son, Jacob, also called Önund, to the throne. But another party continued to support the father, and it was finally agreed that there should be two kings in Sweden, the father and son, Olaf and Önund. After this peace was made between Sweden and Norway.

With a country and with a population such as the Norwegian, the former naturally divided into districts greatly differing in character, the latter strong-willed and independent, and behind-hand in their political education, a single monarch could only maintain his rule by unwearied activity, and by a courage which bordered on cruelty. King Olaf the Saint had owed his elevation, and continued to owe his throne in no small measure to the trusty and highly-trained, well-armed body of mercenary troops that he had brought with him into the country. We see him, surrounded by his guard, making constant progresses throughout his dominions,—now surprising a most dangerous conspiracy of five ex-kings in the upland country,—now making inquisitorial search for traces of heathenism in Throndhjem district, or in far northern regions of Halogaland—regions which his predecessors had left very much to themselves. He owed his after-title of saint to the zeal with which he stamped out heathenism, a zeal for God which, as was contended by his panegyrists, brought about the rise of his discontented bonders, and his own final defeat and death.

In reality Olaf was much less of a saint than of a firm and capable administrator. He had not, we have said, the brilliant person of his namesake, the son of Tryggvi. But he probably surpassed him in solid mental gifts, and in consistency of purpose. Certain it is that, without the aid of Olaf Tryggvason's personal advantages, St. Olaf has succeeded in winning a great place in history. Good luck accompanied the earlier years of his reign. He took advantage of a disputed succession in the earldom of Orkney and Caithness, to obtain the homage of both disputants, to whom he dictated the terms of a settlement. A famine in the fifth year of his reign brought about a relapse towards heathenism. The famine was attributed to the anger of the old gods for the conversion of the extreme north of the country, the part which had till then remained true to them. But Olaf exerted himself successfully to stamp out this reactionary movement.

Olaf had wide-reaching plans; but he was somewhat rash, and not always perfectly honest. He sent messages of friendship to the outlying western islands, which had been always considered in some sort of way dependencies of the Norwegian crown, but most of which were practically independent. The Orkneys he had got himself acknowledged over-lord of. But Thorfinn, one of two claimants to the earldom, before long disposed of his rival Rögnvald; he was not a man to remain in a state of dependence so soon as he should have firmly established himself. This Thorfinn is a striking figure in the history of the Earls of Orkney, whom, had we space, it would be pleasant to speak of at greater length.

The Faroes were a small group, little able to withstand the power of Norway, and Olaf managed in a friendly way to entice some of the leading men of the islands to his court. When he had them there he retained them, in effect as hostages, till the islands accepted the Norwegian law, and agreed to pay 'skatt' to Norway. Olaf tried the same wiles upon Iceland. He invited all the most conspicuous Icelanders over to Norway. But these were too cunning to comply. They sent their sons instead. These in their turn were kept by Olaf practically as hostages. One of them, Stein, killed the king's bailiff, who sought to hinder him from leaving the country; and as he had friends among the leading men of Norway who were ready to take up his quarrel, the matter nearly led to grave troubles.

Olaf could not afford to raise up enemies at home on slight cause. There was always an opposition party, which may in a sense be called the heathen party; for its hostility was in great measure due to the energetic action of the king in rooting out heathenism. Side by side with this zeal for Christianity went in Olaf's mind a love of law and order, to which a large portion of the population were strangers. For, fine as is the Norse character, and brilliant as are the figures which follow one another through the pages of early Norse history, it cannot be maintained that the Norwegians, as a nation, have shown on the whole more coherence, or more power of self-government, than have the Irish as a nation.

We see that during this, the heroic period of her history, there were but intervals during which Norway submitted to the rule of a single king, and allowed him peace enough at home for him to feel himself a match for any of the neighbouring Scandinavian powers. Between these intervals were others during which the country was either partitioned among several rulers, or allowed itself to sink to the lower position of a vassal kingdom to Denmark or Sweden.

As the nucleus of the party opposed to King Olaf the Thick stood the adherents of the Earls of Hakon's line who had lately ruled the country. Two of the chief men of Norway were, we have already said, connected with Hakon's house, Einar Tambarskelfir and Erling Skjalgsson. Both were relatives of Olaf

Tryggvason, and both were connected by marriage with the house of Hakon. The former of the two, after St. Olaf's coronation, left the country for a time; but eventually he made overtures for a reconciliation, which were accepted by the king. Erling remained from the first in Norway, and nominally submitted to the new dynasty, while in reality he ruled his own district almost as an independent lord. Olaf made several attempts to break down the power of Erling, and in these he partially succeeded. Beneath a show of amity there smouldered a continual ill-will between the king and this haughty subject. Erling and his sons had already made offers to transfer their allegiance to Olaf's great rival before the latter was in a position to take advantage of their offer.

This great rival of Olaf Haraldson was Cnut Svendsson, King of Denmark and of England. Cnut and Olaf had always been opposed. Even in his buccaneering days, as we know, the Norseman had offered his sword to the sons of Æthelred against the Danish king. Cnut was now established on the English throne, and so had, in addition to the resources of his native country, those of 'the richest country of the north.' He by no means resigned his claims to Norway in asserting those to England; and he had, some years since, sent an embassy to Olaf, saying that if the latter would do him homage as to an over-lord he would leave him undisturbed in his dominions. But Olaf refused utterly to hold his crown on such conditions. He told the Danish ambassadors that Cnut might eat all the kail in England ere he, Olaf, would place his head in the Dane's hands, or own to him any sort of vassalage. This answer was brought to Cnut. He was not ready to strike yet, but he bided his time.

Olaf strengthened his forces by land and sea, and settled himself in the south of the kingdom opposite to Denmark; for presently Cnut returned for a time to his native land, and was reported to be raising an army. Olaf also sought to strengthen himself by an alliance with the Swedish king Önund (Jacob), the son of his old enemy, Olaf the Swede. Önund favoured the Norwegian alliance, in spite of the fact that the too self-confident Olaf would not consent to bury all thought of rivalry between his kingdom and Sweden for the possession of the border lands, and that Önund received at the same time an embassy from Denmark to bribe him to neutrality.

The expected attack from Denmark was still delayed. St. Olaf went throughout his dominions collecting troops, and preparing a fleet. He held a conference too with King Önund. As still the attack did not come, and the Swedish and Norwegian troops could not safely be disbanded, they determined to take the initiative. Olaf was to fall upon the Danish islands, while Önund attacked the Danish province of Scania, in the lowest bulge of the Swedish peninsula, which, as we have already said, was a part of the kingdom of Denmark. No immediate help being forthcoming from their king, most of the inhabitants of Scania made submission to Önund.

Once more, in the autumn of A.D. 1026, Cnut, having fitted out in England a fleet more formidable, and containing larger vessels, than any that had, up till now, taken the seas, set sail for his native country. With him sailed Earl Hakon, Erik's son, and many another fugitive Norwegian. Of the two great subjects of St. Olaf who figure most in the history of this time, Einar Tambarskelfir, the great bowman, and Erling Skjalgsson, the proud *hersir*, the one chose to sit quietly at home, taking part neither for nor against his sovereign; the other, who had for long hardly been on terms with Olaf, now finally left him and gave in his adherence to Cnut. When Cnut arrived in Danish waters the allied kings Olaf and Önund lay with their fleets off his Swedish coasts—off Scania, as it appears. The Dane at once occupied the Sound between Zealand and Sweden with a force too great to be attacked. Afterwards he sailed in pursuit of the allied fleet.

Cnut came to the Swedish coast, and found that the Norse-Swedish fleet was lying in the mouth of a river, the Helge-Aar (Holy River). This river flows into the sea in the south of Sweden, close to Christianstad. It was now that Olaf gave the second proof of his capacity as an engineer, which he had displayed once before, quite at the beginning of his career, when he found himself blocked in a fjord near Upsala. On that occasion he had cut a canal to the sea, and had escaped by that means. What he now did was to go to the source of the Helge river, that is to say, to Lake Sjövik, from which the Helge river makes but a short course to the sea. At the mouth of the river, we have said, the allied fleet had been lying, and to it the fleet of Cnut was approaching. Olaf, by raising dams, held up the waters of the lake so as to be ready to flood the river. When Cnut came near, Önund, who had been left in command of the fleet, sailed out of the harbour, sounded his war-horns, and bound his ships together to prepare for battle. Cnut arrived at the estuary with a force one-half greater than that of the allies. But as it was evening, and he found the harbour abandoned, he anchored his fleet there, and many of his men went ashore. Olaf and his men now cut through the dams which pent in the waters of the lake; then they hastened to rejoin their own fleet. All seemed safe enough to Cnut and his men. But in the morning the river came suddenly rushing down in a great flood, covering the land, drowning all the crews that had gone on shore, and carrying with it great trees, which were dashed against Cnut's ships and destroyed several of them. All the vessels of the Danish fleet were broken from their moorings, and carried out to sea; Cnut's own dragon-ship, the largest warship that had ever yet been built, drifted out among the fleet of Olaf and Önund. They made great efforts to board it; but it stood so high above their own vessels that these attempts were abortive. This mishap to the Danish fleet gave the allies time enough to withdraw out of its reach; and while the Danes had suffered severely, the Norse-Swedish force found that it had not lost a single man.

This was, however, only an incidental triumph. The case of the allies was really desperate. The kings held a council of war, and eventually decided to part. Olaf was obliged to abandon his fleet, and make his way on foot back to Norway. Many of the Norse crews now left their leader; those who remained true to him destroyed their vessels; and the king, with quite a small following, and after a tedious march through Southern Sweden, returned to the Viken district.

And now all fell from Olaf. The account of the proceedings of the next few months would be unintelligible, did we not bear in mind the peculiarities of Norse scenery, and especially of the Norse sea-coast. We see Olaf lying in one fjord while the Danish fleet is sailing all round the coast of Norway, obtaining the allegiance of the inhabitants of one district after another. Hakon is appointed Earl-Regent of the kingdom, but as a vassal of Cnut, much as his grandfather Hakon had held the country as a vassal of Cnut's grandfather Harald. Then, when the Danish fleet has departed, Olaf sails forth again, goes northward along the coast, and tries to bring back the people to their old obedience. Few respond, and the king's ancient foe, Erling Skjalgsson, comes out with a fleet in pursuit of the royal force. Olaf sails away ; then having rounded an island, he lies in wait for his pursuer, and Erling comes sailing far ahead of the rest of his fleet. So soon as he has got under the lee of the island, the royal ships dart forth and row up to the attack of Erling's single vessel, and, after a desperate resistance, Erling falls. This event took place in December A.D. 1028.

Such isolated successes could do nothing to save Olaf from his fate. He found Hakon settled firmly in the Throndhjem country, the country of his forefathers. And though many of Olaf's followers urged the king to risk an engagement, he felt himself too weak to do so. There was no other course open to him but to make good his retreat over the mountains (the 'Keel') and into Sweden. Only very few of the king's followers remained faithful to him after he had determined to do this. Kalf Arnason, one of the most distinguished of Olaf's men, who had been strongly in favour of an attack upon Hakon at all risks, now deserted his master. We find Kalf, a short time after this, doing homage to Cnut, and receiving large promises from that monarch. Kalf's brother, Finn Arnason, on the other hand, remained to the end St. Olaf's most devoted and most trusted follower. Meantime the Norse king—though, as the account would have us believe, his troubles were alleviated by more than one miracle—had nothing for it but to make good his retreat to Sweden, and eventually to Russia.

Olaf could not rest in his retirement. He still meditated a return, and one more attempt to win back his kingdom; though at other times he would talk of resigning even the royal title, of making a pilgrimage to Rome, and of dying in the Eternal City in the habit of a monk.

One night, when he had been revolving these various schemes, and tossing about irresolute, sleep fell upon him, and there appeared at his bedside a tall and very fair man, in splendid raiment. 'And it came into the king's mind that this was King Olaf Tryggvason who had come to him.' The apparition reproved St. Olaf for his weakness, that he should ever think 'of laying down the kingly dignity which God has given thee. It is the glory of a king to be victorious over his enemies, and it is a glorious death to die in battle. Thou must go back to thy country, and God will give open testimony that the kingdom is thine by right of inheritance.'

This vision determined St. Olaf. He set forth on his return journey from Russia to Sweden, and in the latter country set about collecting an army. Önund, his old ally, gave Olaf four hundred men from his bodyguard, and leave to recruit adventurers in his country. From Norway, meantime, Earl Hakon, who had been set over the kingdom by Cnut, had returned for a while to England, 'where he had a wife,' says the Saga; and, on his voyage back to Norway, he was caught in a storm and drowned off Caithness. Some of Olaf's former subjects thought now of returning to their allegiance; and a body of six hundred men marched over the mountains to join the king's army in Sweden. It was headed by Olaf's half-brother, Harald, son of Sigurd Syr and Aasta, the mother of Olaf, the prince who is called Harald Sigurdsson in Norse history, but is best known to us by his nickname of Hardradi—Harald hard-of-rede. He was now about to take part in a desperate enterprise, and inaugurate a long period of adventure which ended only with his life.

The united Norse army, with these additions, and with its Swedish recruits, amounted to about three thousand men. Olaf's march—his last—was through Dalecarlia to Jemtland, and so over the ridge into Norway. He must have passed pretty nearly over the same ground which is now traversed by the great high-road which leads from Jemtland to the Throndhjem Fjord. During the last stages of his march he descended towards Verdal, where the high land slopes rapidly down through fertile alluvial terraces towards the bed of the fjord. We have ourselves looked down from these high lands, over the long, winding arm of water of the inner fjord, set amidst its pleasant fields and well-to-do farms, until stretched beyond, we saw, or seemed to see, glimpses of the more distant open sea. The time was sunset; that is to say, it was not far from midnight; about half-past eleven, when the sun had just gone down, the red sunset clouds still brooded over the scene and were reflected in the waters of the fjord.

As King Olaf, winding down from the highlands, looked over the same landscape, he became abstracted, and as one who looked and saw not. And afterwards, when questioned by the bishop, who rode at his side, he said it had seemed to him as if the whole of Norway had opened before him, and he saw the entire land, over which he had ruled so many years, and which had been the scene of so many of his adventures, lucky and disastrous. Then it had appeared to him that the scene widened still more, and that he could see over the whole world. No doubt the memory of all his youthful achievements came back to him in these moments which lay—though he knew it not—so near the term of his strenuous and adventurous life. He saw the scenes of those thirteen battles which he had fought in the Baltic, in Valland (France), far down the Atlantic shores, almost to the Gates of Hercules. Or he beheld the places where he had stood by Æthelred, and the sons of Æthelred, against his old enemy and present foe, King Cnut: saw London Bridge as he had stormed it that day, when he had brought up his fleet, roofed with planks, to protect the crews from missiles, and had then moored the boats to the piers of the bridge.

What a life of travel and of activity had his been! He might claim to have seen almost the whole world as it was known to the Norsemen of his day, now that, in addition to those regions of which I have just spoken, he had travelled through Sweden into Russia and back again.

Olaf brought his army to a place called Verdal. There had gone a war-token throughout all the country, and the rugged bonders of the Throndhjem district had collected under their leaders to oppose the king. Cnut himself was not in the country; but some of the chief men of Norway, whom the Dane had loaded with favours, and still more with promises, and brought heartily over to his side, were ready to support his cause. At the head of the army hostile to Olaf was Kalf Arnason. But all the other sons of Arni were in the king's army.[1]

'King Olaf was armed thus:—He had a gold-mounted helmet on his head, and had in one hand a white shield, on which the holy cross was inlaid in gold. In his other hand he had a lance, which to the present day stands beside the altar in Christ Church (Throndhjem Cathedral). In his belt he had a sword, which was called Hneitir, which was remarkably sharp, and of

[1] My notes, written at the time of a visit to the field of Stiklestad, the site of the approaching battle between Olaf and the bonders, and the most interesting battlefield in Norway, give the following directions to the traveller who is going in search of it :—To get to Stiklestad you go by steamer from Throndhjem and land at Tronæs. You follow thence the only road you can take, turning to the right when you come to the telegraph posts, and going along by them. You then pass over a little bridge, and ascend a small hill. You take the first turn to the left after passing the bridge, and at the ridge of the hill. You then walk along a slightly elevated plateau between two watercourses—it is only the further one that contains anything worthy the name of a river—and keep straight on till you see the church of Stiklestad or Verdal rising before you. The position which St. Olaf held is well defined by the slope of the ground, and you see opposite the low hill down which the bonders' army was seen advancing with banners displayed. If in doubt, ask for *Veien til Stik'sta'*.

which the handle was worked with gold. He had also a strong coat of ring-mail.

'Now, when King Olaf had drawn up his men, the army of the bonders had not yet come near upon any quarter, so the king said the people should sit down and rest themselves. He sat down himself, and the people sat around him in a wide-spread crowd. He leaned down, and laid his head upon Finn Arnason's knee. There a slumber came upon him, and he slept a little while; but at the same time the bonders' army was seen advancing with raised banners, and the multitude of these was very great.

'Then Finn awakened the king, and said that the bonder army advanced against them.

'The king awoke and said: "Why did you waken me, Finn, and did not allow me to enjoy my dream?"

'Finn: "Thou must not be dreaming; but rather thou shouldst be awake and preparing thyself against the host which is coming down upon us; or, dost thou not see that the whole bonder crowd is coming?"

'The king replies: "They are not yet so near to us; and it would have been better to have let me sleep."

'Then said Finn: "What was the dream, sire, of which the loss appears to thee so great that thou wouldst rather have been left to waken of thyself?"

'Now the king told his dream: that he seemed to see a high ladder, upon which he went so high in the air that Heaven was open, for so high reached the ladder. "And when you awoke me I was come to the highest step towards heaven."

'Finn replies: "This dream does not appear to me so good as it does to thee. I think thou art fey, king."

'Kalf Arnason then raised his banner, and drew up his house-servants along with Harek of Thiottö and his men. Thorir Hund with his troop was at the head of the order of battle in front of the banner, and on both sides of Thorir was a chosen body of bonders, all of them the most active and best armed in the forces. This part of the array was long and thick, and in it were drawn up the Throndhjem people and the Halogalanders. On the right wing was another array; and on the left of the main array were drawn up the men from Rogaland, Hordaland, the fjord districts, and Sogn, and they had the third banner.

'There was a man called Thorstein Knarrarsmid, who was a merchant and master ship-carpenter, stout and strong, very passionate, and a great man-slayer. He had been in enmity against King Olaf, who had taken from him a new and large merchant vessel he had built, on account of some manslaughter. (A mulct, incurred by one of his misdeeds, which went to the king.) Thorstein, who was with the bonders' army, went forward in front of the line in which Thorir Hund stood, and said: "Here I will be, Thorir, in your ranks; for I think, if I and King Olaf meet, to be the first to drive a weapon at him, if I can get so near, to repay him for the robbery of the ship he took from me, which was the best that ever went on merchant voyage." Thorir and his men received Thorstein, and he went into their ranks.

'When the bonders' men and array were drawn up, the lendermen addressed the men, and ordered them to take notice of the place to which each man belonged, under which banner each should be, who there were in front of the banner, who were his side men, and that they should be brisk and quick in taking up their places in the array, for the army had still to go a long way, and the array might be broken in the course of march. Then they encouraged the people; and Kalf invited all the men who had any injury to avenge on King Olaf to place themselves under the banner which was advancing against King Olaf's own banner. They should remember the distress he had brought upon them; and, he said, never was there a better opportunity to avenge their grievances, and to free themselves from the yoke and slavery he had imposed on them. "Let him," says he, "be held a useless coward who does not fight this day boldly; and they are not innocents who are opposed to you, but people who will not spare you if ye spare them."

'Kalf's speech was received with loud applause, and shouts of encouragement were heard through the whole army.

'Thereafter the bonders' army advanced to Stiklestad, where King Olaf was already with his people. Kalf and Harek went in front, at the head of the army, under their banners. But the battle did not begin immediately on their meeting, for the bonders delayed the assault, because all their men were not come upon the plain, and they waited for those who came after them. Thorir Hund had come up with his troop the last, for he had to take care that the men did not go off behind when the battle-cry was raised, or the armies were closing with each other, and therefore Kalf and Harek waited for Thorir. For the encouragement of their men in the battle the bonders had the field-cry: "Forward, forward, bondermen!" King Olaf also made no attack, for he waited for Dag and the people who followed him. At last the king saw Dag and his men approaching. It is said that the army of the bonders was not less on this day than a hundred times a hundred men.

'As the armies on both sides stood so near that people knew each other, the king said: "Why art thou here, Kalf, for we parted good friends south in Möre? It beseems thee ill to fight against us, or to throw a spear into our army, for here are four of thy brothers."

'Kalf replied: "Many things come to pass differently from what may appear seemly. You parted from us, so that it was necessary to seek peace with those who were behind in the country; now each must remain where he stands; but if I might advise, we should be reconciled."

'Then Finn, his brother, who was with the king, answered: "This is to be observed of Kalf, that when he speaks fairly he has it in his mind to do ill."

'The king answered: "It may be, Kalf, that thou art inclined to reconciliation; but methinks the bonders do not appear so peaceful."

'Then Thorgeir of Kviststad said: "You shall now have such peace as many formerly have received at your hands, and which you shall now pay for."

'The king replies: "Thou hast no occasion to hasten so much to meet us, for fate has not decreed to thee to-day a victory over me, who raised thee to power and dignity from a mean station."

'Now came Thorir Hund, went forward in front of the banner with his troop, and called out, "Forward,

forward, bondermen!" Thereupon the bondermen raised the war-cry, and shot their arrows and spears. The king's men raised also a war-shout, and that done, encouraged each other to advance, crying out, "Forward, forward, Christ-men! cross-men! king's men!" When the bonders who stood outermost on the wings heard it, they repeated the same cry; but when the other bonders heard them they thought these were king's men, turned their arms against them, and they fought together, and many were slain before they knew each other. The weather was beautiful, and the sun shone clear; but when the battle began the heaven and the sun became red, and before the battle ended it became as dark as at night. King Olaf had drawn up his army upon a rising ground, and it rushed down from thence upon the bonder army with such a fierce assault that the bonders' array bent before it, so that the breast of the king's array came to stand upon the ground on which the rear of the bonders' array had stood, and many of the bonders' army were on the way to fly, but the lendermen and their house-men stood fast, and the battle became very severe. The lendermen urged their men, and forced them to advance.

'Then the bonder-army pushed on from all quarters. They who stood in front hewed down with their swords: they who stood next thrust with their spears; and they who stood hindmost shot arrows, cast spears, or threw stones, hand-axes, or sharp stakes. Soon there was a great fall of men in the battle. Many were down on both sides. In the first onset fell Arnliot Gellini, Gauka Thorir, and Afarfasti, with all their men, after each had killed a man or two, and some indeed more.

Now the ranks in front of the king's banner began to be thinned, and the king ordered Thord to carry the banner forward, and the king himself followed it with the troop he had chosen to stand nearest to him in battle; and these were the best-armed men in the field, and the most expert in the use of their weapons.

'Olaf came forth from behind the shield-bulwark, and put himself at the head of the array; and when the bonders looked him in the face they were frightened, and let their hands drop.

'The combat became fierce, and the king went forward in the fray.

'King Olaf fought most desperately. He struck the lenderman before mentioned (Thorgeir of Kviststad) across the face, cut off the nose-piece of his helmet, and clove his head down below the eyes so that they almost fell out. When he fell the king said: 'Was it not true, Thorgeir, what I told thee, that thou shouldst not be victor in our meeting?' At the same instant Thord struck the banner-pole so fast in the earth that it remained standing. Thord had got his death-wound, and fell beneath the banner. There also fell Thorfinn Munn, and also Gissur Gulbraa, who was attacked by two men, of whom he killed one, but only wounded the other before he fell.

'It happened then, as before related, that the sun, although the air was clear, withdrew from sight, and it became dark.

'At the same time Dag Hringsson came up with his people, and began to put his men in array, and to set up his banner; but on account of the darkness the onset could not go on so briskly, for they could not see exactly whom they had before them. They turned, however, to that quarter where the men of Hordaland and Rogaland stood. Many of these circumstances took place at the same time, and some happened a little earlier, and some a little later.

'On the other side of Kalf Arnason stood his two relations, Olaf and Kalf, with many other brave and stout men. Kalf was a son of Arnfinn Armodson, and a brother's son of Arni Armodson. On the other side of Kalf Arnason stood Thorir Hund. King Olaf hewed at Thorir Hund, and struck him across the shoulders, but the sword would not cut, and it was as if dust flew from his reindeer-skin coat.

'Thorir struck at the king, and they exchanged some blows; but the king's sword would not cut where it met the reindeer skin, although Thorir was wounded in the hands.

'The king said to Björn, the marshal: 'Do thou kill the dog on whom steel will not bite?" Björn turned round the axe in his hands, and gave Thorir a blow with the hammer of it on the shoulder, so hard that he tottered. The king at the same moment turned against Kalf's relation, Olaf, and gave him his death-wound. Thorir Hund struck his spear right through the body of Marshal Björn, and killed him outright; and Thorir said, "Thus we hunt the bear (*björn*)." Thorstein Knarrarsmid struck at King Olaf with his axe, and the blow hit his left leg above the knee. Finn Arnason instantly killed Thorstein. The king, after the wound, staggered towards a stone, threw down his sword, and prayed God to help him. Then Thorir Hund struck at him with his spear, and the stroke went in under his mail-coat and into his belly. Then Kalf struck at him on the left side of the neck. But all are not agreed upon Kalf having been the man who gave him the wound in the neck. These three wounds were King Olaf's death; and after the king's death the greater part of the forces which had advanced with him fell with the king.

'Dag Hringsson still kept up the battle, and made in the beginning so fierce an assault that the bonders gave way, and some betook themselves to flight. There a great number of the bonders fell, and these lendermen, Erlend of Gerdi, and Aslak of Finnö, and the banner also which they had stood under was cut down. This onset was particularly hot, and was called Dag's storm. But now Kalf Arnason, Harek of Thiottö, and Thorir Hund turned against Dag, with the array which had followed them, and then Dag was overwhelmed with numbers; so he betook himself to flight with the men still left him. There was a valley through which the main body of the fugitives fled, and men lay scattered in heaps on both sides; and many were severely wounded, and many so fatigued that they were fit for nothing. The bonders pursued only a short way; for their leaders soon returned back to the field of battle; where they had their friends and relations to look after.

'Thorir Hund went to where King Olaf's body lay, took care of it, laid it straight out on the ground, and spread a cloak over it. He told since that when he wiped the blood from the face it was very beautiful; and there was red in the cheeks, as if he only slept, and even much clearer than when he was in life. The king's blood came on Thorir's hand, and ran up between his fingers to where he had been wounded, and the wound grew up so speedily that it did not require to be bound up. This circumstance was testified by Thorir himself when King Olaf's holiness came to be generally known among the people; and Thorir Hund was among the first of the king's powerful opponents who endeavoured to spread abroad the king's sanctity.

'Kalf Arnason searched for his brothers who had fallen, and found Thorberg and Finn. It is related that Finn threw his dagger at him, and wanted to kill him, giving him hard words, and calling him a faithless villain, and a traitor to his king. Kalf did not regard it, but ordered Finn and Thorberg to be carried away from the field. When their wounds were examined they were found not to be deadly; they had fallen in part from fatigue, and under the weight of their weapons. Thereafter Kalf tried to bring his brothers down to a ship, and went himself with them. As soon as he was gone the whole bonder-army, having their homes in the neighbourhood went off also, excepting those who had friends or relations to look after, or the bodies of the slain to take care of. The wounded were taken home to the farms, so that every house was full of them; and tents were erected over some. But wonderful as was the number collected in the bonder-army, no less wonderful was the haste with which this vast body was dispersed when it was once free; and the cause of this was, that the most of the people gathered together from the country places were longing for their homes.'

This battle of Stiklestad was fought on July 29, 1030.

CHAPTER X

HISTORY

Magnus the Good—Harald Hardradi—The End of the Heroic Age.
A.D. 1035-1066.

ONCE more Norway fell under the rule of Denmark. Cnut made large promises to his supporters, especially to Kalf Arnason, who had been the leader of the bonders at Stiklestad, and proceeded to reduce Norway to the rank of a dependency of the Danish Crown. The bonders soon began to regret that they had taken arms against the House of Harald Fairhair in favour of a stranger. Olaf's zeal for the true faith was remembered and exaggerated; and as the Christian party grew in strength a greater and greater halo grew round the memory of Olaf the Thick, who was soon to change his soubriquet and become for all future generations Olaf the Holy.

The heathen party, such as then remained, had no supporters, for Cnut was a firm and zealous Christian. He had had his lesson against any tendency to backsliding towards ancient beliefs, or the showing of any disrespect to Christian saints. Had not his own father, Sweyn (as was the general belief), received his death through the miraculous power of Edmund, the English saint—strong still to revenge a slight, though he had been dead more than a century? Cnut had to humble himself at St. Edmund's shrine. What power had such a king to resist the growing reputation for sanctity which was clinging to the name of the dead Olaf, the continued report of miracles which had accompanied his steps, especially in his latter days of distress and desertion? Popular superstition, like popular fancy, which is illustrated in the folk-tales, always, if it has any excuse for so doing, clings to the losing side.

Kalf Arnason, too, was discontented. Cnut's promises had been fair enough, but he showed no signs of fulfilling them. He had spoken of Kalf becoming the virtual sovereign of Norway in the same way that the Earls of Lade had been virtual sovereigns under Cnut's predecessors on the Danish throne. Hakon, the last representative of that house, was, as Cnut acknowledged, too gentle and too honourable to be intrusted with such power. But it appeared now that the Dane rather thought of keeping the government in his own hands, and Kalf was a no better man than formerly.

Cnut had difficulties in his own kingdom. As he spent most of his time in England his Danish subjects began to long for a king of their own; and it went so far that Ulf, one of the most powerful of the Danish earls, and brother-in-law to Cnut,[1] and Cnut's wife together set up the son of Cnut, Hardacnut, as King of Denmark in the absence of his father. When Cnut came over from England they excused their conduct, and did not venture to oppose the force which the elder king brought with him; but Cnut took an opportunity

[1] He was, through his sister, brother-in-law also to our English Earl Godwin.

before long to quarrel with Ulf, and he had him murdered. Ulf's son, Svend—generally called from his mother Svend Estrid's son—became afterwards a pretender to the throne of Denmark, and the founder of a new dynasty.

Cnut left his own son Svend as nominal regent of Norway; but Svend was only a child; the power belonged to his mother Alfifa. People began to murmur against this state of things, and, as has been said, Cnut had done little to propitiate the two most powerful men in the country, Einar Tambarskelfir and Kalf Arnason.

A pretender presently arose who called himself Tryggvi, and said he was a son of Olaf Tryggvason. He was reported to be the son of a priest; 'but,' says Snorri, 'this praise must be allowed him, that he showed himself more like the son of Olaf Tryggvason; for this Tryggvi was a slaughtering man.' He could get no great following. The fleet which he collected was met by one under the command of Svend (now grown to maturity), and a battle took place very near the scene of Norway's first historic battle, the Hafirsfjord, and there Tryggvi was slain.

But this winter there were consultations between Einar and Kalf at Nidarös (Throndhjem), and early next spring they had apparently decided upon their course, for they collected a great retinue of men, and prepared for a journey. Cnut had sent to demand a tribute 'of axes,' and Kalf had refused flatly, nay, with threats.

The ambassadors left Norway and passed into Sweden. Magnus, the son of King Olaf (whom we may now call St. Olaf), had, since the battle of

Stiklestad been carried away, first to Sweden, afterwards to Russia. There, at the Court of Novgorod (Holmgaard), the followers of Olaf had a friend in King Jarisleif's queen, the Ingegerd who had once been destined for Olaf. Russia had nothing to fear from the King of England and Denmark. This Jarisleif (Yaroslav), the son of Vladomir, was the great-grandson of Rurik or Rorik, who is reckoned the founder of this dynasty of the Russians in Greater Suithiod. Kalf and Einar came first to Ladoga (Aldeigjuborg), and remained there till they had got a favourable response to their invitation to Magnus to come and claim the crown of Norway. They were then invited to Novgorod, and there they did homage to Magnus, or, at any rate, acknowledged him as their king. Magnus then made a triumphal progress through Sweden to the Throndhjem district, and was proclaimed king at the Öre Thing held there.

By this time Cnut was near death. Hardacnut had already received the crown of Denmark. Harald was destined to succeed in England, and Svend in Norway. The latter could hope for little support beyond that which his new subjects were disposed to give him. It very soon appeared that few of the bonders were disposed to take up arms against Olaf's son, and Svend was compelled to abandon the country and sail to Denmark. Thus, without blood being shed, Magnus was restored to the throne of his forefathers (A.D. 1035).

The new king began by driving away many of those who had fought against his father at Stiklestad, and confiscating their estates; albeit he had promised that his reign should be inaugurated by an 'act of oblivion.'

Kalf Arnason, who had been the Monk of this restoration, fell into such disfavour that he thought it prudent to go into exile, and his estates were forfeited. These unjust proceedings caused an insurrection among the bonders, and Magnus, profiting by the timely warning, grew more just and pacific. The latter part of his reign redeemed the outset, and earned him the name of Magnus the Good.

Outside of Norway nothing of great importance was achieved in this reign. At the beginning of it, that is to say, almost directly after the death of Cnut in 1036, the King of Norway collected a fleet and prepared to attack Hardacnut, the new King of Denmark. Hardacnut, on his side, brought his fleet to the mouth of the Göta River, not less ready for battle. In the event, peace was made between the two sovereigns on the condition—the tontine condition, as it really was—that each should reign unmolested by the other, and that the survivor of the two should succeed to both kingdoms. Hardacnut, after succeeding his brother Harold on the English throne, died in A.D. 1039; whereupon Magnus Olafsson collected a large fleet, and prepared, if necessary, to assert by arms his claim to the Danish succession, and for a period he was undisputed ruler of Denmark as well as of Norway.

He appointed as his regent of the latter country—against the advice of some of his wisest statesmen—the cousin of Hardacnut, the son, namely, of that Earl Ulf who had married Cnut's sister Estrid, and whom Cnut, in a fit of jealousy, had caused to be assassinated. We mentioned a few pages above this son of Ulf's and of Estrid's whose name was Svend. He is known in

Danish history as Svend Estrid's son, after his mother, because she was of the old royal line of the Skjoldungs, the time-honoured race that had given kings to Denmark. This Svend was the founder of a new dynasty, the Estridsons. For, the year following his investiture as earl-regent of Denmark, and vassal to King Magnus he deemed himself strong enough to assert his independence, and to take the royal title. Magnus collected a fleet and army to chastise him, but he escaped to Scania, and thence into Sweden. The King of Norway inflicted severe punishment upon the adherents of the pretender.

We see Magnus also upon the German continent, first attacking and destroying the Viking stronghold, Jomsburg; and afterwards marching further inland to meet a large army of pagan 'Vends' (*i.e.* Slavs). The army opposed to that of the Norse king proved to be so much larger than his own that many of Magnus's followers were for persuading him to turn back; but he was very unwilling to do this, for he had never yet shunned an engagement against any odds. At night (when he had ordered his troops and expected to meet the enemy the next day) he lay down in some perplexity and anxiety to sleep. It was Michaelmas Eve. In the night, so runs the graceful legend, his father, St. Olaf, appeared to Magnus in his sleep, and admonished him not to be afraid with a Christian army to attack an army of heathens however great. 'For I,' he said, 'shall be with thee in battle. Prepare to give battle to the Vends when thou hearest my trumpet.'

The king awoke, and told his dream to those about him. The day was just breaking. At that moment all the people heard in the air a ringing of bells; and those of the Norwegian army who had been in the town of Throndhjem (Nidaros) thought it was the ringing of a bell called 'Glod,' which St. Olaf had presented to the Church of St. Clement in that town.

The story makes us think of the magic powers of Michael Scott:

> That when in Salamanca's cave,
> Him listed his magic wand to wave,
> The bells would ring in Notre Dame.

The church bell is always, in mediæval legend, the music of the saint, the trumpet, as we may say, which calls to spiritual battle, to war with the powers of darkness.

It need not be said after this preface that Magnus and his Norsemen gained a signal victory. The battle-field is called in the Saga Lyrskog Heath. It is said to be not far from Sleswik.

The life of Magnus represents him after this fighting two battles against Svend Estridson, who would not resign the title of King of Denmark. In each battle it is said Magnus was victorious, and Svend was driven from his kingdom to take refuge in Sweden, and all his lands were harried. Magnus reigned (nominally, at any rate) as king of both Norway and Denmark, to all appearance the most wide-ruling king who had sprung of the race of Harald Fairhair. But Svend seems never to have laid down his kingly title, while the power of Magnus in Denmark lasted only so long as he had a fleet and an army at hand to support him. Magnus thought of prosecuting still further his claims as the (tontine) heir of Hardacnut; and in virtue of that inheritance he sent to demand the crown of England, which Hardacnut had also worn before he died, of Hardacnut's half-brother, our Edward the Confessor: but he never enforced his demand by arms.

This reign of Magnus in Norway is contemporary with the greatest period in the history of the Earls of Orkney, of which the Jarla Sögur, or Orkneyinga Saga, gives us a vivid account. The possessions of the Earls of Orkney consisted at that time of both the Orkney and Shetland groups of islands, and of Caithness on the Scottish mainland; but the latter county was held from the Kings of Scotland, and belonged without dispute to Thorfinn, called in the Orkney history Thorfinn the Great, one of the joint Earls of Orkney. The other Orkney Earl was Thorfinn's uncle, not much his senior in age, Rögnvald Brusason, a man who had spent much time at the Norwegian Court, and was high in favour with the Norwegian monarchs who claimed to be the suzerains of Orkney, both with Olaf the Saint and his son Magnus. Rögnvald fought by the side of Olaf at Stiklestad, and aided Harald Hardradi to escape from the battle in a way that we shall immediately have to relate. Rögnvald returned for a while to the Orkneys; ruled at first in harmony with Thorfinn, but was eventually driven out by his nephew; he returned and drove away Thorfinn for a time, and was finally slain by the latter.

We now come to the history of that brother of Olaf the Saint who had fought by his side at Stiklestad, the son of King Sigurd Syr and of Aasta, Harold Sigurdson (or as we English know him best), Harald Hardradi,

Harald the Hard. Few figures in Norse history realise better than he does the picturesque character of the old Viking leader. Few men seemed better fitted to draw the Norse nation back to the unity from which it was slipping away; yet none were more unfortunate than this king was; in truth, we may reckon his death as one of the greatest blows ever dealt to Norway.

Harald was but a boy when he fought by his stepbrother's side at Stiklestad. He received a wound there; and when the day had gone hopelessly against his side, he fled up into the kindly shade of the forest with one friend only beside him, Earl Rögnvald, the Rögnvald of whom we have just spoken, and whom the Orkney Saga calls 'the most accomplished man of his day.' Rögnvald left young Harald with a bonder who lived in this forest-country of the border to be healed of his wounds; and, when better, the youth passed on in the early spring through the dense wood of the Markland into Jemtland, and so on to the Swedish court of Upsala. There he met many fugitive Norsemen, among the rest his friend Rögnvald once more. These two decided not to stay in Sweden, but to travel eastward to the Greater Sweden, and to the court of King Jarisleif of Novgorod.

We have already beheld many fugitives from Norway taking the same route. But Harald Hardradi travelled further than most of these. He followed in the wake of those men from Greater Sweden who had found their way as far as the states of the Byzantine Empire, and taking service with the emperor, had formed themselves into a bodyguard, which went by the name of the Invincible Guard. It was also called the Varingian

Guard; for the Greeks called all these men from the north Varingi or Varangi (Pharangi) a name which may perhaps be a corruption of Franks. We are told that this Varingian Guard, which formed a distinct division of the Greek army, often retrieved the day of battle when the rest of the army had been put to flight.

The licentious and cruel Empress Zoe was on the Byzantine throne when Harald came to Constantinople. By her he was appointed to the command of the Varangi. Many are the stories which the Sagas relate of Harald's battles with the Saracens, who were now a great and ever-growing danger to the Greek Empire, and of his wonderful quickness in counsel and readiness of resource. Some of these stories are told of earlier northern heroes of the Viking age. One in particular of Harald's achievements is ascribed likewise to Hasting, a famous Viking of the ninth century. The following story is told also of one of the Norman Dukes of Apulia. Yet, albeit we cannot be sure that it is truly told of Harald, it is worth the repeating.

Harald Hardradi was engaged upon the siege of a strong town in Sicily. He noticed that the sparrows from the town flew out every day into the fields to feed; but flew back at night to nest in the thatched roofs of the houses of the town. Therefore he gave orders that as many of these sparrows should be captured as possible, and, when they were captured, he caused lighted sticks to be tied to their tails. They, of course, at once flew back to their nests in the roofs of the houses and of the citadel; and as these roofs were thatched, they caught fire, and the whole town was burned to the ground.

After the restoration of St. Olaf's line in Norway, Harald Hardradi determined to return to his native country and to claim a share in the inheritance of his nephew, King Magnus. Supposing that his claims were sure to be disputed, he allied himself at first with the pretender to the throne of Denmark, Svend Estridsson, and they proceeded together against Magnus. But Magnus made overtures to Harald, and detached him from the Svend alliance. Eventually the uncle and nephew, who were nearly of the same age, jointly governed the kingdom.

Thus ended the adventurous portion of Harald Hardradi's career, almost the last of the kings of Norway who seemed to partake of the old Viking character. There was one last adventure in store for him. He survived Magnus, and reigned as sole king of Norway. Magnus had left Denmark to his old rival Svend Estridsson, and Norway to his uncle, Harald. The latter refused to admit the right of Magnus to dispose of the Danish crown, and continued the war with Svend. Harald likewise, as we shall see, made the same claims which Magnus had once asserted to the crown of England. Harald Hardradi was not, the historian tells us, very popular with the mass of the population, on account of the severity of his character. He seems, indeed, to have exercised a more personal and tyrannical rule than any preceding king of Norway. But he was respected for his soldierly qualities and his fame in war. After Harald had reigned some years in peace, there came a fresh temptation to him to try once more his fortune as a soldier abroad.

We most of us know, at least in outline, the history

of the last adventure of Harald Hardradi. We know how Tostig, Godwin's son, the brother of our King Harald, who had been expelled from his earldom of Northumbria, sought on every side from the enemies of Harold and of England for aid in the recovery of his forfeited earldom. He applied first to Duke William of Normandy, who was making, as all men knew, preparations for the invasion of England; and he got some men and ships from that quarter and harried the southern coasts of England, but was driven off. Most of his crews deserted him when he tried to make a descent upon Northumberland, and he went next to his ally Malcolm (called Cænmore, or Big Head), king of Scotland. Tostig could not gain all the assistance which he required in this quarter, so he set sail (at least the northern Sagas say he did this) to Norway, to persuade Harald Hardradi to undertake the invasion of England, of which, as we saw, Harald's nephew and predecessor Magnus had claimed the crown.

Harald consented, and made vast preparations for the expedition. We see him reviewing the fleet which he had collected by the Sulen Islands (the Ytre Sulen and the Indre Sulen), which lie just at the mouth of the Sögne Fjord. Strange portents warned men what was to be the issue of this adventure, this death-throe, as it proved to be, of the old heroic Norway.

It is said that one of the companions of the king saw from his ship a huge woman of the troll or demon race, sitting upon the land. She had in one hand a fork, and in the other a bowl, as though for holding blood. And, looking over all the fleet he saw, with the second sight which had come upon him, on each ship perched a bird of prey, a raven or an eagle, as though the crew of each ship was destined to destruction. Another man in the Norse fleet saw in a dream the arrival of their army in England, and the army which they were going to fight; and before the latter rode a demon-woman upon a wolf; it held a human carcase in its mouth, and blood was streaming from its jaws, and as it devoured one man from the Norwegian army, the troll-woman gave it another. Under these gloomy auspices did Harald's fleet set sail in the autumn of A.D. 1066.

The fleet came first to the Orkneys. It was joined there by the two Earls of Orkney, Paul and Erling, the sons of that Earl Thorfinn of whom we have spoken. How it sailed next to Scotland, and then in conjunction with Tostig's fleet down to the English coast, fighting with the men of Scarborough and burning that town, with the men of Holderness, till it reached the mouth of the Humber, readers of English history remember. It sailed up the Humber to the mouth of the Wharf, in which lay the fleet of the Earls of Northumbria and Mercia, the famous-infamous Earls Morcar and Edwine. On Wednesday, September 20, the army of Harald and Tostig met the army of the earls at Gate Fulford. Harald and Tostig gained a signal victory. They then marched to besiege York, which capitulated on Sunday, September 24. Harald took hostages from the city, and appointed Stamford Bridge as the place where the chief men of Northumbria were to come to him and make submission.

But that very evening another English army, under our King Harold Godwin's son, had reached the neighbourhood. It is said that the Norse army was totally unaware of its approach, and that Harald and Tostig had gone forward with some of their bodyguard, but without having donned their armour, when the army of the English Harold came in sight, advancing along the road which leads from York to the river. It is an ancient Roman highway, as the local names Gate Helmsley and Gate Fulford suggest. Tostig was for falling back upon their base; but Harald would only consent to send back messengers to bring up the rest of their force.

The Norse Saga tells the famous story of the message which English Harold sent to his brother, promising him restoration to his earldom if he would make peace. Tostig said:

'This is something different from the enmity and scorn which he offered me last winter. . . . But if I accept of this offer, what will he give Harald Sigurdsson for his trouble?'

The envoy replied: 'He has also spoken of this, and will give him seven feet of English ground, or as much more as he may be taller than other men.'

Then said the earl: 'Go now and tell King Harold to get ready for battle; for never shall the Northmen say that Earl Tostig left King Harald Sigurdsson to join his enemy's troops, when he came to fight west here in England. We shall rather all take the resolution to die with honour, or to gain England by a victory.'

The account of the battle in the Saga is not to be relied upon, except, maybe, for one little touch. As the Norse Harald, it is said, was riding round his army ordering the battle, his horse stumbled under him, and the king fell off. He got up at once and said, 'A fall is lucky for a traveller.' But the English Harold asked 'who the stout man was who fell, with the blue cloak and beautiful helmet.' 'That is the king himself,' they said. Then the English king said : 'A great man, and of a stately mien is he; but I think his luck has deserted him.'

Of the battle of Stamford Bridge, we only know that it was a hard-fought one on either side; but that at the last Harald Hardradi and Tostig fell, and the English gained the victory. But only, alas! to find that Duke William of Normandy had taken advantage of the diversion, and that, his preparations now being complete, he had set sail for England.

We have one other thing to record of this Harald Hardradi beside his career of warlike adventure. This is, that he built the town of Opslo or Oslo, practically the forerunner of the modern Christiania. (Christiania lies almost entirely to the west of the Akers Stream, and Oslo lay to the east of it; that is the only difference between the two sites.) By this act, Harald, the last of the kings of the old order, took one more step towards the bringing on of the new order of things, the more peaceful age which succeeded in Norway.

We may count the death of Harald Hardradi as the end of the heroic period in the history of Norway— the true Saga Age, when the deeds that were done and the skalds that sang or the story-tellers who related them were all alike worthy. Heathenism had now disappeared. But it would seem as if the character of the Scandinavian people were formed upon a heathen model, and could not well adapt itself to a change of faith. As one or two in the great group of Catholic states of mediæval Europe, governed by the beliefs, imitating more or less the social life and the policy of these Catholic states, the Scandinavian countries fall into the background. Their history no longer claims much of our attention. In one of the great-grandsons of Harald Hardradi we see Harald's love of adventure surviving; but now it finds its outlet by the king joining the crusades, and being known to his contemporaries and to all Norse history as Sigurd Jorsalfari, the farer to Jerusalem—Sigurd the Crusader.

Not, indeed, that the Scandinavian peoples—albeit they had now utterly forgotten their Odin worship—showed any unnatural alacrity to follow the precepts of the Gospel of Peace. Their wars continued to go on: but they became of a more petty character from year to year. Once we were able to look upon the whole mass of the Scandinavian nations as forming, in a certain sense, one people, and although they were continually at war with one another, there was at the same time a sort of unity in their life which kept them together, and which kept them distinct from all the nations of Christian Europe. We saw a group of warlike peoples stretching from the middle of Russia up to Iceland, and to the most western of the British Islands. Until the death of Harald Hardradi there seems to be very little change in the character of what we have called the 'Greater Scandinavia.' Such change as there was meant but an extension of the Scandinavian influence in Europe. Our own country lay nearest to the borders of the Greater Scandinavia, almost within the zone of its influence, between it, one might say, and the rest of Christian Europe. It fluctuated for a long time between two opposing forces. Through the immense influx of northern blood which it had experienced in the ninth and tenth centuries it was drawn towards the Scandinavian peoples; by its old Christianity it was chained to Continental Europe. After the Danish conquest of Cnut it seemed to give way to the former attraction, and to become absorbed among the Scandinavian States; but then followed the reign of Edward the Confessor, when the influence of Catholicism and of Catholic Europe again became strong.

This reign brought in a new element, the Norman or French element, into our history. For, of the Scandinavian States which, in a former chapter, we counted as having been born from the great Viking outpouring of the ninth century, one (but one only) had been completely withdrawn from its old associations, had utterly broken with its old traditions, Normandy, namely, the Scandinavian settlement in France. Even during Edward the Confessor's reign a reaction began against this Norman influence. It was expressed by the rise of the House of Godwin and the crowning of Harold. The new king's very name is significant of the influences which had affected England; for this is the first appearance of a thoroughly Scandinavian name borne by a king of English descent. Godwin had married Gyda, the sister of Earl Ulf of Denmark, who himself was the brother-in-law of Cnut; and the influence of Godwin's family and of Harold was to bring back, to re-assert, as it were, the Danish element in English life.

The relationship between England and the Scandinavian lands was shown again in another way : for when Tostig desired to recover his lost earldom, he naturally had recourse to the king of one of the brother Scandinavian states. He went, as we have seen, over to Norway and enlisted the help of Harald Hardradi, with we know what results. The Norse Harald and Tostig fell at Stamford Bridge. The English Harold had no time to raise forces enough to resist the Norman Conquest, wherefore he too fell a few months later at Hastings; and by the Norman Conquest were confirmed the Catholic and Continental influences in the history of this country. That these influences should have been brought in by another Scandinavian nation is curious ; but, as has been just said, though the Normans were Scandinavians by descent, they had utterly thrown off their Scandinavian character; so much so that before the time of William the Bastard the dukes found it difficult even to learn the old language. This was the one Scandinavian nation which separated itself from the rest of the Scandinavian group; but it kept the strength of the Scandivanian character, and when it adopted French ideas and the Catholicism of Central Europe, it adopted them in a more thorough fashion even than the Franks did themselves, and it became the greatest agent in the spreading of these ideas wherever its power extended.

From the time of the Norman Conquest the Scandinavian influence was gradually pushed out of the British Islands. The Norman Conquest, and all that it brought with it, were symbolised by the building of castles and cathedrals, and displayed in the establishment of a stricter discipline in Church and State. All these things we see slowly spreading northwards. The Norman castles and the Norman ways of looking at things made their way into Scotland with David the First; and when that happened the Norse influences in the Scottish Islands were rapidly on the decline. Presently Norway had to give up all her possessions in those parts. Hereafter, therefore, the history of the Norwegians becomes the history of Norway alone. With the other Scandinavian States for many hundred years —that is, until the union of Norway with Denmark and Sweden—we have nothing more to do. And when the union of the three countries does take place, the independent history of Norway comes to an end.

Seeing, then, that we are now bidding adieu to the great age in the history of the northern peoples, and even to all that is of great interest in the history of Norway, let us try and gain some picture of what was the life in this heroic age among the Scandinavians, and especially in Norway proper; now when Christianity had been introduced all over the north, but had not yet seriously affected the character of the people.

We will begin with the domestic life. As we have said, the country as a whole must be looked upon as a collection of farms, larger or smaller. Such it is still, with modifications; such it was then almost purely. The great men, the kings and earls, personally superintended the operations on their farms almost as much as the ordinary farmer in Norway does to-day. They do not seem, moreover, to have had a great number of country houses in different parts of their dominions as the Frankish kings, for example, had, and as our own

Anglo-Saxon kings had also. That great family of Throndhjem earls, for instance, from which came Earl Hakon and his sons, had its country seat at Lade, close to the more modern town of Throndhjem, and we almost always hear of the earls residing there. In the case of one of the small rulers in the south of Norway, that Sigurd Syr, who was stepfather of St. Olaf, we have a picture of the king superintending the *personnel* of his estate at their work, which is delightful and Homeric, and made all the more so by the fact that Sigurd, though he is really only quite a petty ruler, yet bears the title of king.

'King Sigurd Syr was standing in his cornfield when the messengers came to him and brought him the news [of the coming of Olaf, his stepson, who was about to raise the country and assert his claim to the throne]; and also told him all that Aasta was doing at home in the house. He had many people on his farm. Some were then shearing corn, some bound it together, some drove it to the building, some unloaded it and put it in sack or barn; but the king, and two men with him, went sometimes into the field, sometimes to the place where the corn was put into the barn. His dress, it is told, was this: He had a blue girdle and blue hose, shoes which were laced about the legs, a grey cloak, and a grey, wide-brimmed hat, a veil before his face, a staff in his hand, with a silver-gilt head on it, and a silver ring round it. Of Sigurd's living and disposition it is related that he was a very gain-making man, who attended carefully to his cattle and husbandry, and managed his household himself. He was nowise given to pomp, and was rather taciturn; but he was a man of the best understanding in Norway, and also excessively wealthy in moveable property. Peaceful he was, and nowise haughty.'

When the news was brought to Sigurd of Olaf's approach, 'he sat down and made them take off his shoes and put Corduvan boots on, to which he bound his gold spurs. Then he put off his coat and cloak, and dressed himself in his finest clothes, with a scarlet cloak over all, girded on his sword, set a gilt helmet on his head, and mounted his horse. He sent his labouring people out to the neighbourhood, and gathered to him thirty well-clothed men, and rode home with them.'

There is something very *naïf* in this last touch of King Sigurd sending his labourers among the tenants to collect thirty well-clothed men to ride with the king.

This Sigurd was an inland landowner. The larger landowners, whose estates went down to the sea, had nearly all of them one or more boats of their own building, which they might use in various ways, either as vessels of war or as merchantmen. We have said a good deal already about the boat-building of the north. The best descriptions of Viking ships which we have come to us from this period. The boats were not all built on one pattern. There was one kind called a Snaekke, which means a particularly fast boat (fast, that is, for rowing), and which I will guess approached most nearly the ordinary fjord-boat of modern days. Then there was the regular war-vessel, which was called sometimes the long ship, sometimes (purely as a generic name) a dragon, or a worm. I daresay these long ships belonged chiefly to the later Viking age, as in the earlier time before sea-fights began a lighter kind of craft would be all that was required. The mythical story of the death of Ragnar Lodbrok, who insisted on making his Viking cruise to England in one very long ship instead of a number of small ones, rather suggests this. About the longest ships of which we hear mention contain thirty or thirty-two benches of rowers. Now, the Christiania ship, which anybody can see who chooses, contains sixteen benches; and the reader who has seen the Christiania ship may judge for himself to what fine dimensions these largest vessels must have reached. They would not, of course, have been quite double the length of the Christiania boat, but they would have been more than half as long again. However, we read more frequently of boats containing twenty benches; and I daresay this Christiania boat was a very good size for any one under the rank of a king. At this period the king of the whole country—Olaf Tryggvason or Olaf the Saint—generally sailed in some exceptionally large vessel. Olaf Tryggvason had, during the latter part of his reign, his celebrated ship called *Long Serpent*, in which he was when he lost his life at the battle of Svold.

This, we are told in the Saga, was the largest ship of war ever known up to that date. It had thirty-four benches of rowers; the keel, when placed upon the ground, measured seventy-four ells. But, unfortunately, we do not know for certain what was the length of the Norwegian ell at this time—two of our feet, or one and a half. The former would give a hundred and forty-eight feet for the keel of the *Long Serpent*, the latter a hundred and eleven. The lesser number seems the most probable, seeing that the keel of the Christiania boat with its sixteen benches is sixty feet.

The admiration which all the vessels of Olaf excited at Svold among the chiefs allied against the Norse king is told in a graphic manner in the Saga.

They mistook one vessel after another for the *Serpent*, but when the latter did appear it was conspicuous above all others by its size and beauty. 'Many said the *Serpent* is, indeed, a large and beautiful vessel, and it shows a great mind to have built such a ship.

'Earl Erik said, so loud that several persons heard him: "If King Olaf had no other vessels but only that one, King Svend would never take it from him with the Danish force alone."'

The only rivals of the Norse king's ships, in fact, were those of his Norse rival, Earl Erik, the son of Earl Hakon.

'Better were it,' says King Olaf, 'for these Swedes to be sitting at home killing their sacrifices, than to be venturing under our weapons from the *Long Serpent*. But who owns the large ship on the larboard side of the Danes?'

'That is Earl Erik Hakonsson,' say they.

Olaf Haraldsson (Olaf the Saint) had his large ship, which was carved with a man's head and called the *Carlus*. No doubt it represented the head of Charlemagne, who, now that the Northmen were becoming Christians, was beginning to be appreciated as a hero by people of that Scandinavian race to which, in his lifetime, he had been so inimical.

We see, then, that among the ships which were owned by the great landowners, there was always the material ready for the formation of a fleet for either side in any national dispute. These private vessels were by no means exclusively, nay, they were probably not principally, ships of war. It was, indeed, the custom of most of the young nobility to begin their adult years—adult years seem to have begun with these hardy spirits after the twelfth birthday—by one or more voyages of piracy in foreign waters. This was a sort of grand tour for the gilded Norwegian youth. But after they had been so employed once or twice, the vessels might continue to be used, now as pirate vessels, now as merchantmen.

The chief export of Norway in those days must have been fish. In Catholic Europe during the Middle Ages fish was a commodity more in demand (proportionately) than it is to-day. There were beside, furs—peltry—of which the country must have possessed a much greater supply in those days than it has now. It is very easy to see what imports were the most valued. There would first be arms and armour of the best kind obtainable, then clothes of various descriptions. Welsh (*i.e.* French) repps and Welsh swords, says a verse of northern poetry. Before the Northmen learned to smithy the finest weapons for themselves, they must have been a good deal dependent on importation from foreign countries. That very characteristic piece of defensive armour which we read of so often in the Sagas and poems, the ring-sark (chain-shirt) or byrnie (brunia) was a manufacture originally borrowed from the Franks.

For clothes: the Northmen had a great deal of vanity as regards their wearing apparel. In the Icelandic Sagas, for instance, we always hear of the foremost men appearing (at the Thing or wherever else it might be) in very gorgeous apparel. They had a love of bright and shining colours; and it is interesting to contrast the picture we get of their appearance with that of the inhabitants in mediæval Europe, who, we gather, generally dressed in sober-coloured garments. We saw Sigurd Syr just now in his blue kirtle and hose, and afterwards putting on his tanned boots, gold spurs, gold helmet, and scarlet cloak. Scarlet was, of all colours, that which the inhabitants of the northern lands most favoured. In the Sagas people appear constantly in scarlet dress. It was a figure in a scarlet dress which flashed out of men's sight when Olaf Tryggvason sprang overboard at Svold.

The merchant voyages of the Norsemen were, for the present, independent affairs. Each landowner had his own ship, his own private harbour or mooring-place. For as yet congregations of men come to set up a trade in common were hardly known; towns had scarcely begun to rise. Yet in the later days of the history which we have just related, a change had set in. During the greatest part of our history the only approach to a town of which we read is Tunsberg, modern Tönsberg, at the mouth of the Christiania Fjord. But Olaf Tryggvason founded, and St. Olaf rebuilt, after it had fallen into decay, the forerunner of the town of Throndhjem, Nidaros or Kopstat—chapman's town, merchants' town—as it was variously styled. Harald Hardradi, as we saw, built Oslo, which may be called the forerunner of Christiania. The chief events in the following reigns are the building of fresh towns in Norway; and the next era in the history of the country is the era of two things, the establishment of the power of the Catholic Church and the growth of the merchant towns. For both of these things the country is indebted chiefly to foreign influences: to the action of the See of Rome for the one; for the other to the great league of the trading cities on the Baltic and on the North Sea, which went by the name of 'The League,' the Hansa.

CHAPTER XI

HISTORY

The Civil Wars—Sverri—Hakon Hakonsson
A.D. 1066-1263.

HENCEFORWARD we must look upon the history of Norway as divorced from that of the whole group of Scandinavian states, and one to be studied by itself. The heroic age has passed; the ages which follow are far less interesting; they may be dismissed in a much shorter space. It was not for the sake merely of recording events, but of giving a picture of the character of those who made the history of the heroic age, the national character of these Scandinavians during their best days; and again, for the sake of giving some notion of the literature in which their achievements are preserved, that we have dwelt rather lengthily on the first two hundred years or so of Norwegian history. A single chapter now may suffice to cover as much ground as is covered by the four previous chapters.

Harald Hardradi was succeeded by a son, who, in his character, typifies the transition to a new era. His name was Olaf, and he was surnamed during his reign *Kyrri*, or the Peaceful. Harald did, in fact, leave two sons behind him at his death; one, Magnus, he had left behind in Norway; Olaf, the other, had been with his father in England. Magnus took over the government of the country till the return of his brother, but he survived that return only for a short time.

Olaf *Kyrri* is described as a very handsome man, of a silent habit in large companies, but very talkative in small, especially when he was at table; he was a heavy drinker, but even in his cups of a very mild disposition. He may be reckoned as—appropriately enough—the inaugurator of inns or hotels in his country, and on this account he is an interesting figure to the modern traveller. What Olaf actually did in this way was the building of a merchants' house in Nidaros or Throndhjem; a building which served the purpose of an inn or travellers' rest.

We may, perhaps, refer to this period a change in house architecture, of which we have spoken in an earlier chapter, namely, the transferring of the fireplace from the centre of the room to the corner; and the building of chimneys to carry away the smoke. This change would, of course, at first distinguish the houses of greatest pretensions.

Of much greater real importance is it to find Olaf Kyrri laying the foundations of a new town which, during the Middle Ages, was destined to be the most important town in Norway; nay, not only in the Middle Ages, but until quite modern times. This town is Bergen, which, as most travellers would agree, is the most interesting town of Norway; so that its founder deserves to be had in remembrance. Throndhjem had hitherto been the great merchant town of the country; it was founded by Olaf Tryggvason, but practically rebuilt by St. Olaf; St. Olaf also built Sarpsborg, near the modern Frederikstad, which, from that time forward, became the meeting-place of the Thing of the Viken district; then Harald Hardradi founded Oslo, the father of the modern Christiania; finally, we have Olaf Kyrri founding Bergen; and thus the three chief existing towns of Norway are accounted for. Other towns cannot be traced back so easily to their origins; they have grown up gradually from being mere villages or collections of fishermen's huts. Among towns of this class is Stavanger. Another of Olaf's acts was the laying of the foundation of the first stone church in the country, the Christ Church of Throndhjem—in other words, Throndhjem Cathedral.

In a metaphorical, and, to some extent, in a literal sense, the age upon which we have now entered is the age of church building. Christianity has now established itself without a rival. Legend is, during all this age, changing the rough, practical, law-loving Olaf the Thick, into a saint and a martyr, dying for his faith. Before long he will become, so to say, an impersonation of the territory of Norway wiped clean of its old heathenism and reconsecrated to Christ. Then a theory will be established, that Olaf's right of inheritance lives on, though the king is in heaven; so that the legal, the ecclesiastical-legal fiction will be established that the king for the time being holds his kingdom as 'a fief of St. Olaf,' the power of the saint in heaven residing with the ministers of his foundation, the See of Throndhjem, on earth.

The earliest churches built in Norway were, without doubt, of wood. To this day the wooden churches are in a vast majority, and stone ones rare exceptions. We have no wooden structures which go back quite as early as the date at which we are now arrived. But there are one or two wooden churches which belong to a time very little later—the latter half of the twelfth century. These are the churches called *stavekirker*, of which we have specimens still standing at Hitterdal, on the Hitterdalselv, not far from Kongsberg, the terminus of the western railway from Christiania. Another of these stave-churches is at Borgund, near Lærdal, on the Sogne Fjord. This is the one most frequently visited by travellers. These churches give us a picture of the religious structures which, from the time of Olaf Kyrri, began to be raised pretty frequently over Norway. St. Olaf in his day built churches for the principal divisions of the country, and the patronage of these churches lay with the crown. Not seldom some great chief, when he changed his faith, built a church for his own benefit, and the benefit of his household: this was a sort of private chapel. The chief, before his conversion, had been in most cases a priest as well as a leader, and had had a temple of his own, and been wont to assist at the sacrifices. When he went over, it was natural that he should wish to preserve as much as possible of his old status by making himself the patron of a church. Then there were other churches built by districts for their own use; in this case the patronage lay neither with the king nor with any great chief, but rather with the local Thing.

It marks the inauguration of something like true mediævalism in Norway—the nearest approach to it which the country ever knew—that in some cases, notably in the case of the most venerable church in the country, the wooden buildings are replaced by stone ones. The few stone churches in Norway that preserve any traces of Romanesque or Gothic architecture were most of them founded about the time of King Olaf Kyrri, or very soon after his death—that is to say, during the concluding years of the eleventh century. Throndhjem Cathedral stands the first among these, the most interesting architectural monument in Norway. It does not appear that in the building, as it now stands, we have any remains of Olaf Kyrri's work. The oldest parts of the present building were probably erected by the celebrated Archbishop Eystein in the succeeding century: of Eystein we shall have to say a passing word hereafter. Next, after Throndhjem Cathedral, comes the cathedral of Stavanger, which was founded during or soon after the reign of Olaf Kyrri by an English bishop, and was dedicated to the English Saint Swithun—a fair set-off against the fact that we had in the twelfth century, and still have in London, a church dedicated to the Norse St. Olaf. In all the countries which once belonged to the Norwegian crown, and were colonised by Norsemen, we shall find but one example of a stone church which may compare to these two—the cathedrals of Throndhjem and Stavanger. This church is the Church of St. Magnus, in the Orkneys. It, too, is a Romanesque structure, and it bears a close resemblance to the older parts of the buildings at Throndhjem and at Stavanger. Besides being the founder of Throndhjem Cathedral, Olaf Kyrri was a great founder of monasteries. Some of those which Bergen formerly possessed were instituted by him. Olaf Kyrri died in A.D. 1093.

That, however, the old adventurous Norse spirit had not been utterly eliminated from the line of Harald Sigurdsson, was proved by the accession of a son of Olaf Kyrri, Magnus by name, who reverted to the character of his grandfather. His life was a life almost entirely of adventure, chiefly passed in the British Islands, in the Hebrides, or in Ireland. His object was to extend the power of Norway over these various communities in the west, over the kings of the Hebrides, and the islands south of them, over the King of Man, and over the Norse colonies in Ireland, as Olaf and Magnus the Good had established the power of Norway over the Orkneys and Faroes. And for his own lifetime he succeeded—in Scotland at any rate. When this Magnus came back to Norway from his expeditions in the west, he came wearing the dress of the countries in which he had spent so much of his time: a dress something like the Highland kilt,—and from this habit the king earned the name of 'Bare-leg' or 'Bare-foot,' by which he is known in history—Magnus *Berfœtt*. One saying of his is worth remembering: we might call it a last voice from the heroic kingship of old days. When Magnus' friends reproached him for exposing himself too much in battle, he answered, 'Kings were made for honour, not for long life.' He was killed in Ireland at the age of about thirty (A.D. 1103), after he had reigned for ten years, most of which time was spent in expeditions of adventure.

Three sons succeeded Magnus Barefoot, one of whom shared his character: this one is that crusading king, Sigurd Jorsalfari, of whom we have already spoken. But despite the fact that his personal character recalls that of some of his forerunners, the two notable events of Sigurd the Crusader's reign belong to the new era, to the two new tendencies of life in Norway, the growth of the towns, and the growth of the power of the Church. Sigurd built the town of Kongshalla; and while he was in the Holy Land, he vowed that he would establish a metropolitan see in his dominions, and that he would likewise levy a tithe on the whole country for the support of the clergy—in other words, that he would, as the modern phrase goes, bring Norway into line with the more southern states of Christendom, so far as regarded its church-government. These vows were only partially fulfilled. But the position of the Church grew much stronger in this reign, and, indeed, it was growing stronger day by day.

Stronger, also, were beginning to grow the greater landowners, the great leaders throughout the country. Under the Olafs, and their immediate successors, they had fallen much in position. The old race of earls had pretty nearly decayed. The greatest among that body, the Earls of Lade, who so often gave rulers to Norway, had died out at the time that Magnus, the son of Olaf, came to the throne. Of the great chiefs under the two Olafs—Einar Tambarskelfir, Erling Skjalgsson, Finn Arnason, and so forth—some only bore the title of earl. As the old race of earls were the representatives of a still earlier race of independent kings, so now these earls were replaced by a class of aristocracy not new but less imposing in appearance, who went by the name of *lendermen*. The lendermen had been in a manner created by Harald Fairhair. Theoretically they were the collectors of the king's revenue from the different districts of the country. But they were likewise men of noble birth and of great local influence. We may consider them as representing the hersar, the second order of nobility in Norway; and albeit they boasted among their number no houses so imposing as the old Lade house, and that we do not read of any individuals among them so illustrious as Einar Tambarskelfir, yet as a body, they were much more powerful than any aristocratic body that had yet existed in the country. Then the aristocracy became self-destructive by rushing into civil war. This is the history which we have now to follow. It has many points of similarity to the history of the fall of our old baronage in the Wars of the Roses.

During the latter years of Sigurd the Crusader's reign there appeared upon the scene a young man out of Ireland, who declared that he was a son of Sigurd's father, Magnus Bareleg, and by an Irish mother. Magnus had never acknowledged this son; for all men knew he had never heard of him. But the newcomer, Harald by name, underwent the ordeal of fire to prove his royal birth, and Sigurd, Magnus' son, acknowledged him as his half-brother. On Sigurd's death, in A.D. 1130, the kingdom was divided between his son Magnus and this Harald, called Gilli or Gille- christ—'that liar,' as his nephew Magnus called him. The two rulers soon quarrelled, and flew to arms to vindicate their respective claims. Harald had the strongest support. He defeated his (supposed) nephew in a battle fought at Foreleif in Bohuslän.

Magnus was taken prisoner, blinded, and placed in a convent. This is a proceeding most common in mediæval history, the blinding of an unsuccessful rival, and imprisoning him in a convent. It constantly occurs in the history of the Visigoths of Spain, and of the Franks in France; but, strange to say, it is a new feature in the history of Norway, and is worth noting on that account. For one thing Norway was only beginning to possess religious houses. Nobody had built more of them than Olaf Kyrri.

Harald Gilli presents all the characteristics of a mere adventurer. As has already been said, he had never been recognised by his putative father; why Sigurd Jorsalafari recognised him it is difficult to understand. Nevertheless, as we see, he was supported by the strongest party among the lendermen. It may have been that Magnus, Sigurd's son, was personally unpopular, and that Harald was personally liked; there was much of the jovial, reckless Irishman in his composition. But it is probable that the chief reason of the lendermen for supporting him was that they felt that with this stranger on the Norwegian throne they would have more weight in the commonwealth than under an undoubted descendant of St. Olaf.

The man who profits by a state of disturbance in a country may expect others also to take advantage of it. There arose before long in the district bordering on Sweden, a new claimant, a deacon by profession, by character a brave but turbulent, unscrupulous man, little fitted for the clerical profession. His name was Sigurd, and he got the nickname of *Slembidjakn*, or the Bad Deacon. He claimed to be, like Harald

Gillechrist, a son of Magnus Bareleg. He gained little support for his own claims, save among the wilder spirits of the borderland; but, with the help of the small army he raised among these, Sigurd Slembidjakn managed to release the blind Magnus, and the opposition party to King Harald was made up of the adherents of both Magnus and Sigurd.

The aristocracy of Norway were now split up into two fiercely hostile sections, caring in reality little about the rights of the leaders under whom they professed to fight, but each burning for revenge upon the other. The lendermen were, in fact, brought to almost precisely the same condition in which the English nobility were at the time of the Wars of the Roses. Now, if a leader fell, his followers never thought of acknowledging his rival, they simply looked for a new claimant to the throne to lead their party, the best they could find. Harald Gilli at length defeated and slew his two rivals, Magnus and Sigurd, at the battle of Holmensgraa, and for a moment peace seemed to be restored. Harald Gilli was, however, himself murdered in A.D. 1136.

Harald left four sons by different mothers. One of them, Eystein, was in Scotland at the time of his father's death, and the government first devolved upon two brothers, Sigurd and Ingi. When Eystein appeared, and later on a fourth brother, Magnus, the country was divided among all the sons of Harald Gilli.

For a short time there was peace. Then war broke out again between the brothers, or, say, between the lendermen of the four different courts. Ingi, who was physically the weakest of the sons of Harald—he was slightly deformed, and could with difficulty mount on horseback—had among the men of his court two lender-men of great power and influence in the country, two king-makers, as we may call them. The first of the two, leader of Ingi's party till his death, Gregorius Dagsson, had a quarrel with Sigurd when the latter came once to a conference with his brother Ingi at Throndhjem; and Dagsson's men captured Sigurd in a house in the town and put him to death.

Eystein was the next of the brothers to fall. He had collected a fleet and set out upon an expedition to meet Ingi's following in the south; but his ships' crews began to desert him, until he was obliged to abandon his fleet and make his way into the interior. He had still 1200 followers, but the number gradually dwindled, until at last he was caught by one of Ingi's officers, accompanied by one attendant only, and was slain. This was in the interior mountain country, far from where he had abandoned his fleet. Thereupon Eystein's party elected a new pretender—the party, as we have said, now making the claimant, and not the pretender the party—a son of Sigurd, whose name was Hakon Herdibreid. Hakon's reign was inaugurated by a disgraceful defeat inflicted upon him by Gregorius Dagsson, near Kongshalle, the frontier town on the Göta River. Hakon, it is said, had 4000 men in this engagement, and Gregorius only 400. The new king then made his way to Throndhjem, where he had a large following. He collected a fleet there, and sailed to the south. By an artifice he caused the death of Gregorius Dagsson. Gregorius was, says Snorri, 'the most gallant lenderman in Norway that any one could remember.' Hakon next attacked King Ingi himself, who was at Oslo, the precursor of Christiania. It was in winter, and the Christiania Fjord was thick with ice. The ice extended as far as Horedö, the Saga says, that little island about a mile out in the fjord, which is one of the excursion-places from Christiania. There Ingi and his rival met, and the former was defeated and fell (A.D. 1161). He was the last of the rulers of Norway who even suppositiously represented a descent in the male line from Harald Hardradi.

The party of Ingi, which was the party of the greatest lendermen of the country, now looked about for a new leader. There was no thought of reconciliation with their opponents, or of submission to the claims of Hakon Herdibreid. They found their new leader in the most distinguished of their own body. Since the death of Gregorius Dagsson, Erling Skakki stood above all his contemporaries in personal power, in reputation, and in influence. He himself had, however, no tincture of royal blood, and the time had not yet come when that could be dispensed with; but Erling had married Christina, the daughter of Sigurd Jorsalfari, and their son, Magnus, still only a child, was chosen king; the regency and the real kingship devolving upon his father Erling. This was in 1161. In 1162 Hakon Herdibreid was slain by Erling.

The reign of Magnus forms an important epoch in Norse history. At the beginning of it Erling found himself encompassed by difficulties on every side, and threatened by rival claimants of the crown; but the bulk of the lendermen were on his side. They saw in this elevation to the throne of a child king, under the protectorate of one of their own number, the desired opportunity of establishing firmly an aristocratic body in Norway, which might compare with the baronages or Freiheerdoms of the other States of Christian Europe. Thus the effect of the change of faith was now beginning to be fully felt, and Norway came at this time as near as she ever came to adopting the pattern of a feudal and Catholic State, as that pattern had been formed in Continental Europe.

For the Church was much concerned in bringing about the new state of things. We saw how Sigurd the Crusader had sworn to establish a metropolitan See for Norway and its dependencies at Throndhjem. The project was carried out under Harald Gilli: in 1152 Cardinal Nicolas Breakspeare, afterwards Pope Adrian IV., was sent to Norway by the then Pope for this purpose. The one who now held the See of Throndhjem was Archbishop Eystein, a man of marked individuality, and one who had a lasting influence on the history of Norway. Erling Skakki saw that there was little chance of establishing his dynasty upon a firm basis unless, beside the support of the aristocracy, he could win the even more important support of the Church. He entered into an alliance with Eystein, and an agreement was come to which wholly changed the character of the Norwegian monarchy. Instead of being held, as heretofore, as independently as if it were a freehold (odal) possession, it was now said to be held 'as a fief of St. Olaf.' This meant, in the first place, that it was held in fee, or as a fief from the Church; but it meant also, or should have meant, that heredity, in the strictest sense, in the legitimate male line was preserved for it.

Thus the new constitution was both a benefit and an evil to Norway. It was an evil in that it made the monarchy subservient to the Church; it was a benefit in that it put a stop to, or was designed to put a stop to, the continual partition of the country between the sons of the deceased monarch, as this custom had hitherto prevailed. In virtue of what may really be called this New Constitution, Archbishop Eystein consented, in A.D. 1164, to anoint Magnus Erlingsson as King of Norway, a ceremony which had been hitherto unknown to the Norse constitution.

For a while everything seemed to go well with the new dynasty. More and more of the lendermen of the opposition parties gave in their adherence to Erling and his son Magnus. There remained only bands of malcontents hovering in various parts of the country, chiefly in the markland between Norway and Sweden. The Saga gives a picturesque description of how Erling was nearly caught by one of these bands at a place called Rydiokul, on Lake Venner. He was keeping Candlemas there, and the priest of the place, who was secretly in league with the rebels, made Erling and his men drunk, and then sent word to the leader of the outlaws. He, in the hope of entrapping Erling, marched that night forty-three miles, but, through the extreme darkness of the night, eventually failed in his attempt.

Up to now the history of Norway seems to belong chiefly to the coast districts. In the earlier years, from the time of Hafirsfjord Battle down through many centuries, almost all the engagements of importance had been either naval battles, or, if fought on land, they took place between the crews of rival fleets, who landed for the sake of fighting out their differences better than they could on board ship. The reader who has followed upon the map the earlier chapters of this history cannot fail to have been struck with this fact. No real description of these battle-fields is possible on this account. And next after the record of the fights the history of the country consists in the record of the springing up of the sea-coast towns, one after another, round the coast—of the building of Throndhjem (Nidaros), of Opslo, of Kongshalle, of Bergen. In this way the course of history follows the usual course of our travels in Norway. Some travellers never get beyond the coast regions. They may, without doing so, visit the scenes of almost all the events which we have had yet to record, the battles in the Christiania Fjord, in the fjords near Stavanger, the islands near Bergen, the Nord Fjord, the Næs, South More, North More, Throndhjem Fjord, and the regions farther to the north. But now there appears to view, so to say, and takes an important part in the history of Norway, a new region which many travellers never visit at all. I mean the densely-wooded boundary lands which lie below the higher slopes of the 'keel,' and just upon the division line between Norway and Sweden. Here the forests attain their greatest dimensions. The fir-trees tower up to almost inconceivable heights, and among them, stand scarcely less high, the slender *birch*-stems, shining through the gloom like, as has been said, 'silver threads upon a dark green mantle.' We may suppose that culture—civilisation such as it was—had advanced farther and farther inland during all the years of history that we have had to record, so that the wilder spirits who shunned civilisation and quiet had more and more to betake themselves to these inland wooded regions.

Bands of adventurers and outlaws existed all through the Erling-Magnus reign. They represented a perpetual protest against the new ecclesiastical-feudal *régime* of Erling and his son. Presently, out of these scattered elements of disturbance, we see a new band come into existence. They were a ragged regiment. Marching and counter-marching, always pursued, never wholly submitting, they were reduced to the greatest extremities. For shoes they were obliged to betake themselves to the bark of the birch trees which grew abundantly in the forests, so that they gained from the 'respectable classes' the contemptuous name of Birkibeinar or 'Birch-legs.'

The first leader of these Birkibeinar was named Eystein Meyla, or 'The Maid,' so called from his girlish appearance. His command dates from A.D. 1174. (Ten years, we see, had passed since Magnus was anointed king by the other Eystein, the Archbishop.) Meyla had claims to the throne, as good as Magnus', perhaps. He was not wanting in courage, but he had not the resources fitting him to be a great leader, and his period of command was short. He made a descent upon Throndhjem in 1176, and succeeded so far that at the Öre Thing he received the title of king; but soon after this he was met by a body of Magnus' followers, and was killed in the engagement that ensued. Before, however, the troop of 'Birch-legs' could be completely dispersed, there rose to the command of it another man of a much more remarkable build, a sort of Napoleon of Norway, who was destined to change the whole history of the country. This was Sverri. Sverri is commonly reckoned the last of the great Norse kings, and is sometimes placed as a fourth beside the great names of Harald Haarfagr, Olaf Tryggvason, and St. Olaf.

This new leader came from the least-considered of the Norwegian colonies over-seas, namely, the Faroe Islands; and this appearance of Sverri from such an obscure birthplace reminds one of the birth of Napoleon in Corsica. Ostensibly, Sverri was a son of Unas, a farmer in those islands. When he became a famous leader of the ragged regiment, of which he put himself at the head, and which he gradually formed into a troop of invincible veterans, then he let it be known that he was not the mere adventurer that he seemed, but a son of Sigurd, a son of Harald Gilli, Sigurd Mund, as he was called; consequently Sverri was professedly half-brother to Hakon Herdibreid. This enemy and destroyer of the supremacy of the Church in Norway had been brought up for the priesthood, and among his enemies he often went by the name of Sverri Præst—Sverri the Priest; or even Sverri Djæfvul-Præst—Devil's Priest.

As a man, Sverri was as unscrupulous as he was undaunted; and was, on the whole, much more of a Napoleon than of a Cromwell. But there was a certain strain of fanaticism, or may be of genuine enthusiasm, in his character which has led him to be compared to the Great Protector. During the many years of Civil War which had passed, the exasperation of parties had given rise to cruelties which were truly mediæval in character, worse almost than anything that is recorded of the Norwegians in their heathen days. Snorri gives a horrible description of the tortures which were inflicted upon Sigurd Stembidjakn, that unfrocked deacon and warlike adventurer, who opposed himself to the claims of Harold Gillechrist. Certain men were told off to do this wretched work, 'but the chiefs and the greater part of the people went away. They broke his shin bones with a hammer, then they stripped him, and would flay him alive; but when they tried to take off the skin, they could not do it for the gush of blood.' I spare the reader any further details. It is to the infinite credit of Sverri that he showed no trace of this inflamed spirit of revenge; and that, on the whole, his acts were distinguished by a humanity which was remarkable, considering the medium in which his work was cast.

Sverri (whom his partisans called Sverri Sigurdsson) was born in A.D. 1151. His reign is reckoned to begin from the time he became leader of the Birkibeinar in 1177, when, therefore, the renovator of Norway was only twenty-six. There is something strangely picturesque and striking in this youthful figure, who had come from a remote, an unconsidered colony of Norway to overthrow the united powers of the aristocracy and of the Church. Well might men think he worked by magic, and call him the Devil's Priest.

As we have already said, one of the chief features of this war is the place which the inland country now occupies in it. Formerly battles in Norway had been almost entirely connected with the sea-coast. The rival fleets pursue each other round the fjords and in and out among the islands. When people fight they land from their fleets and do battle on some of the islands or some place close by the sea. What is peculiar in the history of Sverri's battles is that we constantly find him making the most wonderful marches in the interior of the country, crossing over in the middle of winter the most difficult heights, and descending places where, in those days, there must have been no road, scarcely even a path. How he induced his men to sustain such hardships is a miracle. But those who know the country of Norway can know how it lends itself to the sort of perpetual guerilla warfare which went on during these hundred years of civil war. It is as easy for an army to lie hidden in one of the valleys as it is for a fleet to lie hidden in any of the fjords or among any of the islands. The country itself seems destined to be split up in factions in the same way that it is split up by nature.

The Birkibeinar had been shattered by the defeat and death of Eystein Meyla, and when we first catch sight of Sverri it is as leader of a band of only seventy men, who have been driven over the border into Sweden, but have now made their way back from Jemteland to the hills which overlook the Throndhjem Fjord—by much the same way as that which St. Olaf took when he returned to fight at Stiklestad. Sverri had caused a proclamation to issue over the country, and before long he was joined by another troop of eighty men from Thelemarken. Presently with only two hundred men or a little more he attacked and conquered an army of 1400 men, and made his way into Nidaros (Throndhjem) and was elected king there, as Eystein Meyla had been eighteen months before. The truth is, the Throndhjem people were, as a body, always opposed to the rule of Erling Skakk and his son. Only the great men in that district were on the side of the existing *régime :* the great lendermen and Eystein, the Archbishop of Throndhjem, who was Sverri's most formidable opponent.

We can account for some of Sverri's easy victories by supposing that the body of the armies opposed to him fought against their will. Often they threw down their weapons at the first onset; and those who asked for quarter very rarely failed to receive it. Sverri's humanity stood him in good stead, and was his best policy, seeing that in many districts the common people were on his side. The Birkibeinar again were, and became ever more so, a terrible body to oppose so long as the lust of battle was on them. Their profession was war.

The new leader was weak so soon as he got to the more civilised parts near the coast. He found he could not maintain himself in the city of Nidaros, and at first sought to make a naval expedition along the coast. But he was soon driven inland again. He made his way to the border-lands, and his next victory was gained near the shore of Lake Venner. After that some desultory fighting continued for a year or two, of which the chief interest is the picture which it gives— first, of the disturbed state of the country, and the difficulty there constantly is in this land of hills and valleys of obtaining any accurate information touching the whereabouts of an enemy; secondly, of the great hardships, the long and difficult winter marchings and counter-marchings which Sverri's troops had to undergo, and which they could only have been induced to undergo by the constancy of their leader, and the faith which he was able to inspire.

In 1179 a sudden change came to the fortunes of the hunted troop. For the third or fourth time they made their way over the mountains to Throndhjem, and there succeeded in surprising the army, under the command of Earl Erling Skakki in person. Erling's army was far the larger; but it had been feasting the day before, and when the pickets brought the news of the approach of the Birch-legs, the greater part of the men were too drunk to answer the call to arms. About six hundred of them gathered round the standards; still were they superior in numbers to their opponents; but they were no match in valour for the Birkibeinar, and after a sharp engagement Erling's army was put to flight, and the earl himself was slain. Henceforward Fortune generally attended the standards of Sverri. We find him entering Bergen after his victory over Erling, and wintering in that town, which was now becoming, or had become, the chief city of Norway, Nidaros (Throndhjem) falling to the second rank.

In the year 1181 a hard-fought naval battle took place at Bergen between the fleet of Sverri, sixteen sail, and that of Magnus Erlingsson of thirty-two sail. The battle took place off the Nordnæs, the promontory which lies between the two harbours; and along which runs the Strandgaden. In this the Heklungs, as Magnus' party was now called, were defeated by the Birkibeinar. But while the latter were still rejoicing in their victory, Magnus returned upon them from Stavanger, to which place he had fled. It was now the turn for the Birch-legs to take to flight, for they

were quite unprepared for battle. Sverri accordingly
betook himself with all his followers to Throndhjem.
Thither he was before long followed by Magnus; who,
however, could not force his way into the town. But
he could largely diminish the supply of provisions, and
Sverri was obliged to carry a portion of his army across
country to Oslo (Christiania).

In this forward and backward fashion the war went
on, until the year 1184, when the rivals came to a
decisive naval engagement in the Sogne Fjord. As
usual it was a case of surprise. Magnus had been driven
away, and had gone to Denmark. Now he came sailing
up from the south—fought a battle at Bergen, and then
came to the Sogne Fjord, within which Sverri was known
to be, with but few ships. There had been one evil
omen for Magnus. A flight of crows (rooks?) alighted
upon his ship as it sailed out of Bergen. Magnus
heard that Sverri was in the Nore Fjord, a branch of
the Sogne Fjord, and eventually the two fleets came
into action near Femreite. Magnus' fleet was not much
the larger; and, on the whole, the two parties were fairly
equal in strength, and they were animated by almost
equal animosity against their enemies, and determination not to yield. Magnus desired, above all things,
to come to a personal encounter with his rival; and
he made dispositions that his own ship and three others
should surround Sverri's ship, a vessel of unusual size
and strength. 'I was but five years old,' Magnus
thus addressed the comrades in arms who stood by
him as he gave them his final orders, 'when I was
chosen to fill the throne; and only seven when Archbishop Eystein anointed me king. I had no care about

reigning. And up to now, that I am twenty-eight, I have had but little pleasure of my royal state.' These last words of the young king give a certain pathetic individuality to his character; just as those words of his namesake and great-grandfather Magnus Barfod, 'Kings were meant for honour but not for long life,' give an individuality to his. This Magnus Erlingsson was to prove the truth of the latter saying. He had upheld his cause with distinguished courage, and proved himself worthy to be the son of the great Earl Erling, or to be the descendant through his mother of Sigurd the Crusader, of Magnus Bare-foot and of Harald Hardradi. Yet his rival, a mere adventurer, probably of ignoble descent, was no less distinguished. If Magnus was only twenty-seven, Sverri, though he had already lived through many years of constant battle, was only thirty-three. The fight raged from early in the afternoon till past midnight. Magnus carried out his plan of bringing four ships to attack Sverri's huge vessel. But the latter kept the space clear between herself and the land, and Sverri could land when he pleased. Sverri left his ship to go among his fleet, and to encourage his men; when he sought to rejoin his own vessel it was under so fierce a fire of darts and stones that he could not do so. At last, however, one after another the ships of Magnus' fleet were taken or sunk. So many crowded on board those that remained that they began to sink under the weight of their own crews. Magnus' ship was one of these. The king jumped overboard, and was drowned. Thus ended the lofty ambitions of the house of Erling Skakki.

Sverri did not win peace by thus putting an end to

the family which rivalled his own; but he won a
firmer place on his throne. He had already begun to
carry out changes of government which were to effect
a revolution in the constitution and the destruction
of the old aristocratic lenderman class. He had begun
to establish a bureaucracy, dependent entirely on the
support of the crown. The new officers who were to
oust the lendermen from almost all their power were
called Syssel-men—District-men. The difference between them and the lendermen was that the latter had
been great landowners, and owed their consideration,
first of all, to their family and their estates, only in
a very secondary degree to the functions—of tax-
collecting, etc.—which they performed for the crown.
The Syssel-men, on the other hand, were officials and
nothing more. The difference may be illustrated for
us to-day by the difference between the unpaid and
the paid magistracy in England. For the unpaid
magistracy—the county justices of the peace—represent the last relics of aristocratic government in this
country.

Sverri, through all his years of adventure, had shown
himself—or professed himself—a man of almost fanatical piety. We constantly see him stopping to pray,
all exposed to the darts of his enemies, at the beginning
of a battle, or in its course. In his great battle in the
Sogne Fjord, it was at his raising the *Kyrie Eleison* that
his foes saw that the battle was going against them. For
all that, Sverri was the deadly foe to the pretensions
of the Church. We might call him a sort of Middle-
Age Puritan; it is on this point that he comes nearest
in character to Cromwell. It was the object of the new

king to do away altogether with the claims of the Norwegian Church, founded upon the compact between Archbishop Eystein, on the one side, and Erling, for his son Magnus, on the other, the well-known compact of A.D. 1164—just twenty years before this battle in the Sogne Fjord. The kingdom was not to be held any longer 'as a fee of St. Olaf' from the Church. But men were to go back to the old 'Law of St. Olaf;' and the crown should once more be a freehold possession, as it had been of old. Sverri, moreover, as we have seen, took measures that, through the bureaucracy which he established, the position of the throne should be much firmer than it had been in old days. And no doubt he intended that the law of primogeniture should be still preserved.

It was his attempts to wrest the kingdom from the hands of the Norwegian Church which raised for Sverri his most formidable opponents. And though a number of different parties sprang up to contest his position, it is only one of these which calls for mention here. This was the Church party properly so called. It was founded in 1196, not by the Archbishop of Throndhjem—the great Eystein was dead before the foundation of the party—but by Nicholas Arnason, Bishop of Oslo. This party got the name of *Baglerne*—the *Bagler*, i.e. Crozier Party. It gained great strength from the support of Pope Innocent III., who in A.D. 1198 excommunicated Sverri.

By this time, however, Sverri had so firmly established himself in the affections of his own followers that nothing could shake him. The Birkibeinar were no longer a poor and ragged regiment; they were half the people of Norway, with a fixed tradition and policy, and a feeling on matters of Church and State which, allowing for the vast difference between the ages, may be not unjustly compared to the feeling of the English Puritans under Charles I. The indomitable king died in A.D. 1202, fighting to the last, after his twenty-five years of so-called reign.

The civil war continued, but not so vehemently. Sverri was succeeded by his son Hakon. But, unfortunately, this prince only lived two years after his accession. He had approached the Church party with offers of a compromise, and everything seemed to hold out hopes of peace. Greater confusion than ever supervened upon Hakon's death, confusion so great that it is in no way our business to trace it or its causes. At the time of this Hakon Sverrason's death, his own child, an illegitimate son, Hakon, was not yet born. But at last this young prince succeeded in raising his head above the storm of faction, and he was in 1217 recognised as king at the Throndhjem Ore Thing, and later in the same year at Bergen. Bergen was now the chief city of Norway, and it was the election of Hakon (IV.) Hakonsson at the Thing held in this city which gave the final seal to his title. It is this scene that forms the opening one in one of Ibsen's plays, *Kongsemnerne*—'The Rivals.' After 1240, and the death of a certain Skuli Jarl, long a rival of Hakon and a friend of the Bagler party, complete peace was established.

The old aristocratic party had been rooted out as completely, and much in the same way as the old baronage of England was rooted out by the Wars of the Roses. Honour to both though fallen; for they

T

fell because they knew that the business of leaders is to lead; because they were ready to say, like King Magnus, 'noblemen were meant for honour but not for long life.' The result is that the house of Sverri steps upon the scene much as the house of Tudor does in English history, founding an almost autocratic power through a well-ordered bureaucracy on the ruins of the aristocracy and of the Church. Sars, a living Norwegian historian, compares Hakon Hakonsson to Louis XIV. of France. This reign was a period of restoration for Norway. Hakon used his triumph with the greatest moderation, and the passions of faction, fanned by a century of civil war, did at last die down. It is not an eventful reign; rather one of those long periods of rest when a nation is happy in having no history.

Outside the sphere of home politics Hakon accomplished one thing of importance, and made a conspicuous failure in another, which as a failure was of even more significance and importance.

During these years of civil war in Norway, Iceland had imitated the mother state by embarking upon a period of civil war at home. This is not the place to speak of those internecine quarrels by which the old aristocracy of landowners in the Icelandic Republic brought about its own ruin. To a very large extent the rivalries in Iceland followed the rivalries of parties in Norway. The history is interesting enough, and it is interestingly told. It is bound up closely with the literary history of Iceland and Norway, for the family which was most largely concerned in these feuds was that of the famous Sturlungs, whose most illustrious member, Snorri Sturluson, is the historian of Norway, and one of the greatest literary men that Scandinavian countries have produced. We have already said how he was murdered at the instigation of Hakon, one year after the fall of Earl Skuli in Norway. The result of the long period of civil war in Iceland was, that when Hakon had established himself firmly on the throne of Norway, he found this daughter country utterly exhausted, and had no difficulty in incorporating it in his dominions. Iceland had, in early days, been theoretically a tributary country to Norway. We see that when Olaf Tryggvason is doing his best to establish Christianity in his own country, he takes measures, almost as a matter of course, to introduce it likewise into Iceland as into the Orkneys, and to the former country he sends that Saxon priest Thangbrand, 'a great man-slayer,' who used more force than persuasion in his missionary work. But the tie between Norway and its daughter republic remained of the loosest, till Hakon really incorporated Iceland with Norway, a union which has lasted ever since. He did the same with Greenland, that little adventurous colony which was still flourishing, but was destined in the following century to come to a sad end. The Orkneys and Faroes were already counted among the possessions of the country.

What of those other parts of the Greater Scandinavia which lay among the British Isles? Let us take one final glance at them.

The Danish and Norse conquests in England had long since been merged in the English nation. Opposite the Orkneys, in Caithness, there was still, probably, a large Norse population, but they were now subjects of the kings of Scotland as much as the men of Northumbria were the subjects of the English king. The Norsemen in Ireland, too, who had once put themselves at the head of a federation of Scandinavians in the western parts of Great Britain, who sent out rulers to govern Man and the western islands of Scotland, these Irish Norsemen (Ostmen, as they were called) had likewise become, since the days of Strongbow, the subjects of the English king.

But there still remained Man and the western islands of Scotland; these were independent of the Scottish king; they were still essentially Norse colonies. We saw how Magnus Barefoot had spent his energies in trying to revive the Norse power in Scotland; he lost his life in trying to do the same in Ireland. The names of one or two of the rulers of these Scottish islands and of Man who lived subsequent to Magnus' time have been preserved for us; one of these is the well-known Sumerled or Sumerleda, from whom so many of the heads of clans in the west of Scotland claim descent, the family of Argyll among the number. The western Scottish islands were now divided into two groups, the dividing point being the most western point of the Scottish mainland, the point of Ardnamurchan. The expression Sudreyar, which had once been the designation of the whole of the western islands of Scotland, the Hebrides, *par excellence*, was now applied only to the islands south of the Hebrides. These *sudreyar* (in the latter sense) probably formed with Man a single kingdom or earldom. This latter kingdom it is which corresponds to the diocese of the

Bishop of Sodor and Man. The Hebrides, now the Nordreyar, formed another kingdom.

As the power of the kings of Scotland increased, and the adventurous spirit of the Norsemen declined, it must have become clear to these lesser kings and earls that no prospect lay before them but of becoming feudatories of the Scottish king; well for them if, on these terms, they could preserve their possessions. Of some of them homage was obtained by the kings of Scotland at the price of a grant of further territory on the mainland, the undisputed possession of the Scottish kings. Alexander II. sent an embassy to Hakon offering to purchase the claims of suzerainty over these islands of the Norwegian crown; and the offer was repeated by Alexander III., but each time decisively rejected by the King of Norway. Such a proposal was enough to put him on the alert; and presently there came news to Hakon that the Scots had been making forays in these western islands, and had committed all sorts of atrocities there.

It was time for him to stir if he would not let drop for ever the claims of Norway to the suzerainty of these, its ancient colonies. Hakon determined, as the crowning achievement of his life—it was in the forty-sixth year of his reign—to strike a great blow against the power of the King of Scotland, and for the re-establishment of the influence of Norway on that side of the Northern Ocean. In the winter of A.D. 1262 he sent messages throughout the country for the collecting and arming of a fleet. It assembled the following summer to be reviewed by the king, one of the largest fleets which had ever sailed from Norwegian waters.

Hakon embarked in it, and sailed first of all to the Orkneys.

There was a young king, Alexander III., upon the throne of Scotland. He was only twenty-two, and his reign since he succeeded as quite a boy had been not a little troubled by rival factions at home, and by interference from England in the south. It cannot be said, therefore, that Hakon's time was ill-chosen; and, in fact, he never did encounter any direct opposition on the part of the King of Scotland.

The enterprise failed rather through its own inherent weakness. Hakon sailed from the Orkneys to the Hebrides, and found in that kingdom a King John, from whom he demanded homage and furtherance. But John replied that he held more territories from the King of Scotland than from the King of Norway, and that he was bound by his oath not to take arms against him. Another king, Magnus of Man, and the lord of the southern islands, were more amenable, and Magnus did no small amount of ravaging on the western coasts of Scotland, which is described in inflated terms by the poet of this expedition—of whom more presently.

At length Hakon brought his fleet round the Mull of Kintyre, and anchored between Arran and Ayr. Messengers came from the King of Scotland to negotiate a peace. They even offered—according to the Norse account—to restore to Norway the supremacy over the western islands that she had possessed of old. But Hakon asked for more. He must have the islands, such as Bute and Arran, which were enclosed by the mainland, and which had never formed part of the Scandinavian group. Then the Scots began to spy hopes of help from another quarter. The summer had passed; the equinox was near. They may have seen signs that it was likely to be a stormy equinox. So they prolonged the negotiations; and suddenly, as Hakon's fleet was riding at anchor, the storm broke upon it.

Many vessels dragged their anchors and drifted to the north. A certain number of crews were obliged to land at Largs. They were attacked by the Scots. Hakon sent more boats' crews to their assistance. But a larger and larger hosting assembled on the hills above the beach. At length it came to something of a pitched battle, which in the Scottish chronicles is known as the Battle of Largs. We have, for any details, only the Norse account of this battle. According to this the Norsemen were victorious; but over what? Only over a local hosting, which the government of Scotland, properly so called, had no share in organising. And half of Hakon's fleet had been destroyed by the storm, which still continued to blow. The Norse king had no choice but to sail away to safer waters. At last he got to the Orkneys with the residue of his fleet. His expedition had failed miserably, and he, an old man, had been worn out by the fatigues of it. He died in the Orkneys, and was buried in St. Magnus Cathedral there.

Hakon's son, Magnus, formally renounced all the claims which his father had sought to make good. He retained only the supremacy over the earldom of Orkney, to which, as yet, the Scottish kings had made no claim.

This expedition of Hakon's is always considered

epochal, in the sense that it is the last flicker of the Viking spirit before it finally expires. Magnus Barefoot's expeditions at the end of the eleventh century fell far behind the achievements in the same parts of the world of his forerunners of the ninth and tenth centuries. But, compared to Hakon, in spite of the vast preparations which had preceded the voyage of the latter, Magnus Barefoot might be reckoned a successful leader.

It is appropriate enough that we find a bard of these later days celebrating Hakon's expedition in the inflated style and false imagery to which the Norse poetry had now descended, since, for many generations, it had ceased to be really national, and had become merely an affected versification, patronised at courts and kept up for the glorification of its patrons. This last breath of the old Norse poetry may be placed side by side with the last flicker of the old Norse spirit of adventure.

CHAPTER XII

HISTORY

Magnus the Law Reformer—The Union of Calmar—Transition to Modern Times.

HAKON's son, Magnus, had remained behind in Norway when his father set out to the west. He saw the uselessness of prosecuting the claims which his father had put forward, and, as we have said, ceded by treaty all his rights in Scotland, except that of the suzerainty of the Orkneys.

Henceforward, save as a trading country, Norway had little to do with foreign affairs.

What we have now to note is the confirmation of a sovereign power built upon the ruins of the old aristocracy—the ruins of the adventurous and turbulent spirit of bygone days; and in place of these a new industry at home, a new attachment to the works of peace, and a longing on all sides for a reign of law and order. To meet this longing rose Magnus, who is known in history as Magnus *Lagabætir*, or Magnus the Law-Reformer (1263-1280). As we are not concerned with constitutional history, it is not necessary to enter into the details of Magnus' law reforms. The general effect of them was to carry on the work of centralisation which had been begun by Sverri, and continued by Hakon Hakonsson. The efforts of these two had been chiefly in the direction of administrative centralisation the efforts of Magnus Lagabætir were directed towards legal centralisation. Up to now the law had been different for different parts of the country. There were four great Things, and each administered its own laws for its own district. That is to say, latterly two of the three districts, those of the Eidsvold Thing and the Borgar Thing, had the same laws and customs, but these differed from those of the other two Thing districts.

It will be understood that none of these laws—or but very few—were codified; so that the law administered at the Things was what we should call 'case-law.' The law (according to the old custom, at any rate) was administered for the peasants by the peasants. Generally the most venerable and the most respected bonder was elected for life to be the exponent of the laws and customs of the district. This man was called the lawman (Lagamadhr). His business was to recite from memory the known laws, what formed, in effect, the code of the country, to decide the case-law, and to be a sort of speaker for the local Thing in the presence of the king or of the earl of the district—which is precisely what the speaker of the English Parliament originally was. This peasant-law of the Things did not directly apply to the king or the higher aristocracy, the earls; but they were bound to respect it, and in the government of their own estates they were bound by its provisions.

Across this district law there lay, so to say, a band of church and king law, which had been introduced

with the new religion by Olaf Tryggvason and St. Olaf.
It was not so much the formal change of faith which
awoke opposition to these innovators as the Church
or canon law which they introduced therewith, laws
relating to slavery, to ecclesiastical and moral offences,
such as sacrilege, adultery, and so forth. These reforms
had long been incorporated with the Thing laws; but
they came from outside, and were uniform for the whole
country.

The first task which Magnus undertook was the codi-
fying of the traditional law; the second, was the introduction of a uniform code for the whole country. This
was the essential of his work. But incidentally certain
changes were introduced which had the effect of enlarg-
ing the kingly power, while it secured the greater independence in many respects of the peasant class, but
destroyed the remaining power of the old aristocracy.

The chief of these latter changes was the abolition of
the picturesque and terrible blood-feud which plays so
conspicuous a part in the history of the northern races
during their heathen or almost heathen days. We have
only to read the Icelandic Sagas to see how large a part
the blood-feud occupied in the life of families in those
days. The law of private revenge, which was involved
in the theory of the blood-feud, always lay rather outside the regular Thing-law of the country. That is to
say, it was recognised by law, but the chief efforts of
the Thing legislators were directed to limiting its appli-
cation. In Magnus' laws this right of private revenge
was abolished; and with it was abolished the right
which families claimed of determining for themselves
the blood fine for a murder, the compensation money

(as it in fact was) for which they would consent to abandon their right of revenge.

Other changes related to the free holding of land. Free possession, or what was called odal or udal right, only vested in a family which could establish its possession of the soil on which it lived through a number of generations; failing that, the land by Harald Fairhair's law theoretically belonged to the king. He might bestow it upon any among his servants or nobility, and it was in this wise that some of the greater estates had been acquired, and the powerful landed aristocracy of lendermen had been formed. By Magnus' law sixty years' possession established a title to an odal estate. This law limited the power of the crown. But it also tended to reduce the power of the aristocracy. The result of all these reforms was that the greater aristocracy of Norway (the *lendermandsaetter*) practically disappeared, and the lower aristocracy (*holdernesaetter*) became little distinguishable from the peasant class.

In Denmark and Sweden the yeoman class had separated from, and raised out of itself an aristocratic order; and this, in these countries, had in its turn reduced the bonder class to a lower level, a level not much above that of the peasants of Germany. In Norway, on the other hand, the peasant class had absorbed or re-absorbed the aristocracy which a warlike age had evoked from it.

The future history of Norway alters little in this social condition of things. For though after its union, first with both Sweden and Denmark, afterwards with Denmark alone, these countries imposed upon it some of their own political and social ideas, their influence came from without and never much affected the people. Thus when, in 1814, Norway once more obtained a constitution of its own, it reverted instinctively, as it were, to the condition of things to which it had been brought by the warlike efforts of Sverri, his son and his grandson, and by the statesmanship of Magnus, the law-reformer.

The Church in Norway was more successful in holding its own than the aristocracy. Sverri had succeeded in spite of it. Hakon Hakonsson, though he made peace with the Church, and was crowned by a papal legate, receded very little from the attitude which his grandfather had taken up towards the privileges of churchmen. But his son Magnus came to an agreement with the ecclesiastical body, and a sort of Concordat was signed between the two powers, whereby the king virtually gave up all jurisdiction in Church affairs, conceding that very point which Becket had attempted in vain to wring from Henry II., which the Constitutions of Clarendon were especially framed to reject—that priests should be removed altogether from lay jurisdiction.

Such was the condition of things in which Magnus left the country. The two sons who followed him tried their best to shake the power of the Church, to revoke the Concordat which Magnus had established, and to return to the condition of things which Sverri had bequeathed to Hakon. Magnus' immediate successor, his eldest son Erik, was for this cause constantly embroiled with the priesthood, and so got the name of Erik the priest-hater (Praestehader). This Erik,

Magnus' son, is interesting as the father of Margaret, the Scottish princess, who is known in history as the Maid of Norway. He reigned from A.D. 1280-1299. He was succeeded by his brother Hakon Magnusson (Hakon v.), who reigned from A.D. 1299-1309. Hakon left only a daughter Ingeborg, and thus the house of Sverri became extinct in the male line. Ingeborg was married to a Swede, Erik, Duke of Sondermanland, the heir to the throne of Sweden. Their son Magnus, who is known as Magnus *Smek*, Magnus 'the Luxurious,' became King of both Sweden and Norway, and the union of Norway to other Scandinavian lands began (1319).

This union was broken again when Magnus was deposed in 1355, and Hakon his son elected King of Norway. Hakon's father continued for some years to govern Sweden. But at last the Swedish nobles determined to offer the crown to Albert, Duke of Mecklenburg (1363). The troubles which ensued upon this placing of a German upon the throne of Sweden belong to the history of that country.

Hakon, the son of Magnus, married Margaret, the daughter of Waldemar, the King of Denmark—that illustrious Queen Margaret whose reign shines out as a brief period of prosperity in the troubled history of the Scandinavian countries. The son of these two was Olaf, under whom the crown of Norway was united with that of Denmark; and this union proved the permanent one. Eventually, after Olaf had died (1387), his mother Margaret was made first regent, and then sole monarch of both these countries. And when the Swedes, growing tired of Albert and of his German proclivities and German favourites, expelled him from his throne, Margaret became regent of Sweden likewise, and the three countries were practically united under one sceptre.

The actual and legal union of the three Scandinavian countries, known as the Union of Calmar, took place in 1397, when Erik of Pomerania, whom Margaret had adopted as her heir, had been elected to the throne of each of the three kingdoms. Margaret continued to be the actual ruler of them until her death in 1412.

The history of Norway as a separate kingdom ends with the union of Calmar, ends practically, in fact, with the earlier union under Magnus *Smek*. The country was left for the most part at peace, and its old heroic character seemed to have deserted it. It had lost its aristocracy, and had achieved the modest comfort of a people among whom there was no great wealth and no abject poverty. But at the same time it had lost the proud, the restless and adventurous spirit of former days. It submitted without shame to be treated as the mere appanage of one or other of the two larger Scandinavian kingdoms. The political centre of gravity now leaves this country, and if we wanted to know anything of the outside influences which affected Norwegian life for succeeding centuries, until in 1814 the country once more sprang into virtual independence, we should have to follow the histories of Sweden and Denmark.

This, of course, we have not space to do. And it is the less necessary to do so, that even then we should have only a picture of the side influences on Norwegian history. It is enough for us to notice some of the great movements in Europe by which the life of the Scandinavian countries, and Norway with the others, was deeply affected.

The first great movement is the growth of the Baltic trade, more especially of that great league of the trading towns of Germany which were concerned in the commerce of the north, and which succeeded in absorbing it almost altogether. I mean the association which went by the name of the League—the Hansa.

The growth of the Hansa is an example of one of the revenges which time brings about. For it had been the Viking piracies in the first instance—the inveterate marauding which generations of sea robberies had engendered, which laid the germ of the great association of the leading Baltic towns.

Not but that, as we have seen, there had been Scandinavian merchants alongside of—nay, we may say identical with—the Scandinavian pirates. When speaking of the earliest days of Northern history and of the doings of the Vikings in Europe, we took occasion to point out how the adventurers who came from Norway had a character and a career somewhat different from those which they had who came out of the other Scandinavian countries, Denmark or Sweden; how while the two last were conquerors and colonisers of Northern England, of Normandy, of Gardariki in Russia, the Norsemen were *par excellence* conquerors and tradesmen; so that what Ireland owes to its Norse conquerors is not any great admixture of Scandinavian blood, but the founding of seaport towns in the island and the first introduction of a coinage into the country.

Later on, when we were picturing to ourselves the domestic life of the Norsemen in the heroic age, we saw how every landowner of any consideration, if his estate lay near the coast, was sure to possess one or more vessels built and armed by himself and manned by his house-carls, which might be used as occasion required either as merchant vessels or as ships of war. They were used as both. Long after the true Viking age was over the custom obtained in families of the higher class of sending the young son or sons of the house upon expeditions half of warlike adventure and half of trade. As our young gentry used a century ago to signalise their entry into manhood by making the grand tour, so used these young sprigs of Norse nobility to set out upon their voyage of trade or war.

In this wise the Norwegians very early began to reap some of the benefits of commerce. But it was likewise this early proclivity towards trade which arrested the development of Norway as a commercial nation. For it prevented the growth of a distinct trading class, such as had ere now developed in Europe proper, especially in Northern Germany; a class which from generation to generation had increased its power in the teeth of feudalism, which through initial weakness had learnt the need of union, until now through that union it had grown so strong that it could set the kinghood and the chivalry of many nations at defiance.

It so happens that the time when the great Viking expeditions came to an end, and were succeeded by a series of petty raids directed by one of the northern nations against another, or between rival parties in the same state, was precisely the time when Norway might have reaped greater commercial advantages than have since fallen in her way. For in the full flower of the Middle Ages, when the fasts of the church were rigidly observed, fisheries, such as the northern cod-fisheries, were of the greatest value in the economy of Europe. There was no article of commerce from countries with a seaboard to inland ones for which there was a more constant demand than fish. Undoubtedly the northern fisheries developed largely under the stimulus of this demand. If at the same time a special merchant class had grown up to stand as middlemen between the getter and the consumer of this necessary article of diet, Norway might have attained a high degree of commercial prosperity.

But what was not supplied from within the country was supplied more or less forcibly from without. The Hansa, or 'The League,' which had been hatched by terror of the northern pirates, was now grown great enough in its turn to be a terror to the Scandinavian nations.

The town of Wisby, in Gothland, bears traces of the great prosperity which it attained when it was the chief Scandinavian city of this famous Hansa. There are in that one city more Gothic churches of stone than are to be found in all Norway. All along the southern shore of the Baltic we come upon towns, strong-walled towns as they were in the Middle Ages, with their walls still standing, which were members of this mighty League: Dantzig, for instance, which still contains the immense warehouses which were built in the Middle Ages. Stolpe is another of these towns which to-day is half forgotten; but its old walls remain. Then we come to a group of the Western Baltic cities, Stralsund,

Rostock, Wismar, Lübeck (the most famous of all the Hansa towns), which, with Hamburg, which had an outlook to the German Ocean, were the founders of the League. Other more inland towns, such as Cologne, joined it. But originally it was designed to protect or to command the trade of the Baltic. Its greatest establishment out of Germany proper was Wisby. It soon began to have corresponding places of business or factories, Kontors as they were called, in Russia, in Scandinavia, and in England. In Norway it had them at Oslo and at Bergen. Bergen had, during the civil war, grown to be the most important town in Norway; and the Bergen Kontor of the Hansa soon began to absorb all the trade of the country.

The Hansa did not establish its power unopposed. There were frequent quarrels between the Germans and the natives in Bergen. But the latter were so little supported by their government that the foreigners soon began to show the greatest insolence, and to act as if the whole city were theirs. Then, about the middle of the fourteenth century, the Hansa gave such a display of its power that all the Scandinavian countries were reduced to a virtual submission to it.

This state of things was provoked by the action of the King of Denmark. During the fourteenth century, while Norway was sinking more and more into a position of dependence, and was preparing to be united to the other Scandinavian countries, Denmark, after a long period of internal struggle and consequent weakness, once more rose to power under its king, Waldemar, called Waldemar Atterdag or 'Day again.' It was Waldemar who conceived the idea of getting possession of Wisby, the city of Hansa creation, the nucleus of the Baltic trade of the League. He did take the city; but his action brought about a warlike union of all the Hansa cities, the like of which had never been seen before. Hitherto the League had been apparently only a peaceful corporation. It was its peaceful attitude which deceived Waldemar into despising its power. Now, under the leadership of Lübeck, the League showed that it could put into the field an army superior to any that the Scandinavian countries (once the scourge of Europe) could oppose to it. How completely has the whirligig of time brought its revenge, when we see this league of northern traders defeating the children of those adventurers who had in their day attacked and taken half the chief cities of Europe!

After this famous war, which took place in the years 1368-9, so far as Norway was concerned, the unquestioned supremacy of the German traders was established. Bergen may be said to have been given up to them. It was not for two hundred years, till, that is to say, the middle of the sixteenth century, that Norway succeeded in wresting back again the trade in her own productions.

Up to the time of the monopolising of Norse trade by the 'Lübeckers,' as the Hansa merchants were often called in Norway, the commerce with the British Isles, which the Viking age had first introduced, continued to be one of the chief branches of Norwegian external trade. According to the legend, one of the boats which came to Norway on this errand, brought with it a strange and awful freight. The boat—a cock-boat it is called in the history—came from England, and put

in at Bergen. It had several persons on board. But
before they were able to unload the ship all these
people fell dead, one after another, on the landing-quay.
People did not like to see the cargo lying there useless, so
they set to work to carry it up to the town. They likewise died. Then the pest spread over the whole city.
It was the 'Black Death,' or, as the Norwegians call it,
the Mænd-död, the 'Mens-death,' '*The* Death.' Men
began dying in thousands here in Bergen; and presently
the death spread over all the country. It was said that
two-thirds of the population of Norway died from this
plague. This is no doubt an exaggeration. One-third
would be a fairer reckoning. But at this lower estimate
the history of the disease is strange and terrible enough.
It seems to be a fact that whole villages were depopu-
lated: that sometimes the sites of them were re-absorbed
into the primeval forest, and lost to memory. There
are even stories of the emergence of a sort of race of
wild men of the woods, the grown-up children from
places where the whole adult population had died, and
the inhabited country had been, as it were, restored to
the empire of Nature.

The political events which affected Norway during
the fifteenth century arose from the rivalries of Sweden
and Denmark. The former of these two countries never
peaceably accepted the state of things sanctioned by
the Calmar Union. That meant that Sweden was to
be in effect governed from Copenhagen, from Denmark, and, therefore, in accordance with Danish ideas.
For Denmark was by far the most civilised of the three
Scandinavian kingdoms. It was, too, in much closer

relationship with Germany than either of the other two. Soon the time was to come when a dynasty would ascend the Danish throne, whose founder could not speak a word of Danish, so that, for a time, no Scandinavian tongue was spoken at the court of Copenhagen.

It was not likely that Sweden would submit to be governed on such terms. And the whole of the fifteenth century, and down to the year 1523, is the history of the struggles for mastery in Sweden between the legitimate royal line of Denmark, with the prestige of legitimacy and royalty behind it, and the leaders of the Swedish nobility, who, sometimes with the kingly title, sometimes with the name of regent only, but with the power of kingship, succeeded in raising themselves to the supremacy in Sweden. The Swedish national party is, during this century, generally led by members of a single family, or, say, by a succession of leaders allied by blood; by Carl Cnutson, regent in 1436, king from 1448 to 1450, and again, 1464-66, 1467-70. Greater names than this of Carl Cnutson are those of the members of the Sture family, Sten Sture, the Elder, who had not the royal title, but as regent and marshal enjoyed a firmer rule than Cnutson's from 1471-1497, and again from 1500-1503, and conferred greater benefits upon his country; Svente Sture, regent between 1503-1512, and Sten Sture, the Younger, 1512-1520. The battle of Brunkebjerge, near Stockholm, in which Sten Sture, the Elder, defeated Christian I. of Denmark, the founder of the German Oldenburg line (1471) is celebrated in Swedish history.

Norway during this period trod timidly in the steps of Sweden. It cannot be believed but that she desired at all times to shake off the Danish yoke, and that if it was necessary for her to be attached to either nation she would have preferred that that nation should be Sweden. For a period Sten Sture the Elder added the regency of Norway to that of Sweden, but the country remained Danish subsequent to the first defeat of Sten in 1497.

Then arose in Denmark the remarkable Christian II., that wise ruler of his own country, and cruel oppressor of the Swedes. How his horrible execution or massacre of eighty-two of the heads of Swedish houses, known in history as the 'Stockholm Blood-bath,' led to the rise of a new dynasty in Sweden, the dynasty of Gustavus Vasa, under which that country was to attain the summit of its glory, is known probably to most readers. At any rate, it is not a part of Norwegian history. In 1523 Gustavus was crowned King of Sweden, and the Union of Calmar was for ever dissolved.

A play of Ibsen, *Fru Inger til Österaad* (Lady Inger of Österaad) gives a picture from Norse history at this time. It shows a party in Norway longing after a reunion with Sweden, or, at any rate, after a severance from Denmark, a party which represents the scattered remnant of the old aristocratic houses, and which has also the sympathy of the more patriotic among the peasants. We see also how an intrusive aristocracy of Danes—resting upon the firm support of the court— has made its way into Norway, and by marrying the heiresses of Norwegian houses has settled itself upon the soil, and grown to be the strongest support of Danish rule in the dependent kingdom. Doubtless the picture presented to us is, in its main outlines, a true one:

though the actual characters, who cross the stage of the play, and the actual series of events, may have been changed to suit the requirements of the playwright. The story turns upon the existence of a descendant of the Stures, who is living concealed in Norway, and whom it is the intention of the disaffected party to bring forward at a fitting moment as the leader of the peasantry.

For the Scandinavian nations altogether there is one more great movement to be taken account of, and then their history may be allowed to sink into the obscurity and forgetfulness which hang over it during modern times.

This movement is the Reformation. The condition of the Catholic Church in the north corresponded generally with its condition in other parts of Europe during the fifteenth century. It made, in many ways, a greater display of power than ever; but it was slowly, but inevitably, losing its hold upon the mass of the population. Consequently in this age the first open collisions occur. The first trial and execution for heresy in Sweden belongs to this century. We may put it side by side with the executions of the Lollards in this country. Christian the Second, in his Swedish wars, appeared as the friend of the Church, as the supporter of the Primate, Archbishop Trolle, who had been deposed by the patriot party for his traitorous correspondence with Denmark. The trial—a mock trial—which ended in the horrible 'Blood-bath of Stockholm,' was conducted almost exclusively by ecclesiastics. It was the last important exercise of ecclesiastical power in Sweden, and it must have struck a deadly blow at that power.

At home, in Denmark, Christian the Second was a reformer. The Reformation in Denmark began under his auspices in 1520. It was carried out in a tolerably high-handed manner; and with as great an admixture of impure and worldly motives as were displayed in the English Reformation under Henry VIII. and Edward VI. There is much in the character of Christian II. which resembles that of Henry VIII. Still, no doubt, the mass of the people were thoroughly prepared for the change, and gladly welcomed the Lutheran preachers whom Christian brought into Denmark. In Sweden the Reformation began with the rise of the House of Vasa in 1523. There was an attempt made to restore Catholicism by Gustavus' grandson, Sigismund, who was King of Catholic Poland, as well as of Sweden. But he and his schemes alike were defeated by Sigismund's uncle Carl (Victory of Stangebro, A.D. 1599); and when the latter ascended the throne as Charles IX., the 'Peasant's King,' as this champion of the third estate was called, the Lutheran faith was firmly established in Sweden. Norway was the least ready of any of the three northern kingdoms to change its creed: showing in this respect a conservatism in religion which often characterises the people of a mountainous country.

Then arises the Thirty Years' War, and with it the great Champion of Protestantism, Gustavus Adolphus (1611-1632), the son of Charles IX., steps upon the scene. Beside the greatness to which he and his ministers raised their country, the rival Scandinavian State the Dano-Norse kingdom, sank into insignificance. Jealousy of the brother Scandinavian State was henceforward the chief motive force in Danish policy. The balance between Denmark and Sweden was, to some degree, redressed in favour of Denmark by Christian IV. But in the following century there arose another Swedish hero far inferior, indeed, to the great Gustavus, but great enough to make his country once more—and for the last time—blaze before the eyes of Europe, and once more thoroughly to humiliate Denmark. I mean, of course, Charles XII.

May it not be, as was suggested in an earlier page, that the Swedish people were only now beginning to enter upon their inheritance of victory, now that the nations of the Danes and the Norsemen had burnt out their heroism and achievement; that during the old Saga era the Swedes had been, compared to their brother Scandinavians, a peaceful people, and that they had held their strength in reserve till now?

However that may be, in all this history of the rivalry between Denmark and Sweden, it is obvious that Norway has no part.

For all the important period of our historical sketch the Scandinavians have been for us what they seem to be constituted by the formation of their country, the youngest of the nations of Europe. But during the latter years which we have rapidly run through—just those years when Norway has, in fact, passed off the historic stage—it is interesting to notice how a new nation, a younger one still than any of the Scandinavians, steps upon the boards—Russia. At one time, we know, Russia had been part of the Scandinavian confederacy; and it had, as a rule, been the most powerful of all the members of that group. That Jarisleif (Yaroslav), to whose court came Harald Hardradi and the Orkney Jarl Rögnvald, is an important person in Russian history, for he is the first legislator for Russia. Not long after his time ends what has been called the heroic era in Russian history, which, like the heroic era of Norway, is simply the Saga age. Then the old Scandinavian stock becomes more and more mixed with Slavonic elements, and finally, there comes the long dominion of the Mongol Tartars, during which Russian nationality, though not extinguished, lies under a cloud. During this period there had been some relations between the Swedes and the Russians, chiefly of a hostile character, and when Norway came to be united with Sweden she sometimes suffered from attacks from Russia.

We read of one, just before the union, in 1316, which fell upon Halogaland, in the north of Norway; of others in the succeeding century.

In the middle of the fifteenth century comes the consolidation of the Grand Duchy of Russia, under Ivan; and it is from this time forward that the country begins to be known by trade, and otherwise, to the other nations of Europe. We find in the reign of Ivan the Terrible an Englishman of the name of Horsey, going to Russia as Ambassador from Queen Elizabeth, in order to arrange a sort of commercial treaty between the two countries. From this time forward the Russian trade was a very important element in the trade of the Baltic.

After the death of Ivan there followed civil war, during which Russia once more became insignificant; but at the end of this period there arose the monarch, who was the founder of modern Russia, Peter the Great. We need not dwell on the history of the wars between the last great king of Sweden, Charles XII., and this great Tsar. But it is interesting to note that the fall of the last famous Scandinavian ruler, the last man whose personality recalls in any way that of the old Saga heroes, is brought about by the first great monarch of the Russian empire.

Charles XII. of Sweden lost his life, as every one knows, in an attack on Norway, and in the siege of Frederikshald, in that country (December 11, 1718). Frederikshald lies in the part of Norway which tourists rarely visit, that is to say, in the country which stretches east of the Christiania Fjord, between it and the Göta river, and close to the Swedish border. It is near Frederickstad, the site of that interesting old town of Sarpsborg, which was built, we know, by St. Olaf, and where the Borgar Thing was held. This, too, is the country of the Bohuslän stone-carvings, of which we spoke in the earlier chapters of this volume. So that, altogether, we can trace more of the footmarks of time here than in any other part of Norway. For we may say that, with Frederikshald, the light went out from the history of Scandinavia.

In Sweden a time of foreign rulers supervened, men of German family, for a generation men not even born in Sweden. The higher classes used the interval to reduce the royal power almost to a shadow. When Gustavus III. arose, a native-born king, and tried to win back something of what his predecessors had lost, the nobles conspired his overthrow, and he was shot at a masked ball by Ankerstrom, one of their number. The nobility themselves were divided into two parties, fiercely opposed, like the English Whigs and Tories of the last century. They went by the names of the Hats (Hattar) and Nightcaps (Nattmössor).

The one thing constant in Scandinavian history during these later centuries was the enmity between Sweden and Denmark. Towards the end of the seventeenth century Denmark recovered somewhat from the position to which it had been reduced by Gustavus Adolphus and his immediate successors. In the war between Louis XIV. and Holland, as Sweden was the ally of the French, Denmark joined the Dutch, and the armies of the two Scandinavian countries (under Christian V. and Charles XI.) met at Lund in 1676. It was Frederick IV. of Denmark who provoked the hostility of Charles XII.; and Denmark and Sweden were again at war, almost continuously from A.D. 1709 to 1720. After this, there is nothing worth recording in Danish history till the French Revolution, and the wars which sprang therefrom, which affected every state in Europe. In one respect, Denmark anticipated the French Revolution by the liberation, in 1788, of the peasant class from the oppressive taxes and services to which it had become liable.

At the beginning of the revolutionary war, Denmark preserved a neutral attitude, a condition of armed neutrality, in which she protected her own merchant fleet, and carried goods to countries of either party. This condition of things was viewed with a very evil eye by England, and when, in 1800, Russia, Prussia, and Sweden, seemed inclined to adopt the same attitude, and made overtures to Denmark to form a league with them, England determined to strike the latter country at once, and to destroy its fleet. This led to the celebrated battle of Copenhagen (A.D. 1801), Nelson's first great naval victory, and one of the hardest he ever gained; one too, it must be said, of the least justifiable acts that England ever committed. Bad, however, as this was, it was not so blameworthy as the bombardment of Copenhagen, and the seizure of the Danish fleet by England again, in 1807, on the mere suspicion that the country was going to form an alliance with France.

This simply threw Frederick VI., the King of Denmark, into the arms of Napoleon. The Danish king had no force at his command for the defence of his country, which Sweden was once more threatening. Wherefore Napoleon despatched to Denmark General Bernadotte with an army of 30,000 men. But these troops did nothing for the defence of the country, and Denmark found herself obliged by the Treaty of Kiel to cede Norway to Sweden, then the ally of England.

Sweden had left the French alliance. That same Marshal Bernadotte, Napoleon's general, had been selected as a successor to the reigning king of the country, and received into the royal family. The choice was made to flatter the susceptibilities of Napoleon. But the latter soon became jealous of his late subordinate, and even proposed to the English and the German powers the dismemberment of Sweden.

When, by the Treaty of Kiel in 1814, Norway was

taken from Denmark, and handed over to Sweden, the Norwegians roused themselves to once more assert their nationality. The Swedes appeared in force, by land and sea, upon the frontiers of Norway. It was not, however, until the latter country had been guaranteed complete national independence that she consented to a union of the countries under the one crown. The agreement was made, and the constitution of Norway granted on the 17th of May 1814, at which date the contemporary history of Norway begins.

CHAPTER XIII

MODERN NORWAY

Constitution—Religion—Education.

On May 17, 1814, as we have seen, a Constitution was granted to Norway. The Fundamental Law of the constitution (*Grundlöv*), which almost every peasant farmer now-a-days has framed and hung up in the chief room of his house, bears the date the 4th of November 1814. The Act of Union with Sweden is dated the 6th of August 1815.

The union of the two states is a union of the crown alone, as, I suppose, every one now knows, seeing that the union of Sweden and Norway has been one of the most frequent examples cited in favour of the Home Rule Bill for Ireland. (And the instance is more in point, from the fact that we have already noted, namely, that the political history of Norway has many points of resemblance to the political history of Ireland.) Sweden and Norway form, like Great Britain, a hereditary limited monarchy. One of the clauses in the Act of Union provides that the king of the joint countries must reside for a certain part of the year in Norway. But, as a matter of fact, this period is a short one.

In his absence, the king is represented by the Council of State (*Statsraad*), which must be composed entirely of Norwegians, and consist of two Ministers of State (Cabinet Ministers), and nine other Councillors of State. As with us, the king personally can do no wrong; the responsibility for his acts rests with his ministers. Of the State Council, or Privy Council (above spoken of), three members, one a Cabinet Minister, and two ordinary members of the Privy Council, are always in attendance upon the king, whether he is residing in Norway or Sweden. The rest of the council forms the Norwegian Government resident in the country. All functionaries are appointed by the king, with the advice of this Council of State. The officials, who form what we should call the Government (as distinguished from what we should call the Civil Service), together with the préfets (Amtmen) and the higher grades of the army are, nominally, removable by the king; but, if removed, they continue to draw two-thirds of their salary until their case has come before Parliament (the Stor-thing, Great Thing), which decides upon their pensions. The king is commander of the military and naval forces of the country, and these cannot be augmented, except by permission of Parliament. No foreign troops may be brought into the country in time of peace; not even Swedish, except for the quite temporary purpose of joining the Norwegian troops in military manœuvres.

In the same way, the Norwegian navy is quite separate from the Swedish navy, and may not be manned by other than Norwegian sailors. Neither army nor navy can be employed in offensive operations without the consent of Parliament.

x

This Storthing or Parliament of Norway consists of a hundred and eleven members. The system of election to it is different from the system of election to the English Parliament, and resembles more nearly that of the Congress of America; that is to say, it is indirect. In the rural electoral districts, each parish chooses according to its population a certain number of electors; and the college of electors, thus nominated, proceeds to choose a representative. The chief towns of the country have one, or more, representatives of their own; the lesser towns are formed into groups, which elect a representative among them. But in the towns, as in the country, the first business is the election of the college of electors. Two-thirds of the Storthing (seventy-four members) are elected by the rural constituencies, and the remaining third (thirty-seven members) by the urban constituencies.

The franchise is enjoyed by the following classes:—(1) In the country, those who have been in the use of—as tenants or proprietors—land on which they have paid taxes for five years; (2) those who, in the towns, possess a certain, although very small, amount of real property, or who have a patent as tradesmen, or artisans, or as captains of ships; (3) those who have held any of the public offices, the nomination to which rests with the king. The possessors of real property, it will be understood, are, in proportion, enormously in excess of the same class in England; forming, in fact, about two-thirds of the cultivators of the soil.

The Storthing is a triennial Parliament. Its sittings are annual; but they cannot, without the king's consent, last more than two months of the year. Until lately, it was supposed to be part of the Constitution of Norway that the ministry could not be members of the Storthing, and could not be present at the debates of Parliament, nor in its committees. But in 1884 the Storthing brought in a Bill abrogating this law, and making the ministers more directly responsible to Parliament than they had been hitherto. The ministers at that time were Conservatives, but the Storthing was Liberal; and it was on the motion of the Liberal leader, Svedrup, that this Bill was introduced. The Constitution of Norway (which in many ways follows the lines of the French Constitution of 1791) allows the king a suspensive veto on all legislation, but with regard to Svedrup's Bill it was maintained by the Conservative ministers that it effected a change in the Constitution of the country; and that the king might exercise not a suspensive, but an absolute veto upon it. Again and again the Bill was brought in, again and again it was vetoed. The excitement in the country rose to a great height. The present writer was in Norway at this time, and he remembers one person who talked about the crisis to him, comparing it to the contest between Charles I. and the Long Parliament. It must be said, however, that all this political excitement lay beneath the surface of life visible to the ordinary traveller; and, probably, not one per cent. of the tourists in Norway during this year was aware of what constitutional questions hung in suspense. Finally, the king or his ministers gave way, and the Bill was carried. It does not seem to us a matter of enormous importance; but it was the most exciting political contest that Norway has passed through for many years.

A recollection of this time of ferment has been preserved in Henrik Ibsen's social drama *Rosmersholm*. It is said that the writer, returning to his country about this time, was painfully impressed by the bitterness which, through party feeling, had crept into all social life. He, from the standpoint almost of a foreigner—for he does not reside in Norway—is for ever satirizing the pettiness, as he conceives it, of the life of his fellow-countrymen. A strong Liberal himself—like Björnson, his contemporary—it is his object to rouse the Norwegians from their contentment with their parochial life, and with their traditional religion, and from their fear of innovation. Thus it is the Conservative schoolmaster, Kroll,[1] who is responsible for all the ill-feeling and misrepresentation which embitters the lives of Rosmer and Rebecca in this drama.

In 1876 the number of electors to the Storthing were under a hundred and forty thousand, not more than 7·7 per cent. of the whole population. So that the franchise was by no means a very wide one. Out of the electors, nine-tenths were proprietors of some kind. What is perhaps more curious, is that out of these hundred and forty thousand voters, only a little over eighty-four thousand had, before the previous election, got themselves placed upon the register, and of these only a little over thirty-seven thousand actually took part in the election. So we see that that Parliament was actually elected by only about two per cent. of the population.

---

[1] *Rector* Kroll, he is called in the play, the title Rector being given in Norway, not to the clergyman (who is Præste or Pastor), but to the schoolmaster.

In foreign affairs only does Norway not act as an independent nation. There is a single foreign minister for the two countries, and he is usually a Swede.

For the purposes of internal administration, Norway is divided into twenty districts, called *Amter*—which we may best translate 'Prefectures.' Of these, the two chief towns of the country, Christiania (with its population of 150,000) and Bergen (population about 50,000) form each a separate Amt. The remaining eighteen prefectures include both towns and rural districts; all, that is, except one, Söndre-Bergenhus, which is entirely rural. These eighteen prefectures are divided into fifty-six *Fogderier* (*arrondissements*), which among them contain twenty-two ports; and into thirty-nine towns, each of which has its own *sous-préfet*, who is also a magistrate.

The thirty-nine townships and eighteen of the ports before mentioned constitute together fifty-seven urban communities.

On their side, the rural districts throughout the country are sub-divided into four hundred and fifty-nine rural communities, or *Hæreder*; and in these are included the four remaining small ports. The boundaries of the Hæreder are very generally coincident with those of the rural parishes.

We have thus five hundred and sixteen communities, or, as we may fairly call them in the English sense, townships, each one having its own electoral body and two representative bodies. The larger of these two is the Municipal or Parish Council (*Repræsentantskab*), which consists of from nine to thirty-six members; and a smaller body consisting of from three to twelve persons, called *Formandskab*—literally Body of Chief Men. We may translate it Local Government Board. This, like our late County Boards, has the administration of most of the local affairs; but the budget, or, let us say more simply, the local rates are settled by it in conjunction with the Municipal Council. The last body exercises no administrative functions separate from those of the Local Board.

The matters committed to the care of these local bodies are the maintenance of the roads and highways (of most of them, that is to say), of quays, churches, schools, hospitals, and other public buildings; free education, hygiene, and the administration of the public hospitals; the regulation of the water supply, scavenging, and police—though of these last only the main body of the force: the officers are paid by the State.

These three last items apply only to the urban administrative bodies. For, strange to say, there is no police in the rural districts: and this fact shows that, however turbulent and difficult to govern the Norwegians were in the earlier years of their history, they are very amenable to law and order now. In the country districts the authority of the law is represented by the Fogder and the Lensmænd. But, as we have not yet spoken of the executive authorities of either town or country, we will devote a separate section to explain what these are.

In most towns the executive authority is confined to a Borgemester or a Raadmand. The larger towns have one or two of these functionaries, their magistrates;

the smaller towns have but one in each. In certain cases the magistrate is required to act on the advice of the Municipal Council and the Administrative Board.

In the country there are three functionaries on whom fall the duties of police and magistracy. The lowest of these is the Lensmand, of whom there is one for each rural township. He is not a magistrate, but should rather be described as a police officer. But he is a police officer without subordinates; to carry out the orders of the executive he has the right to call upon the assistance of every private citizen, as indeed have the police in this country; and this power in Norway is found sufficient. The two superior officers, who are both magistrates, are the Amt-men (Prefects), and their subordinates the Fogder (bailiffs), whose sphere of administration are the Fogderier, as those of the Amt-men are the Amter. The Lens-men are appointed by the Amt-men.

The revenue of the communities is derived from rates, both upon real property and upon income. But a very large source of their receipts come from the liquor traffic, concerning which Norway has adopted a system almost peculiar to the Scandinavian countries. The main lines of it are nearly identical with that which, in this country, is familiar under the name of the Gothenburg system. And the essential part of the system is, that the manufacture and sale of spirituous liquors is not left to local enterprise. It is made a monopoly of the township. The public-houses or inns have no licence for the sale of spirits, which, as a rule, can be purchased only in bottles, and only in the licensed shops of grocers and so forth. It has been found that, in effect, these simple regulations have almost put an end to excessive drinking in Norway; at any rate, that the country, which was at one time the most intemperate in Europe, now holds a good place for sobriety among the nations. The traveller is sure to come across instances of drunkenness. These take place generally on some occasion of special festivity, such as a wedding. But the kind of continual drinking in the public-houses and the streets, which we are used to in our towns and villages, will not be found.

It is curious that the Scandinavian countries, Sweden and Norway, have been among the last to keep up a system of religious intolerance, almost of religious persecution. Until quite lately domicile was not allowed except to the members of certain recognised creeds, of which the Roman Catholic was not one. I do not mean that there were no Roman Catholics in the country, but that they did not enjoy the rights of citizenship. Even to-day these rights are not extended freely to all denominations; still, only certain sects, Evangelical (Lutheran), Roman Catholic, Jewish, one or two forms of 'orthodox' dissent, are recognised. And still no important public office is open to any one but a Lutheran.

There are probably few countries in Europe in which the ministers of religion have a greater influence in the administration of the country and in the control of the education of the people than they have in Norway. Belgium may, perhaps, be parallel with it on the Roman Catholic side. However great the reluctance of Norway to receive the Reformed Faith in the sixteenth century, she has become deeply attached to it now. Of the amount of power intrusted to the clergy in matters of education, etc., we shall show some instances hereafter. That they do not misuse their powers or interfere overmuch with the liberty of the people, may be judged from the fact that there can hardly be said to be in the country an anti-clerical party.

There is nothing exciting or outwardly attractive about the religious observances of Norway. The only beauty that the modern Norwegian churches possess at service time is imparted to them by their congregations, the women in their picturesque bright dresses, long fair hair, the men in their jackets and buttons and their knee-breeches. But this dull decorum suits the Norwegian peasant. Church-going with him is an ancient custom; and it implies much more than a religious ceremony. It affords the time and place of meeting for men and women from distant parts, many of whom lead very quiet and almost solitary lives. In the intervals between the services they exchange gossip, and even settle questions affecting the township—for the township is generally identical with the parish. Thus the traveller will see on Sundays the boats stealing across the fjords on every hand, and the steamers crowded with peasants in their Sunday dresses.

A few of the *illuminati*, such as Ibsen, who have taken their ideas from abroad, may rail against the narrowness and the formalism of the average Norwegian priest (as Ibsen does expressly in *Brand* and indirectly in many of his social dramas); but no party in the country is eager to curtail the authority of the Church.

The low standard of sexual morality in Norway

might be cited as a proof that the pastors do not do their duty by the people; but there are many quasi-accidental circumstances in Norwegian social life which tend towards a low standard of morality, and cause the large number of illegitimate births which mark the social life of the country districts.

Free compulsory education obtains in Norway; but it does not begin from such an early age as in England; in fact, it begins at a later age than in almost any other European country, namely, at eight years. The reason for beginning it so late is no doubt the difficulty which children have in attending school, the distances they have to walk, etc.,—owing to the sparseness of the population. Parents are allowed to send their children at seven, if they choose. The limit at the other end is later than with us, and with most other countries. It is made by the Confirmation, and this, in Norway, generally takes place at the age of fifteen.

The free public schools are, of course, under State inspection. There are other schools which are not free. Some of these are also State foundations; some have been founded by the townships; and some are kept by private persons. The masters of these private schools are not obliged to obtain a licence to teach, nor to undergo any examination by the State; but, on the other hand, the children instructed at these private schools periodically undergo government inspection, and, if the education they receive is not up to the proper standard, the parents can be forced to send their children to one of the public schools. If they choose to continue likewise to pay fees to the private schoolmaster they can do so, but it is not likely that they will. Parents neglecting to send their children to school (either public or private) are fined; and if they persist, or if the children are ill-treated at home, or receive a bad example there, they can be taken away and placed in other families, the parents still being forced to pay for their maintenance.

The Board Schools, as we may call them, are maintained by the townships or parishes. And they are governed by a Board, of which the chairman is the pastor of the parish; or, in the towns, one of the pastors nominated by the bishop. This fact shows how strong is the position which the State Religion holds in Norway. A considerable part of the cost of free education is defrayed out of the revenue of the Church lands, which were alienated at the time of the Reformation. The balance of expenditure is made up partly from what may be called rates, partly from State grants, or, in other words, out of taxation. The object of the primary education has been described as ' to complete the home education; to sow the seeds of a true Christian knowledge, and to give the minds of the children such a formation as befits every citizen of the State; and to impart such elements of knowledge as may enable the children to continue their education in later life according to their means.'

The subjects taught at these primary schools are reading, religion, Bible history, according to the authorised manuals, reading of the Bible and of the Psalms, reading from some appointed books, which treat principally of physical geography, natural science and history; writing, and the reading of writing, arithmetic, singing; and, if circumstances permit, gymnastics and military exercises. To these subjects the Board may, if it thinks fit, add grammar, higher geography, history and science, drawing, surveying, and, for the girls, housework.

Even with us in England, with our dense population, and by consequence the comparatively small area of our school districts, a certain amount of hardship is entailed in country places by the distances which children have to walk to attend the board schools. In many parts of Germany, where the education-acts are more strictly enforced than they are here, these hardships are sensibly increased. I remember myself once, in North Germany, stopping to rest at the lodge of a keeper in one of the great royal forests, which are so numerous in East and West Prussia, and in Posen. The children of this keeper had every day to walk four or five miles to school at the nearest town; they had to remain there the whole day, taking their dinner with them, or buying it at a shop, between the morning and afternoon school, with, perhaps, no sheltered place in which to eat it. Then, summer and winter, they had to trudge their four or five miles back through this dark and intensely lonely pine forest. The father was a splendid man (an old soldier, of course), and the children looked charmingly healthy. But this discipline must have been a severe trial, both of body and mind.

In Norway, with its narrow valleys, its numberless forests and uncultivated mountains, and its solitary farmsteads, the difficulties and hardships of this kind would be increased a hundredfold, if there were not some way of meeting them. The only course that can be adopted is, that the master, instead of the children, should travel from place to place. He could not, of course, do this each day, and teach the families one by one. What has to be done is, that the families of each district, under the charge of one master, are grouped into much smaller districts; that the master travels round to each in succession, and that, instead of there being one school and one residence for the master, the farmers of the lesser districts have to take it in turns to give him board and lodging for the time that he is with them, and to put at his disposal a room for a schoolroom. This curious peripatetic life of several of the board schoolmasters limits very much the possibilities of receiving instruction on the part of their pupils. In fact, the limit of compulsory attendance in many country districts is only nine weeks in the year—nine weeks of six days and thirty-six hours in the week. In the majority of country districts the compulsory attendance is limited to twelve weeks. How the children taught on this plan can retain any of their instruction, how, during the remaining forty weeks of the year, they can possibly remember what they learned during the golden twelve, must be a matter of wonder and speculation to any one who knows what the English child is like.

As a rule, one master is appointed for every fifty or sixty pupils. Manufacturers, etc., who employ as many as thirty families, or heads of families, are compelled to build a school for the instruction of the children of their employés; and groups of neighbouring small manufacturers are formed for the same purpose up to the same number of hands.

The public examinations, or inspections, take place yearly; and the inspectors are not appointed by the school board. Boys and girls are generally taught separately, but, as a rule, by the same master. Board schoolmistresses, however, are beginning to be introduced in the towns. Training colleges have been established for schoolmasters and schoolmistresses.

At the end of 1875 the number of children of an age to receive primary instruction in the towns and in the country was 270,780. Of these 213,842 were attending the fixed schools; 31,156 were being instructed by the peripatetic schoolmaster in the manner that has been described above; 3000 were receiving in private schools an education as good as that in the Board schools; in addition to these, 18,000 were attending the higher, or secondary schools, or receiving private instruction of a higher grade: 4769 children were receiving no education at all. The masters and mistresses employed in this work were 3942. The number of fixed schools at the same time in the country was 4591. Of these, 2100 were buildings constructed for that special purpose; the remaining 2491 buildings hired, only temporarily, for the purpose. The number of peripatetic schools was about 1860. The number of children taught in both was 209,461. This for the country; in the towns, instruction was given during the same period to 35,537 children by 670 masters and mistresses. The number of school buildings used for this purpose I have not been able to ascertain. The cost of educating the 209,461 children taught in the rural districts was 3,950,000 kroners, or rather less than fifteen shillings a head; a cost which seems incredibly small—

a cost calculated to make the English ratepayer's mouth water when he compares it with the cost of education per head in this country. The 35,537 children educated in the towns cost somewhat more, a fraction over £1, 3s. 9d. a head. But that was not a very ruinous charge.

Still, this difference of cost is significant. It shows the superior educational advantages of the towns beginning to display itself. The superiority is more marked when we pass from the primary or elementary school to the secondary schools. Attendance in these secondary schools is not compulsory. Beside these State secondary schools there have been established of recent years a number of High Schools, called by that name (Höiskoler), the plan of which, like that of our High Schools, is, of course, derived from the German *Hochschule*. From schools of this class there were in 1875 only 780 country pupils who received instruction. In the towns, on the other hand, there were 2529 pupils educated at the secondary schools, and 6574 educated at the High Schools—9103 in all. From this point the superior educational advantages of the towns manifest themselves decisively. Following upon those numbers, we have in the towns 2390 pupils receiving a still higher education, fitting them for entry into the university.

The University of Norway has its seat at Christiania, and is commonly spoken of as the University of Christiania. It is, it need scarcely be said, a university of the continental pattern, an establishment for the conferring of degrees and giving of lectures, not a collection of colleges such as are Oxford and Cambridge.

CHAPTER XIV

MODERN NORWAY

Land Tenure and the means of living.

In the earlier chapters of this book we have spoken about the way in which the land of Norway was settled, and the system on which it was held, that system of free tenure or udal right which Harald Harfagr sought to convert into a semblance of the feudal system. We saw how his efforts failed in essential particulars; and that his successor, Hakon the Good, obtained his crown at the price of restoring to the bonders their free tenure of the land. Attempts were made by succeeding princes to go back to the policy of Harald Harfagr, but their measures were generally revoked by the next successor. When Norway was under the rule of Denmark more persistent efforts were made to introduce feudality, and in certain parts of the country, in some which lie near Christiania, others which lie near Bergen, there existed until almost the other day one or two large manors (counties or baronies) which bore witness to the partial success of these efforts.

In travelling by rail from Christiania to Tönsberg—that oldest of Norwegian towns which the traveller interested in history ought not to miss seeing—we see on the right, a few miles before reaching Tönsberg, the old castle of Jarlsberg, which is a reminiscence of the last which remained of these feudal earldoms. Other feudal manors were the Earldom of Laurvik on the Laurvik Fjord—that eventually devolved to the crown,—and the barony of Rosendal, which lies on the Hardanger Fjord. The owners of this barony bore the title of Barons of Rosenkrone.

All titles of nobility were abolished in Norway by an Act of 1821. This, as was said in an earlier chapter, is rather a return to the condition of things which existed before Norway had any political connection with Denmark than an absolutely new departure. The other side of the feudal system, serfdom, has never existed to any great extent in Norway.

The house-carls who figure so much at the courts of kings and earls during the Saga-age were but the development for purposes of war and state of the ancient race of *husmænd*, which is represented still on the estate of each considerable farmer. The house-men of to-day were probably the thralls of a former age; now they are in much the same position as many of the peasant proprietors in North Germany, that is to say, they possess and cultivate land of their own; but they are compelled for a certain number of days to work upon their master's farm. This is too, of course, the corvée of the French peasant previous to the Revolution. The number of these house-men in Norway does not very sensibly increase.

The system of udal tenure (*odalsret*) as it exists in Norway, though it implies the free holding of the land, does not include free sale. In fact, a proprietor cannot, properly speaking, do more than mortgage his landed possessions. He or his descendants have the right of re-entry on the repayment of the purchase-money, if this payment is made within three years of the sale. Even when this is not done the new holder does not acquire udal right in his tenure until he has held it for twenty years.

The inheritance of property in former days vested in equal shares in the sons of the house; but the daughters, as a rule, inherited personal property only. Later on, the share of each daughter in the real property of her father was half that of each of the sons. But since 1860 the rights of all children have been equalised. The power of testamentary disposition moreover is limited to one-fourth only of the property of the testator. It will be seen that in framing these laws concerning property, as in framing its constitution, Norway, while it has in many ways done not much more than legalize the customs which already existed, has yet in effect run pretty closely on the lines of legislation in France since the Revolution.

This law of the compulsory partition of estates, of course, tends to the splitting up of properties into very small divisions. But it is partly modified by a certain option of purchase accorded to the inheritors in order to prevent the farms being further divided. This power of purchase goes by the name of *Aasædesret*.

As it is, however, the land often becomes subdivided in a most ridiculous manner. For the Norwegians, like peasant proprietors in all countries, are very jealous of their rights, and by no means very reasonable in asserting them. The extreme variableness in the character of the soil too, throws difficulties in the way of valuation and exchange; so that each proprietor is disposed to cling to his own little patches. A traveller along the Norwegian roads cannot fail to notice some curious evidences of this subdivision of the land; for by law the peasant proprietors are obliged to keep in repair the roads which their properties adjoin. The result is, that you may see a constant succession of posts along the roadside with such inscriptions as 'Thor Andresson, 3 metres,' 'Knut Fogelberg, 10 metres,' 'Præstegaard (the glebe lands), 100 metres.' Then may come again Fogelberg with 6 metres more, then a new proprietor with 50 metres, then Andresson with another 4 or 5 metres, and so on. In former times there existed restrictions on this continual division of property; but these restrictions were all abolished before the end of the last century.

All landed property formerly paid a land-tax, except that in Finmark, which was excepted, it may be presumed, on account of the extreme poverty of the soil. But in 1836, this impost, which had undergone successive reductions, was finally abolished. There still remain succession-duties, and a certain number of what we should call rates levied on land.

Although, as was said, the system of what has been called the village community did not exist in Norway to the extent that it existed in other European countries, there has been at different times, and still is, a good deal of agricultural land held in common. This is, of course, chiefly the uncultivated pasture-land. In 1870 13·4 per cent. of the landed property of Norway was common land. Holdings of this type obtain chiefly in the west, from Lindisnæs, in the extreme south, as far as the Throndhjem Fjord. Over this district the proportion of common properties rose as high as 30 per cent.

Those again of the forests of Norway which were not crown land were originally common land. And when the rights in them came to be distributed they were often settled in a very curious and complicated way. Over the same area one man might possess the right of pasturing his cattle beneath the trees; another, of stripping off the birch bark, which in old days had so many more uses than it has to-day, being used, for example, to make leaves to write upon, and sometimes being used for clothing; then a third might have the right of felling these birch-trees, but these trees only; a fourth might have the right of cutting conifers—the firs, and pines. The legislature has tried hard to remedy the inconveniences caused by the stripping up of the land into fragments, and by the complication of common rights.

The great land hunger which exists in Norway, and is quite as strong there as it is in Ireland, will have been already suggested by the facts which we have detailed. During the whole of this century the proportion of proprietors to tenants of the land has been constantly on the increase. Thus in 1825 the proprietors constituted 66 per cent. of the cultivators of the soil, and in the succeeding five decades they increased successively to form a proportion of 70, 76, 81, and 85 per cent.

Equally marked has been the absolute increase in the number of the peasant proprietors. Thus, in the thirty years between 1840 and 1870, the number of landed proprietors in the country grew from 109,154 to 149,013, or by 36 per cent.; about an average increase of 1 per cent. per annum. The amount of reclaimed soil increased between these dates at almost exactly the same rate.

The chief productive industries of Norway are three—Fishing, Agriculture (including with that what is the chief industry in Norway of this kind, cattle-breeding), and the Felling of trees. I cite them in this order, not because it represents the scale of their importance, but because it is the order in which they first strike the attention of the traveller. Probably one of his first experiences in Norway will be a visit to the fish-market at Bergen, where the women in their picturesque dresses and headgear, looking as if they had come straight out of some drawing by Holbein, are to be seen bargaining from the quay with men in round, rough caps, in short jackets, and fishing-boots, who stand in their boats just below them. Immediately on our landing in any part of Norway, the rich hill-pastures, the cattle on the mountain-sides, suggest the second industry of the country. But in all the neighbourhood of the sea-coast the trees are weather-worn and stunted. We have to travel into the interior of the country, into the upland region, which lies between the two Scandinavian countries, before we come to the scene of the third great industry of Norway, tree-felling.

This order, too—Fishing, Agriculture, Wood-cutting—which is the order of our acquaintance with them, is likewise the order in which these industries have become known to the people of Norway. The thought of fishing carries us back to those extremely ancient prehistoric people who, thousands of years before the Christian era, lived dotted about on the sea-coast of the Baltic, in Denmark, in Southern Sweden, in a few places in Norway. These primitive people lived chiefly on the shell-fish which they found in their neighbourhood. But they did venture out sometimes into deep water, for some bones of deep-sea fish have been discovered among their remains. In later ages fishermen settled all along the sea-coast of Norway. Long before there was much cultivation of the interior, there were, no doubt, colonies of them scattered far up the coast. These gained their livelihood by fishing in the fjords, and their frail boats were protected from storms by the belt of islands outside.

Then came the time of agriculture and of cattle-breeding, and at the beginning of the historical era these were so far developed that the two most fertile parts of the land, the region which lies behind the Christiania Fjord and the region which lies round the Throndhjem Fjord, were the most thickly inhabited, and were politically the most important parts of the country.

It is just at the dawn of the historical period that we begin to hear of adventurers penetrating into the forest regions, and clearing out from the midst of them space for a fresh settlement, which sometimes grows into a little kingdom. Tree-felling of this kind was for the sake of clearance merely, and was not in itself a productive industry. We have to come down to the sixteenth or seventeenth centuries, before the exploitation of the forests takes its place as a branch of industry and commerce. Of late it has proved a more productive industry than the fisheries.

1. *Fishing* remains an industry of very great importance, without which the coast population from Stavanger to the far north could not be supported. The fisheries are chiefly of two kinds of fish, cod and herring. Both sorts can rarely be carried on in the same district: where the cod are numerous the herrings soon begin to disappear. Then the cod, their nourishment failing, take their departure, and the herrings come back. This alternation has been very curiously illustrated near the island of Karmö, by Stavanger. In the far north the chief food of the cod is the *lodde* or capelan (*malotus arcticus*), an arctic fish of the salmon species. The codfish (*torsk*) fished in Norway are of two sorts, the *fjord-torsk* and the *hav-torsk*, sea-cod or *skrei*. The taking of the fjord-cod goes on throughout the fjords, the taking of the sea-cod is limited to certain places and to certain seasons, the scenes and times for the spawning of the fish. The chief locality for this sea-cod fishery are the Lofoten Islands, and the mainland opposite. There are to be seen the great fleets of fishing boats of antique build, which are so like Viking fleets of the Saga-age.

There are two methods of preparing the cod for exportation, and according to the way it is prepared it is called *klipfisk* (splitfish) or *stokfisk* (stickfish). The making into *stokfisk* is much the oldest method of preparation. The name comes from the fish being (after cleaning) hung upon sticks and dried in the wind. The 'splitfish' method, which was introduced into Norway from this country, is simply that of splitting and salting, as is practised with herrings and haddocks among ourselves. At the time that the fish is cleaned the liver is sold for the manufacture of cod liver oil.

The herring fishery (*sildfisk*), which comes next in importance to that of the cod, is not so widely spread as the former. The herring is scarcely found in the Skaggerak, and not in great quantities north of Stattland, the promontory which lies between the Nordfjord and the Voldenfjord. There are three seasons for this fishery—spring, summer, and winter, of which the last is the most important; and there are two distinct varieties of herrings fished on the Norwegian coast: the ordinary herring and the large herring, called *storsild*, which is only found in the extreme north.

The cod and herring fisheries are the ones which are chiefly made for foreign exportation, and are distinguished as the great fisheries of the country. Beside these there are the fisheries for home consumption, of which the chief are mackerel and haddock.

The salmon fishery stands somewhat apart now that it is so much sought by English (and in a less degree by Americans), who occupy almost all the salmon rivers of the country. The capital which the pursuit of this sport incidentally brings into Norway must be very great. The immediate yield, since the rivers have been more carefully preserved, has been sensibly diminished. Till within comparatively recent years there seemed a danger that the salmon would become extinct in Norwegian waters, so reckless was the way in which the fish were netted. And further restrictions are still required on this practice if the breed is to be kept up.

2. *Agriculture* was the industry Norway developed next after fishing; and its earliest developments were, so

far as we can judge, in the countries of the Christiania Fjord, and of the Throndhjem Fjord. And it is a curious fact that, at this very day, it is in these two districts that the greatest advance in agriculture has been made; in these that steam winnowing-machines have almost entirely superseded the old-fashioned flails, and that steam ploughs and harrows are coming into common use.

We use here the general term agriculture to include all means of raising products for consumption from the soil. But anybody who has travelled in Norway, or indeed heard any description of the country, does not require to be told that the chief employment of the farming population is in tending and breeding cattle and horses.

The general principles of farming in Norway closely resemble those in Switzerland. The following are perhaps the chief points of difference : Like Switzerland, Norway is essentially a pasture and grazing country. The extreme moisture of the climate and the constant supply of water in the northern country makes the preservation of the water of much less importance there; the result is that we see much fewer water-meadows in Norway than in Switzerland. On account, likewise, of the abundance of rain in Norway, the making of hay is attended with great difficulties. The result is that there has been adopted there a system of haymaking which is peculiar to the Scandinavian countries, and is the first feature in their agriculture which is likely to attract the attention of the traveller. He will probably, indeed, have previously heard how the Norwegians are accustomed to dry their grass, not by leaving it upon the ground, but by packing it between the bars of hurdles, which remain constantly standing in their fields for this purpose. The pasture in the low-lying meadows is often extremely abundant, though it is very apt to be coarse, and is generally full of wild flowers. It is chiefly in the lower pastures that we find water-meadows, and in them that we see hay-making going on. In order that the grass may be allowed to grow for this purpose, the cattle are transported to higher pastures among the mountains, where they are kept all the summer months. This, again, is a custom which has its parallel in the farming of Switzerland; but nowhere does it exist to such an extent as in Norway, to the life of which country it has given one of its most characteristic features.

The mountain pastures of Norway are known by the name of *sæters*. It is on account of the long duration of winter there, and of its heavy snows that these sæters have such a rich and short-lived vegetation, of which it is necessary to make full use. To the sæters the cattle of the lower lands are transported for the whole period during which they are available. This involves driving the beasts up steep mountain paths which it would be impossible for them to frequently ascend and descend. Wherefore a colony of attendants on the cattle is formed from the farm in the valley; and these attendants transport themselves to the sæters practically for the whole summer. Cottages are built for their accommodation. We have already spoken of these one-roomed sæter-houses, which are often not even provided with a chimney. It is the fact that they are only designed for summer use, which allows the most primitive type of house building to be retained here, when it has long since been abandoned in the plains.

The sæter system is so engrained in the farming of Norway that it is common for even the smaller properties to include a portion of mountain pasture as well as of land in the plain or the valley. The larger farms have generally their own sæters. But many sæters consist of a combination of small holdings, whose owners act almost as if the property was held in common. Sometimes the portions of land are individually too small to maintain a single head of cattle; and the owners combine to maintain a certain number of beasts among them. The life in these sæters forms probably the most agreeable episode of Norwegian country life. The men and women are occupied together in tending and milking the cattle and in cheese-making, the great industry of this sæter-life. They carry down their produce into the valley in enormous baskets, which are strapped upon their backs, and which none but mountaineers could carry up and down such paths; and they return to the sæter at night with their baskets full of provisions. The tourist who toils up these steep mountain ways, a guide, maybe, carrying his knapsack for him, is put to shame by quite old men, or quite young girls who trip past him laden with what appear enormous burdens.

Cattle-breeding is by no means carried on to the exclusion of that of sheep, for which the mountain pastures likewise afford great facilities. Goats are also cultivated, but not in numbers at all comparable to those in Switzerland. Horses, too, are bred in considerable numbers, for almost the sole means of transport inland is by road, and they are the only beasts of burden. Asses and mules are practically unknown in the country; and only in a very few districts—some of those bordering on Sweden—are cattle used for ploughing.

3. *Forestry.*—The third productive industry of Norway is the felling of trees, chiefly soft-wood trees, fir or pine. Her exportation of the wood (deal) from these trees forms the chief commercial link between Norway and Sweden and our own country; so that it is this wood-felling that we naturally think of as the characteristic industry of Scandinavia. No part of Europe does more in that way, in proportion to its size, than this. Our word 'deal' is derived from the Swedish *dæl*, a piece; deal properly signifying the planks of wood after the tree-trunk has been cut up, as distinguished from the mere trunk itself, and having nothing to do with the material of which the pieces are made. But, as a matter of fact, all the planks which come from Scandinavia to England, being made out of soft-wood trees, deal has come with us to stand for wood of this kind.

In early historic days there was no thought of exporting wood from the country; but the houses were then, as they are to-day, built almost entirely of wood, and tree-felling was required for this purpose as well as for the supply of firewood. In the earliest days the Norsemen had no idea of cutting peat or turf for their fires. The first Norseman who ever thought of doing this was Einar, the second Earl of the Orkneys. He learnt the art no doubt from some of the Celts of the islands. Since Einar's days the practice of peat-cutting has been quite naturalised in Norway; and the traveller will not have made many drives in the country without having seen instances of this turf-cutting in progress. For there are many parts of Norway which are very scantily supplied with trees. The extreme north of the country produces no firs; nothing but a little scrub birch. Then, again (to go farther south), the Lofoten and the Vesteraalen islands, Bergenhus (farther south still), and the 'Amt' of Stavanger, have not enough wood for the construction of their houses, and are obliged to purchase it from districts farther east.

It is when we get to the lands sloping up towards the backbone of Scandinavia, and those near the Swedish border, that we meet with the largest forests and the finest trees. The total forest area of Norway is reckoned to be a little more than one-fifth of the whole area of the country. This forest district includes, however, large tracts which are marshy and swampy and bare of trees, or only produce stunted bushes.

Theoretically after the days of Harald Harfagr the forest rights in Norway belonged to the crown; for Hakon's restoration to the bonders of their udal possessions did not affect the unsettled portions of the country. But the crown rights were very little enforced for many centuries; and the forests were very little protected. They sometimes suffered the most fearfully destructive fires; and this was especially the case during the civil wars of the eleventh and twelfth centuries. Certain rights, moreover, were preserved to the people, such as the right to cut wood for building purposes; a right which was obviously liable to a great deal of abuse, because it was impossible to say in cutting down a tree what portion of it would prove to be available for building purposes and what refuse there would be which must be sold as firewood. Only since 1884 have serious attempts been made to put restrictions upon the felling of trees. Even now the regulations are not, properly speaking, in the hands of the State.

Common rights in the forest have been revised and re-arranged, and now these rights have become once more really the property of the Communes. They are regulated by a commission composed of representatives both of the proprietors of forest lands themselves and those who have only forest rights. These last take precedence of the rights of the proprietors of the soil. The commission of the Commune (*Bygdealmenning*) has full powers to regulate the felling of trees, and to take measures, by planting, etc., to preserve the forests. At the present moment about eight-ninths of the forest land of Norway is under the regulation of the representatives of the Bygdealmenninger. The remaining one-ninth consists chiefly of forests belonging to the State or to the fund of public instruction (what was formerly Church land). The State sets aside the small sum of £3600 per annum for the purchase of forests.

The life of the forester while he is at his work of tree-felling is an extremely hard one, and is not without its spice of adventure. For the time at which the trees have to be cut down is after all their foliage has withered and the sap which it contained has returned to the trunk of the tree: then is the wood at its hardest and in best condition. Thus all the tree-felling goes on in late autumn and winter. The wood-cutter goes by himself far into the depths of the forest, and lives in a little hut which he himself has made, and whither he carries a good store of provisions. If he is reasonably near the inhabited parts of the country he may make frequent returns to his family and friends; but this is not always possible, for the distances to which he removes are often very great. The ground during all this time is probably covered with a garment of snow, and has the intense stillness which belongs to this condition; a stillness, however, which is from time to time broken by the roaring sound of the wind, which in pine forests can be heard from an immense distance. The great distances over which the woodman may have to travel, if he goes back to the inhabited country, and the roughness of the ground over which he passes, are both lessened for him by this friendly covering of snow. For he does not walk over it, but skates on his snow-skates or *skés* (*skier*)—instruments very unlike the skates with which we are acquainted. Their runners are of great length, much longer even than those of Dutch skates, and likewise much broader, and they are made of wood. In the intense cold of these winter nights the woodcutter has to keep a fire continually burning in his hut to prevent himself from being frozen to death. He does not, however, keep himself warm by drinking spirits to the extent that a labourer similarly situated would do in Great Britain or North Germany. His chief beverage is coffee. The horses that are used to drag the felled trees sometimes suffer extremely from the cold; and probably no other horses but the Norwegian could endure it. As it is, they are often obliged to be worked in the night to prevent them from being frozen to death. It is a curious fact that it is found that hay and not oats is the diet best suited to give the animals warmth sufficient to resist the cold.

The horses drag the trunks down some prepared route which ends at the side of a mountain stream. By the bank huge piles of 'lumber' are made; these are visited by the proprietors, and each trunk marked or branded with the proprietor's mark. During the winter months the piles accumulate (they are called *Tömmervælter* or *Tömmerlunder*, 'lumber piles'); but when the spring comes round and the snow melts, commences the difficult and dangerous operation of floating the lumber down the stream. When, as frequently happens, the tree-trunks get caught on their way down stream and accumulate in large masses, the woodmen who superintend their passage have to jump upon them to free, with the boat-hooks which they carry, the log which bars the passage, and then jump ashore again before the whole mass is once more whirled down by the stream. It need not be said that this work requires great agility, and is attended by no small danger. On some of the streams where waterfalls or rapids would absolutely debar the passage of the wood, canals have to be made to give it transit.

The life of the woodcutter is thus not only very solitary, but is attended with considerable hardship and danger. It is, however, a great resource for the Norsemen during the long winter months when the ground is covered with snow, and all agricultural occupations would be impossible. It is an occupation most suited for unmarried men, and the great majority of the woodmen belong to this class. The value of the Norwegian forests has been estimated at £22,000,000 sterling. Including those employed in match-making, preparing the birch-bark for paper, etc., from sixty to seventy thousand persons are supported by industries connected with the tree-felling. The annual value of the exportation of wood from Norway is about two and a quarter millions.

The traveller may be left to himself to discover the peculiarities of Norwegian life; the appearance of the houses; their position and size; the people, their dress and their food; the modes of conveyance by land and by water; only remembering what we have already said which touches these subjects, and adding thereto the following incidental observations which may direct his attention to some points which he would otherwise have missed.

His guide-books will have explained to him the method of inland conveyance by posting. The present system of posting dates from the year 1816, at which time a law was passed creating what are called the 'fast' stations (properly fixed stations—*Faste Stationer*) on certain routes. At these stations (certain specified farmhouses) the farmer is compelled to keep horses in constant readiness for use in posting, for which service he is indemnified at a rate fixed by the State. The conveyances used in this inland posting are of three kinds, the well-known cariole or *kariol*, a two-wheeled conveyance for one person only, the *stolkjærre*, which is only an enlarged cariole fit for holding two persons, and the *vogn*, which is a four-wheeled conveyance resembling a smaller fly or drosky.

On the fjords and lakes there exist water stations, which supply four-oared boats on much the same conditions and terms as the conveyances are supplied by land. But, owing to the increase in the number of steamers which ply along the coast, this kind of water-posting is, comparatively speaking, very little used.

In the appearance of the Norse people themselves, the traveller who is full of reminiscences from the Sagas, or has heard much talk of hardy Norsemen, is liable to be disappointed. The men are generally thickly and strongly built, but they are certainly not men of exceptional height. The Swedes are on the whole, a much finer race; indeed, the Swedes are said to have the greatest average height of any European nation. In North Germany, again, the men are much finer-looking than the Norsemen; and they are so too, I think, in Yorkshire, and indeed in most of the northern counties of England (at any rate in the eastern ones), and in the eastern counties of Scotland. Probably the finest men of the nation are drained away by emigration. Certainly it has been my own experience that the only Norsemen of exceptional size that I have met in the country were returned emigrants.

With regard to two other matters, the national costume and the food, the casual visitor to Norway is somewhat liable to be deceived. As is the case in Switzerland, the national costume is kept up in Norway to a great extent for the benefit of travellers. The tourist finds the picturesque Hardanger costume very prevalent among the hotel waitresses throughout the country, thus extending into regions to which by right it does not belong. Nevertheless, there are many specimens of national costume still to be found, and these are well worth noticing. For the men the characteristic dress is a short round jacket, buttoned below the neck only, and made picturesque by two rows of metal buttons, which, in the case of the richer peasants, are often of silver. The material is a thick home-spun cloth. They have waistcoats to match, ornamented with smaller buttons, and knee-breeches, generally of home-spun, but sometimes of leather; coarse woollen socks, and shoes, which occasionally have buckles. Their head-dress is generally a round skin cap, of the kind that in our imagination we generally think of as Russian or Polish. In some parts a tall cylindrical felt hat is worn, not unlike the hats which Welsh women used to wear.

The picturesque dress, especially the head-dress, of the Bergen women should be noticed. The *ensemble* reminds one of the women whom Holbein drew. In Bergen, too, we should notice the number of people wearing *sabots*, for this kind of *chaussure* is rare in Norway. The full costume of the women of the Hardanger district is the most beautiful which is worn in Norway, and is the one usually adopted in fancy-dress balls, or in festivals wherein the national costume has to be represented. It consists of a dark skirt of green or blue; of a bodice of scarlet, edged with ribbon or with gold lace, over a muslin shirt, with full sleeves, and much plaited in front. The married women wear caps of exquisitely white muslin; the unmarried women go bare-headed. Round the neck and round the waist are worn specimens of the beautiful 'old silver' (frequently gilt), if any heirlooms of this are left in the family; but the high prices which foreigners are willing to give for this 'gammel sölv' is bringing an immense quantity into the market. All of this, of course, goes out of the country. The present writer found that in an interval of seven years the price of the old silver had gone up enormously.

The casual traveller must not expect that in the hotels to which he very likely will confine himself he will find any true representative of the food of the people, any more than he found one of the national costume. There he will get salmon and fresh meat in abundance. But in the interior of the country, in many parts, at any rate, the people only rarely eat fresh meat or fresh fish. The meat which they do consume has been smoked or dried and kept for months —for a year may be—hung up in their *stabur* or storehouses. To our taste it is uneatable. Salt herrings are very much consumed in the country. But farinaceous food forms the staple of the national diet. It is usually eaten not in the form of bread but of porridge, called in the Norse gröd. In the rural districts the bread is generally of two kinds, black bread made of rye, and resembling in almost every particular the German rye bread, and a curious very thin biscuit-bread no thicker than mill-board, which goes by the name of flat bread (*flatbrød*). It is made of barley or oatmeal, often with a little potato-meal added. Potatoes, though they were not introduced into Norway till the middle of the last century, have become a favourite article of food.

In the constitution and the domestic life of the country, as we have described it, we seem to have reached the ideal of a republic where there is no great wealth and no abject poverty, where the abolition of titles should secure that there shall be as much equality among men in social life as there is in the eye of the law. It is interesting, then, and it is instructive to ask how far the condition of Norway justifies the hopes and efforts of those who are striving constantly to bring about a similar condition of things among ourselves.

If we were to take as an answer to this question the picture which Ibsen presents us of social life in Norway, we should say that the result was wholly unsatisfactory; that the only effect of the strivings of Norway after republican equality had been to produce a people who, in their private life, were sordid, selfish, by no means very moral (the proportion of illegitimate births in Norway is very large), and in their public life were narrow, self-interested, conventional, hypocritical. But this estimate of Ibsen's cannot be a fair one. One of the things which proves that the Norwegians are capable of a wise and far-sighted self-government is the way in which they have dealt with the liquor traffic, and have succeeded in cleansing the nation from one of its greatest vices—excessive intemperance.

The absence of anything like abject poverty is, again, a remarkable and a most pleasing feature of the social condition of the country; and a still more remarkable and more pleasing one is the almost total absence of serious crime in the rural districts; so that, as we have already pointed out, there exists in these country districts no regular police. It must be acknowledged by any one who has conversed with the better sort of members of the *bonder* class, that for education and intelligence they compare favourably with the small proprietors of other countries. It is true that they are not very energetic; and that, though (like the Irish, with whom we have more than once compared them) the Norwegian peasant proprietors interest themselves a good deal in politics, they have no very extended political views, and they have never been able for many hundred years—perhaps never in the course of their history—to form any wide political combinations. But if Ibsen in *Peer Gynt* gives a poor and unlovely picture of the Norwegian peasant, what a picture does Zola give of the French one in *La Terre!*

On the other hand, it cannot be said that the abolition of titles, and the social equality of all citizens in the eye of the law have had the effect of bringing about a real feeling of equality, or of obliterating the mean ambitions which belong to small communities. On the contrary, there are few places (outside Russia) in which the smaller government offices are more sought after for the sake of the distinction which they confer than they are in Norway, or where official titles of distinction, such as chamberlain (*kammerherre*), are more the objects of petty striving and petty jealousy. This state of feeling produces the narrow bureaucracy which is characteristic chiefly of the town communities of Norway; and it is this which is the subject of endless animadversion and satire in Ibsen's social dramas.

CHAPTER XV

NORSE LITERATURE

THE Saga literature, of which we have already spoken fully, and given so many examples of in the course of the historical chapters in this volume, is not in the proper sense a literature of Norway, but of Iceland. When this Saga literature comes to an end there follows the true mediæval period of Norse history, during which the country was, as we have seen, a prey to civil war, and when there was no room for literature to flourish. We saw a sort of last echo of the old Saga literature in the account of Hakon's expedition to Scotland, and in the verses which were composed as a record of it. After this period comes the time of union between Norway and Denmark. The latter country was much ahead of Norway in point of culture; and therefore throughout all the period of union it impressed its character on the writings of the Norsemen of the epoch. All the Norsemen who wished to educate themselves had to go to the University of Copenhagen, and to imbibe there the culture of Denmark.

It was only after the creation of a native University at Christiania (1811), and the severance of the connection with Denmark, which followed almost immediately after (1814), that a genuine Norse literature once more arose. It is usual to date the beginning of it from the appearance of the patriotic effusions, pamphlets, and poems which celebrated the proclamation of a separate constitution for Norway. The poetry, especially, which this event called forth, was voluminous in quantity; but of a quality which left much to be desired. The date of the proclamation of the Norse Constitution was the 17th of May 1814. Wherefore this class of poetry went by the name of 17th of May poetry ('Syttendemai Poesi'). The authors were called 'Syttendemai' poets.

This literature attained its zenith in the writings of a poet of much higher inspiration than the others, Peter Wergeland by name, the father, as he is generally reckoned, of modern Norse poetry. Wergeland's writing is distinguished by the sort of graceful and facile optimism which is most popular with the half educated; and the reading class in Norway was then—nay, it still is—composed mainly of the half educated. To compare Wergeland to Longfellow will perhaps give the English reader the best notion of what I mean by the facile and graceful, but it must be also added rather cheap and conventional poetry of this author. The best known of Wergeland's poems is 'Den Engilske Lods,' 'The English Pilot.' It gives a series of travel-pictures very largely of English coast scenery in graceful and agreeable verse.

Welhaven is the writer next in importance after Wergeland, of whom he was the contemporary, and to whom he presents in many points an almost exact antithesis. Welhaven has little sympathy with the 'syttendemai' movement. He is severely cultured and critical; and he looks back with a certain amount of regret to the days of the connection with Denmark, and of a higher culture which existed at the Danish capital as compared with the somewhat raw enthusiasm of Christiania. The best of Welhaven's poems are of a satirical kind, and are contained in a volume entitled *Norges' Dæmring* (Norway's Dawn—the title is satirical). He is the intellectual godfather of Henrik Ibsen. Two other poets of this earlier period are Andreas Munch and Jorge Moe. This early Norse poetry is filled with allusions, rather stagey some of them are, to the heroic days of Norse history and to the heathen beliefs of the past; of these last the writers show a very inadequate knowledge. When they are not dealing with these subjects they write of the pastoral life and picturesque beauties of the country itself. Many of these writers of the earlier years of the century are extremely graceful; but there is not one who can fairly be called powerful. Anybody who has acquired the Norse may read them with pleasure; there is no one of them whom it is the least necessary for us to read, if we are in search of the finest fruits of European culture.

It is different with two other Norse writers who are now living, and of whom we shall have to speak presently; I mean Ibsen and Björnson.

Side by side with this very decided, though not very deep vein of poetry which the earlier Norse literature of this century reveals to us, we see growing up in prose a school of very painstaking historians and antiquaries, some of whom rise to a very high place in their class. The Scandinavians have, during the present century, been eminent in antiquarian and historical studies. The names of the Danish antiquaries Nielsen, Thomson, Worsaae, and others of a past generation, will be familiar to many readers. They will know that it was due to the researches of these men that the records of the past, contained in the buried implements of prehistoric men, were first brought to light and made the subject of serious and scientific study. To them was due the first division of the prehistoric ages into the now familiar Stone, Bronze, and Iron Periods. The two Steenstrups, father and son, the two Müllers, father and son, our countryman George Stephens, are other distinguished names in Denmark; and in Sweden the two Hildebrands, Montelius, Pederson, and many others. Norway has produced Unger, Holmboe, Schive, Bugge, Bang, and Storm. But the most distinguished among the antiquarian-historians of the north was Peder Andreas Munch, the author of *Det Norske Folks Historie*, 'The history of the Norse people.' It is a work of immense research, conceived upon the German pattern, but wanting in the graces of style which mark the best English and French histories. A contemporary Norse historian whose work may be strongly recommended to the Englishman (with a knowledge of Norse) who is studying the history of the country, is J. E. Sars.[1]

We now come to speak of the only two writers who can claim a place in the Walhalla of the higher European literature, Björnson and Ibsen. I will speak of Björnson first, because, though he is the younger of the two, it is best to leave Ibsen, as the greatest name in Norse literature, to be spoken of at the end.

[1] *Udsight over det Norske Historie* (1873, etc.).

Björnstierne Björnson is a most voluminous writer, and has written in almost every department of light literature—lyrics, dramas, novels, comedies—besides political pamphlets and addresses. He is a man of superabundant energy and self-confidence. He is the optimistic spirit of Norse literature, as Ibsen is the pessimistic. Intellectually, these two may be compared and contrasted as the Schiller and the Goethe of Norway. Each one is, of course, inferior to his prototype. But each of them is under a deep debt of gratitude to German literature; and this they have repaid by gaining as high appreciation almost in Germany as in their own country. But it is Björnson who, in his plays, has gained most from Schiller, and Ibsen who has modelled some of his finest work upon the poetry of Goethe.

In another way Björnson may be called the Muscular Christian of Norway. His writings remind one sometimes of the utterances of the Muscular Christian school in England, especially of those of Charles Kingsley. He has something of the robust self-confidence and versatility of the English writer. But as a name in literature, the Norseman stands much the higher.

Björnson was the son of a Norse pastor, and was born (in 1832) in the wild and barren Dovrefjeld. But a great part of his childhood was passed in the Romsdal. And the traveller who has read Björnson's beautiful descriptions of Norse scenery should especially bear them in mind when he goes up this lovely valley. In this country and in America Björnson will always be known as essentially the novelist of Norwegian country life. Probably it is as this that he will go down to posterity. He seems by his character, his physique (he is a man of powerful and robust frame), and the circumstances of his birth, to be the poet not only of Norse scenery, but of the Norse peasant, and of his rough and strenuous life seen at its best. Björnson's finest work in this kind is to be found in what may be called the novels of his early and middle period, such as *Synnöve Solbakken*, *Arne* (Arne is a poet-peasant, illegitimate son of a drunken father, a fiddler who has a touch of genius in him along with ferocity and even semi-insanity), *En glad Gut* (The Happy Boy), *Fiskejenten* (The Fisher Maiden). This last is more psychological, and has a wider scope than the preceding ones. It is a transition towards the novels of Björnson's later manner, of which we have to speak hereafter.

It is to be noted that here again in the peasant tales, there was a prototype for Björnson in the German peasant novel, the *Bauerngeschichten* of writers such as Auerbach and Werner.

There are, beside, the numerous plays which Björnson has written. One is of great length, a 'trilogy' on *Sigurd Slembe* (Slembidjakn, the rival of Harald Gilli), which, we may assume with confidence, has taken Wallenstein for its model. Another of Björnson's historical dramas is *Mellem Drabningerne* (Between the Fights), a one-act tragedy, which is concerned with the picturesque time of the rivalry between Sverri and Magnus. This was one of Björnson's earliest dramatic efforts. He has also written *Kong Sverri* and *Sigurd Jorsalfar*, the last, in my opinion, the least successful of his dramas, and, not fearing to associate his name with that of Schiller, *Maria Stuart i Skotland*. *Halte Hulda* (Lame Hulda) is a powerful drama, not strictly speaking historical, *De Nygifte* (The Newly-Married Pair), *En Hanske* (A Glove), *Geografi og Kjærlighed* (Love and Geography), *En Fallit*, show him in a lighter vein. Some of the dramas, *Halte Hulda*, for instance, and some of the novels, are interspersed with beautiful lyrics. We have also from Björnson a volume of *Digte og Sange* (Poems and Lyrics), and *Arnljot Gelline*, a story in verse.

Of late Björnson has come much under two influences; first, that of the Naturalistic school of writers, and next under that of Ibsen. Under these influences his writings have become, not in the strict sense books with a purpose, but what the Germans call *Tendenz-Schriften*, books which illustrate certain particular leanings or tendencies in human nature. One of his plays, *Redaktøren* (The Editor), is modelled on Ibsen's social dramas, and his two latest novels *Paa Guds Veje* (In God's Way), and *Det flager i Byen og paa Havnen* (Literally flags are flying in the town and harbour),[1] are books of tendency. *Det flager* deals with the effects of heredity, and shows how, by careful training, they may be eradicated. It deals also, in a modern sense, with the question of the relation of the sexes, the same question which has exercised the pens of so many contemporary writers of fiction in the east and north of Europe, as (for one instance) Tolstoi in the *Kreutzer Sonata*. It is the same question which reappears in many of Ibsen's plays, as in 'Love's Comedy,' the 'Doll's House,' and 'The Lady from the Sea.'

[1] *Paa Guds Veje*, the latest of Björnson's novels, has been translated in Heinemann's *International Library*. A translation of *Det flager* is promised for the same series.

We now come to the greatest name in Norse literature, the only one, perhaps, which is of very great weight and of importance for the literature of Europe generally; I mean Henrik Ibsen. In this country Ibsen is only beginning to be generally known. When a translation of 'The Doll's House' (*Et Dukkehjem*— literally 'a Doll's house') was put upon the stage in London in 1889, this was the first time that the majority of the public, and even of writers for the press, had heard Ibsen's name. Even then he was generally spoken of as an eccentric rather than a great writer. The acting of *Hedda Gabler* last year brought one of his works into pretty general notice; and since then it is probable that the volumes containing his prose dramas, translated by Mr. William Archer, have been a good deal studied.

As long ago, however, as 1873, Mr. Edmund Gosse contributed to the *Fortnightly Review* an article on 'Ibsen, the Norwegian Satirist,' which turned the attention of the more literary to Ibsen; and induced some persons to learn Norse in order to read him. The article was written before Ibsen had begun to write his prose dramas of social life.

In Germany Ibsen is much better known, and much more highly appreciated than in this country. No plays by living German authors are played there more frequently than Ibsen's are. That the Norse poet and dramatist should find a cordial reception in Germany is only right; for certainly in many respects his muse can trace its parentage to the best muse of Germany.

Ibsen is associated in our minds almost exclusively with his realistic dramas of modern social life. But to confine our attention to them is to have gained but a limited notion of this writer's achievement.

We have said that Ibsen shows, in his work, as marked traces of the influence of Goethe as does Björnson of the influence of Schiller. This is especially patent in two long dramatic poems of a didactic-satirical kind, *Brand* and *Peer Gynt*. These are, in my judgment, the finest of Ibsen's works. No fair estimate can be formed of the powers of the writer of *The Doll's House* and the rest of the social dramas, unless the critic is likewise acquainted with these two poems. They are written chiefly in octosyllabic verse, with irregular rhymes, in character varying from passages of great lyrical beauty to others of a doggerel versification: this is as much as to say, that their versification is modelled upon that of the greater part of *Faust*. In *Brand*, Ibsen satirises the formality and sloth of the average Norse parish *præst*, and draws a picture of one of an ideally high type. *Peer Gynt* is a more grotesque satire upon the average Norse peasant, and may be reckoned a counterblast to the fulsome praise which the majority of writers, from the days of the 'syttendemai' poets to those of Björnson, have lavished upon him.

Other of Ibsen's works are:—

> *Cataline* [sic], a drama in blank verse. This was Ibsen's earliest work. It was written, Ibsen tells us, in the winter of the revolutionary year 1848-9. Its object is to whitewash the man whom Sallust and Cicero describe as a conspirator, but who, according to Ibsen, was a reformer, with ideas far in advance of those of

his age. There is no great beauty in the versification of this play.

Fru Inger til Osteraad (Lady Inger of Osteraad). A prose historical drama of the early years of the sixteenth century. The characters—or at any rate the *names* of the characters—and the general setting of the play are historical. But there is little historical in the development of the plot. It is a work of great power.

Gildet paa Solhaug (The Feast of Solhaug). A mythico-historical drama in verse.

Hærmændene paa Helgeland (The Heroes of Halogaland). This is the finest of the historical or quasi-historical dramas which belong to Ibsen's earlier period. It is in prose, and the plot is chiefly founded on the Volsunga Legend, with a touch borrowed (and not well borrowed) from the Njáls Saga, and another, better adapted, from the Flyting of Loki (*Lokasenna*) in the Edda.

Kjærlighedens Komedie (Love's Comedy). This drama in verse puts forth views against love-marriages, resembling those to which Tolstoi has given expression in the *Kreutzer Sonata*.

Kongs Emnerne (The Rivals for the Throne). Another prose historical drama. The period in which the action takes place lies in the early years of Hakon Hakonsson, the grandson of Sverri.

De Unges Forbund (The League of Youth), the forerunner of Ibsen's social dramas. These social dramas turn mainly upon the play of two forces (tendencies) in social life: the force of public opinion (especially as this is wielded by the press), with the consequent dread of scandals and exposure; and the relations of the sexes; these last are considered as modified by what Ibsen considers conventional rules, and thus by the other tendency, the force of public opinion. *Hedda Gabler* and 'Ghosts' (*Gengangere*) do not come under these two categories.

Keiser og Galilæer. A long prose drama, of which the action falls in the reign of the Emperor Julian. It is, in fact, inspired by the well-known (if mythical) exclamation—*Vicisti Galilæe.* It is not a piece of great merit.

Then come the rest of the Social Dramas, namely—

Et Dukkehjem (The Doll's House). The story, with which most readers are probably familiar, of a young wife treated as a child or a puppet by her husband, who learns to despise him and decides to live her own life.

En Folkefjende (The Enemy of the People). The plot of this drama, as of the Pillars of Society, turns very largely on the narrow self-interest, and at the same time terror of public opinion (especially of newspaper opinion) which, according to Ibsen, forms a leading characteristic of Norse town life.

Fruen fra Havet (The Lady from the Sea). This play is concerned chiefly with the question of the tie of marriage as against that of love. The heroine loses her husband, and forms a connection with her earlier love. The husband (a sailor) has not died, and appears again upon the scene. She has to decide between the two men.

Her husband leaves her to her first love. But she changes her mind, and goes back to her husband.

Samfundets Stötter (The Pillars of Society). The Pillars of Society are persons who, for their own interests, but professedly for the good of the community (Samfund), are busy in promoting certain industrial schemes, shipbuilding, railways, etc. They live in dread of the local press, and of any exposure of the misdoings of their youth; though, in fact, such exposure need imply no unfitness for their present position; and they are even ready to commit crimes simply to avoid the scandal. The chief character is a less criminal Bulstrode.

Vildanden (The Wild Duck). This is the one of Ibsen's plays perhaps the least suited to the general reader. It is concerned with the combination of the two forces spoken of above, sexual relations, and the unequal severity with which the sins of the two sexes are dealt with.

Rosmersholm. This was written at the time of the political crisis of 1884 (spoken of in Chapter XIII.), and it represents the bitterness of political feeling at the time.

Gengangere (Ghosts). A tragic, and it must be said repulsive, picture of the inheritance of disease by the son of a dissipated father.

Hedda Gabler. The typical girl of the period made tragic through her utter self-absorption.

The first thing which strikes us in reviewing Ibsen's work as a whole is—in no offensive sense be it spoken—its essentially bourgeois character. We have already said how, when literature revived in the country, men were at first led to go back for inspiration to the great days of Norse history. Moreover, Europe generally was in the beginning of the romantic revival. Thus the early Norse literature is romantic too; and when it is lyric or pastoral it is full of enthusiasm for this land of heroes, for the beauty of the Norse scenery, the constant interchange of hill and valley. As Ibsen's critic and biographer, Jæger, says, when you read these poems you think that Norway is never to be seen save in the summer; or if a winter picture do intervene it is a picture only of the delights of the season, of sledge drives, of the beauty of the forests under their burden of snow. In a word, the literature of the revival of letters in Norway is mildly romantic, and above all it is optimistic. Into the midst of this circle of writers there stepped the strange figure of this new poet and satirist. He is scarcely a Norseman. At any rate he has a large immixture of Danish and Scottish blood. His name Ibsen is Danish. Born in 1828 in the small, though ancient, town of Skien (near Laurvik), and passing his youth in the smaller one of Grimstad (where, like Keats, he was apprenticed to an apothecary), Ibsen really knew little of Norway in his early years, save its narrow bourgeois life. These towns are on the southern coast of Norway, far away from its grander scenery. At the age of twenty Ibsen went to Christiania to go through the University course. At a later time he lived in Bergen. But though this writer had in his early years none of the same sort of inspiration which produced the poems of the old skalds of

Norway, he had in his character all the energy and all the perverseness which marks their works. We might give him the title which was applied to a bard of Olaf Tryggvason's court, and call him Vandræda Skald, the perverse poet.

Refusing absolutely to go by hearsay and tradition or to accept anything on authority, this apothecary's apprentice with the spirit of the viking, soon set himself to work to destroy all his country's illusions about the simplicity and beauty of Norwegian society, the hardiness and worth of the people. He began, it is true, like his predecessors, with historic and mythic dramas, such as the *Heroes in Helgaland*, of which we have spoken. But he very soon changed from that tone to one of criticism and satire; and in this tone he has continued ever since, with scarcely any break, whether he express himself in verse as in *Brand* and *Peer Gynt*, or in prose as in the social dramas.

Ibsen is generally spoken of as a realist. But we must use the word, which is employed in so many different senses, in rather a peculiar one if we apply it to him. His characters are all natural. But the object of the writer has not been merely to follow the bent of his own imagination, and to mirror nature from out of his own experiences. What has been said of Björnson's later work must be said of all Ibsen's social dramas, that though not precisely works with a purpose, they are works with a 'tendency,' which has been mapped out for the characters by the author. We hardly see character moulding destiny as upon the whole it does in real life; more, at any rate, than it fulfils any fixed destiny prescribed for it by fate, or heredity, or social tendencies. I hardly think that when they are stripped, as time must strip them, of the rather adventitious aid of their connection with burning questions of the day, Ibsen's social dramas will hold a very high place among creative works. But a certain place they will hold; and they are far above the average dramas of our age.

Two more recent writers, who have scarcely yet come to the knowledge of English readers, are Jonas Lie and Alexander Kjelland. Both are voluminous writers, who have given to the world novels and dramas. The best of the novels of the former are those which deal with the life of the sea, such as *Lodsen og hans Husfru* (The Pilot and his Wife), *Rutland*, *En Mælström*, *Træmasteren Fremtiden* (The Ship *Future*). Kjelland is a friend, and in a large degree a disciple of Björnson, a strong liberal, ready to use his pen for the propaganda of his social and religious views, but at the same time deeply impressed by the methods of the French realists. Two of his best novels are *Garman og Worse* (The Firm of Garman and Worse), and *Skipper Worse* —the second to some extent a continuation of the first. Both deal, rather after Björnson's later manner and that of Ibsen's social dramas, with the provincial town life of Norway in its prosy aspects.

CHAPTER XVI

THE WILD FLOWERS OF NORWAY

By Eva Tindall

Part I.—*Peculiarity of Distribution*

The most casual observer will have noticed, whilst travelling in Norway, the unusually large size and brilliancy of colouring of even such common wild flowers as the Harebell (*Campanula rotundifolia*) and the Pansy (*Viola tricolor*), besides the frequent occurrence of specimens hitherto totally unknown to him. To one more deeply interested in the study of botany, the peculiarity of the distribution of the Norwegian flora will suggest matter for consideration. He will have observed that the flora of one locality differs greatly from that of another, and that for no apparent reason. If he has not confined his excursion to the coast, but travelled inland, and crossed on foot mountains varying from 3000 to 5000 feet in height, he will have found one mountain-top covered with greyish yellow lichens, whilst at a similar height on another mountain, especially on slaty ground, he will have met with a profusion of alpine plants, some few inches in height, particularly distinguished by the largeness of their flowers, and the purity and brilliancy of their colour. He will have seen masses of the lovely white blossoms of the *Ranunculus glacialis* (Glacier Crowfoot), intermingled with the handsome yellow corolla of the *Ranunculus nivalis* (Snow Crowfoot), and the brilliant pink flowers of the *Saxifraga oppositifolia*, and, probably, as on Knudshö in the Dovrefjeld, one or two specimens to be found here only in the Old World.

Professor Blytt, the distinguished scientist and professor of botany at Christiania University, explains this seeming incongruity in his interesting pamphlets—which are published in Christiania, and unfortunately have no circulation in England—entitled 'On Variations of Climate in the Course of Time,' and 'Essay on the Immigration of the Norwegian Flora during alternate Rainy and Dry Periods.' The former pamphlet begins as follows:—'If we examine the meteorological charts of Norway, we observe at once what a great influence the sea and the mountains exercise over the climate in various parts. Nearly all the climatological lines run more or less with the shape of the coast, so that we encounter far greater variations when proceeding from the centre coastwards, than from south to north. In keeping with this peculiarity are the variations of the flora.'

He then proceeds to call attention to the following facts:—

The alpine flora of the slaty tracts in the mountains of Norway is also found in Arctic regions, and is therefore of an Arctic character. As these plants naturally put forth shoots at a low temperature, they cannot stand the mild and variable winters of the coast, and are therefore found in patches separated by long distances, *but always sheltered from the sea-wind*, which patches, from the fact that the sea lies principally to the south and west, and the ruling winds in Norway are from those quarters, are found on the east and north-east of the highest mountains and largest glaciers, those acting as barriers against the mild climate of the coast. In such patches the botanist might fancy himself transported to Spitzbergen or North Greenland, and, if he follows the Arctic flora to Spitzbergen, he will find that there it also shuns the sea.

But besides the mountain plants, there is a lowland flora which shuns the coast, and which, like the mountain flora, has a scattered extension. It is richest in the tracts round Christiania, gradually becomes poorer along the coast westwards, almost entirely disappears on the coast of the province of Bergen, but reappears at the bottom of the Sogne, Hardanger, and along the Throndhjem Fjords, which fjords are separated from the eastern districts by high mountains. Plants belonging to this description of lowland flora grow in the finer *débris* found in the higher parts of screes, consisting of different kinds of rocks, and facing the south, screes which so frequently occur under precipitous mountains. In such places flourish a number of highly-scented Labiatae, and several Papilionaceae, besides deciduous trees and shrubs, such as the elm, lime, maple, wild apple, dog-rose, etc.

Near the open sea the flora becomes poorer in species, and of a less interesting character. On a map coloured according to the places where certain groups are most abundant, we find the same colours occurring in smaller or larger patches, but those of the same colour separated by great spaces of a different tint.

The explanation of this problem seems to have been solved by Edward Forbes. He, as well as many other modern botanists, maintains that 'The climatic variations of the past are reflected in the fauna and flora of the present,' and was probably the first to demonstrate that the Glacial Age has left its distinct mark on the flora of the present day. During the Glacial Age, the Arctic species which are now found on mountains in temperate climates, grew in the plains; but as the climate became milder, they receded to the far north and the high mountains, their places in the plains being taken by new species.

It has been already said how, not long since, geologically speaking, the whole of Norway and Sweden was covered with an inland sea of ice, above which only solitary mountain-tops arose, at which period the majority of the present flora could not have existed in Norway. But it is proved by the fact that specimens of the present flora are found in coal strata older than the Glacial Period, that the flora itself is older. For instance, yew, fir, and spruce, hazel, willow, etc., have been found in old peat-bogs of England and Switzerland, which are covered by the bottom moraine of the inland ice. The present flora must have existed, therefore, in other countries which were free from ice during the Glacial Age, and have immigrated to Norway as the climate became milder and the ice receded.

But to account for the variety of species existing in

Norway, we must suppose that there were repeated changes of climate, several thousands of years of a severer climate, during which the northern and eastern species immigrated, followed by thousands of years during which the milder climate favoured the immigration of the flora from the south and south-west, compelling the older flora, less suited to this change of temperature, to retreat. In this manner the climate must have changed several times since the Glacial Age, and the distribution of plants must have changed in accordance.

Professor Blytt gives, as proof of alternating dry and rainy periods in the climate of the Scandinavian Peninsula, the result of his investigations in Norwegian bogs—besides referring to those of Professor Steenstrup in the Danish bogs—in the oldest of which he has, by boring, found four layers of peat, separated by three layers of stumps of trees, some standing upright, showing four wet periods during which the four layers of peat were formed, separated by three drier periods, when the growth of the peat was arrested, and the bogs covered with trees.

When a dry period was succeeded by a moist period, the continental species, that is, the species which shun the coast, became rarer, and when a moist was followed by a dry period, the plants which love moisture became scarce.

The mode of immigration is still a matter of surmise, but it is probable that the migration of the greater part of the present flora, during the gradual change of climate, has proceeded slowly and step by step across connected tracts of country.

As the struggle for existence, the struggle between rival species, has exerted so much influence in the distribution of the Norwegian flora, the following extract from Professor Blytt's 'Essay on the Immigration of the Norwegian Flora,' pp. 35 and 36, may be interesting:—

'The struggle between rival species has an essential influence in deciding the nature of the locality where any species can grow; for we frequently see that plants, when exempted from that disadvantage, are very independent of the conditions of such locality. Thus I have found *Parnassia palustris* (Common Grass of Parnassus), which otherwise is a marsh plant, on the dry shifting sand of Jaederen, thriving excellently in company with *Carex arenaria* (Sand Sedge). *Iris pseudacorus* (Yellow Flag) is usually a water plant—I have found it several times on dry sand-shores, once even in flower. These species could have scarcely been able to grow on the dry sand, if the covering of the vegetation on the sand had not been so thinly spread; that is to say, *had there been other species to dispute the place with them.* Several species grow naturally only where they are moistened with snow water; many species are naturally bound to a salt soil, many to marshy places; when cultivated, they are found to thrive remarkably well under conditions which we should think would be anything but favourable to them. Thus, in our botanical garden, *Catabrosa algida* is cultivated, and thrives excellently without snow water; it is known that shore plants can thrive, when cultivated, without requiring salt; species which naturally only grow in very marshy places, are cultivated in the botanical garden in dry ground, and are not more watered than the others, but thrive nevertheless remarkably well; for instance, *Veronica Beccabunga* (Brooklime), *Anagallis scutellata* (Shielded Pimpernel), *Carex chordorhiza* (a sedge), *Epipactis palustris* (Marsh Helleborine), *Naumburgia thyrsiflora* (Tufted Loosestrife), etc. The explanation of this lies in the fact that the gardener who removes the weeds takes on himself the functions of the snow water, salt and swampiness, the keeping off the competitors for a place in the soil. When, therefore, the climate changes, for instance from dry to wet, all the species which like moisture will be able to extend themselves at the expense of the others; because many places which before were dry, will, in the humid climate, become moist. Even if the climate does not absolutely prevent any species from growing on a given substratum, it may yet happen that the climate favours certain rivals to such an extent as to enable the latter to appropriate the soil.'

Part II.

Localities in which the various groups are found.

From the foregoing it will be seen that there is no hard and fast rule as to the distribution of plants in Norway with regard to latitude, or elevation above the sea-level, but that the greatest variety of the alpine plants is found in rubbles and shale rocks, which are best sheltered from the sea-winds, and in places more or less inaccessible to the other species of flora.

We will turn our attention first to this mountain

flora, to which the name of the Dryas formation is applied, from *Dryas octopetala* (Mountain Avens) (2),[1] the most frequent and most conspicuous of the species which distinguish it. The other three species which characterise this flora are *Salix reticulata* (Willow), *Thalictrum alpinum* (Alpine Meadow-Rue), and *Carex rupestris* (Rock Sedge). Dryas often forms on the ground a shining white flower-carpet, variegated with, may be, the pretty blue of the *Veronica saxatilis* (Blue Rock Speedwell), the yellow of the *Potentilla nivea* (Snow Potentilla), and the violet of *Oxytropis lapponica* (Lapland Oxytropis) (11). *Dryas octopetala* (Mountain Avens) (2) grows on the mountains of Norway, especially above the birch limit, from the most southern part of the province of Christiansand as far as to the North Cape and Varanger. In the southern parts of the country it is *occasionally* found in the lower regions, growing, for instance, abundantly on the limestone and argillaceous slate rocks at Sangesund, 59° north latitude, nearly on a level with the sea; also at Varaldsen in the Hardanger, and on the shore cliffs at Frosten in the Throndhjem Fjord, living side by side in these low-lying places with a more southern flora. But it is not until we come to the islands in the sea at Helgeland (about 66° north latitude) that the Dryas group, which in Southern Norway is generally limited to the mountains, descends to the sea.

Beginning in the south, we find on the black shining shale around Grananuten and Haarteigen, in the

---

[1] The figures refer to corresponding ones in Part III., where the flowers, which are numbered, are fully described, some of them for the first time in English.

Hardanger tract,' *Latabrosa algida* and *Koenigia Islandica* (Persicaria Tribe) (1), which have here their southern limit in Europe, and *Alsine stricta* (a Chickweed) and *Arenaria ciliata* (Fringed Sandwort), which are not found farther south in Scandinavia.

Further north in the Urland Mountains in Sogn, especially at Ravonanaasi, are similar shales, with a rich alpine flora. *Carex rufina* (Pink Sedge) has here its southern limit in Europe, *Potentilla nivea* (Snow Potentilla) its southern limit in Norway, *Arenaria ciliata* (Fringed Sandwort) and many other rarer alpine plants, grow here. On Vasendlifjeld, at Helinstrand, in Valders, on the shales, are found a similar vegetation. *Ranunculus nivalis* (Snow Crowfoot), *Draba nivalis* (Snow Whitlowgrass), and *Papaver nudicaule* (Iceland Poppy) (10) have here their southern limits.

In Lom and Vaage are found for the first time *Campanula uniflora*, *Draba alpina* (Alpine Whitlowgrass), *Alsine nirta*, *Sagina nivalis* (Snow Pearlwort), *Salix polaris* (Polar Willow), *Rhododendron lapponicum* (Lapland Rhododendron), *Phaca frigida* (Frigid Mountain Lentil) (9), *Astragalus Oroboedes* (a Vetch), *Saxifraga hieracifolia* (a Saxifrage), several of which have here their southern limits in Europe. But by far the richest district of all Norway in rare alpine flowers is the Dovrefjeld, where the shales of Gula and Throndhjem occur; besides, most of the species already mentioned there grow here: *Artemisia Norvegica* (Norwegian Wormwood) (8), *which is not found elsewhere in the Old World*, *Luzula arctica*, *Saxifraga stellaris* (Starry Saxifrage), variety *comosa* (6), *Carex misandra*, *Poa stricta*, *Primula stricta*, which have their southern limits here, and many others. Some few of the rare alpine plants are also found, but only in small numbers, in Beieren, Salangen, Ofsten, Sorreisen, at Sylfjeldene, Bygdin, and Horungerne.

'If we arrange the localities named according to the number of the rare alpine plants found in each of them, the order of the series will be as follows. (By rare is meant such species as have special localities indicated for them in the flora) :—

Lapmark of Lulea,	50	Tromsö,	29
Dovre and Foldalen,	46	Maalselven,	28
Lapmark of Tornea,	45	Ranen,	28
Vaage and Lom,	44	Tonset,	16
Salten,	43	Urland,	14
Lapmark of Pitea,	40	Vasendli,	14
Alten,	37	Haarteigen,	8

Here we see clearly how the number of *rare* species decreases towards the south and west; the richest regions lie farthest from the ocean, or are the best protected from it.'

Our limited space will not allow us to mention all the species of Arctic flora found far north, but we will content ourselves with saying that no place is known which can be compared with the Dovre for richness in rare plants, nor do we again find a rich mountain flora before arriving nearly at the Arctic Circle. We would strongly recommend any interested in the mountain flora of Norway to make a stay at Kongsvold, which lies at the foot of Knudshö, a mountain justly celebrated for its rich Arctic flora. During the months of June and July this comfortable 'station' in the Dovre is visited by Norwegian, Swedish, and German botanists, of whose kindness in imparting valuable information, and giving invaluable help, experienced by myself in the summer of 1890, I cannot speak too highly. Within the last few years many rare new species have been discovered there, which are fully described in Professor Blytt's condensed *Norsk Flora*, to be published within the next few years.

We will now turn our attention to the lowland flora, which has a nearly uniform distribution throughout the whole country, and is for the most part poor in varieties of species. This is especially the case with the flora of the pine and birch forests, which consists principally of *Vaccinium* (Bilberry), *Calluna* (Ling), and *Empetrum* (Crow Berry); and in a less degree with the flora of the luxuriant grass-covered moist slopes, often found in the belts of willow, birch, and pine flora, consisting of *Cirsium heterophyllum* (a Thistle), *Mulgedium alpinum* (Alpine Sow-thistle), *Ranunculus aconitifolius* (Aconite-leaved Crowfoot) (3), etc. The unwooded west coast is mostly carpeted with monotonous heather.

But there are localities which are exceptions to this general uniformity. Under steep walls of rock are often seen dry rubbles of fallen stones, and when these rubbles are exposed to the sun, we find growing in them a remarkably rich and diversified flora. A great many of the more delicate deciduous trees and shrubs (for instance, lime, elm, hazel, oak, sycamore, apple, etc.) form in such places small groves and brushwood, sheltering amongst others the following:—*Convallaria polygonatum* (Solomon's Seal), *Daphne Mezereum* (Spurge Laurel), *Dentaria bulbifera* (Bulbiferous Coral-root),

Echinospermum deflexum (Viper's Bugloss), and *E. Lappula*, *Orobus vernus* (Spring Vetch), and *Vicia pisiformis* (a Vetch). The flora of such rubbles is very similar in all parts of the country, and is not affected by the chemical composition of the rock.

The flora of the dry limestone and shale rocks has the greatest resemblance to that of the hard rock rubbles, especially in the part of the country west of the mountains. In the less elevated Silurian regions east of the mountains the flora has a still more diversified character, and in the limestone and argillaceous slate in the lowest regions—as in the Skiens Fjord and the Christiania Fjord—are the richest flora in Norway. Besides most of the species found in the rubbles, sheltered by deciduous trees, are to be found *Phleum phalanoides* (a Grass), *Libanotis montana* (Mountain Meadow Saxifrage), *Fragaria collina* (Hill Strawberry), etc.; and the rare species, *Cirsium acaule* (a Thistle), *Ononus campestris* (Rest Harrow), *Trifolium montanum* (Mountain Trefoil), *Cephalanthera rubra*, and several others.

The sand and detritus on the shores have also a peculiar flora. In the shore region of northern Norway are found *Carex arctica*, *Plantago borealis* (Northern Plantain), *Gentiana serrata* (a Gentian), *Primula Sibirica* (Siberian Primrose), *Stellaria numifusa* (a Stitchwort), which are wanting on the mountains. Mountain plants have also been found on the shores in other districts, which are not elsewhere found in the lowlands. Thus *Peristylis viridis* and *Saussurea alpina* grow on the sandy beaches of Jaederen, *Sedum villosum* (Hairy Stonecrop) on the shores of Sogn, *Gentiana tenella* (Tender Gentian) in Salten. On the shores are also found some of the species of the rubble-slope and of the Silurian formation.

Several uncommon species occur in sandy and gravelly river-banks, such as *Vahlbergella affinis* on the banks of the Alten river; *Arabis petraea* (Alpine Rock-cress) on the river-banks in Sogn; and in other places, *Hippophaë rhamnoides* (Sea Buckthorn), *Myricaria Germanica* (German Myrtle), *Salix daphnoides* (Laurel Willow), etc.

We see, therefore, that the physical condition of the substratum, as well as the climate, exercises great influence on the distribution of plants in Norway. Generally speaking, the flora of the western parts resembles that of the Scottish Highlands, whilst that of the mountains, besides consisting of the greater number of alpine flowers to be found in Switzerland, is rich in Arctic species.

Part III.

Description of Flowers.

Amongst the numerous interesting and beautiful flowers found in Norway, it is most difficult to select a limited number for description. A preference has been given to those peculiar to Norway, and to alpine flowers found also in the mountainous parts of Switzerland, but the number described is necessarily limited. They are arranged according to the colour of their corollas. The reason why figures are prefixed is explained in Part II.

FLOWERS GREEN.

1. *Kœnigia Islandica*, a mountain plant belonging to the Polygonaceæ. It is smooth and succulent, and of stunted growth. The stem is from ½ to 3 inches high, either undivided or with straggling stalks. The leaves lowest on the stem grow opposite each other, those higher up are alternate, the highest of all almost entirely surround the flowers; all of them have short stalks, are inversely egg-shaped, entire and thick. The flowers are very small and green, and bloom from July to September.

FLOWERS WHITE.

2. *Dryas octopetala*, in Norwegian, Reinblom, *i.e.* Pure Flower. A mountain plant also found in Switzerland and belonging to the Rosaceæ. It is easily distinguished by its oval, roundly-toothed, *deeply-furrowed* leaves, which spring from the root, and are of a shiny dark green on the upper side and downy beneath. The pretty shiny white flowers are usually the size of a shilling, and have eight petals. The stamens and pistils are yellow. It flowers in July and August.

3. *Ranunculus aconitifolius*, in Norwegian, Hvid Soleie, *i.e.* White Ranunculus. The upright stem is from 1 to 4 feet high; it is round, smooth, and branched at the top. The leaves are shiny and veined, either entirely smooth or somewhat hairy at the margins. Those from the root have long stalks, are palmate and divided into from 5 to 7 segments; those from the stem have short stalks, and are less deeply divided; those from the flowers are narrow and entire. There are numerous

flowers which grow singly at the end of smooth or slightly hairy stems, which are from 2 to 4 inches long. The oval sepals fall off immediately after the buds have opened. The petals are white, inversely egg-shaped, and are about $\frac{3}{8}$ of an inch long, which is double the length of the sepals.

4. *Ranunculus glacialis*, Norwegian, Is Soleie, *i.e.* Ice Ranunculus. A mountain plant found at a great height, often close to everlasting snow, also met with in Switzerland. The flowers are either solitary or in pairs, and grow on a stem from 4 to 6 inches high. The root leaves are stalked, and divided into three lobes, the stem leaves are sessile (*i.e.* without stalks). The large white flowers turn a pale reddish violet when about to fade.

RANUNCULUS GLACIALIS.

5. *Saxifraga cotyledon*, the most beautiful of all the saxifrages, for which the Norwegian country people have many names, amongst others, Mountain Rose (Fjeldrose), Mountain Bride (Bergfrue). It grows in clefts of the rocks, and varies from 6 to 12 inches in height, or

even more. It is branched throughout, and bears on its stiff stems numerous pretty white flowers, which have five petals, and an equal number of sepals. At the root it has a rosette of thick, fleshy, serrated leaves, which are ever-green. It is also found in Switzerland.

6. *Saxifraga stellaris*, Norwegian, Stjernesildre, growing from 3 to 5 inches high. Its leaves are oblong, wedge-shaped, toothed towards the ends, and grow round the base of the stalk. The flower consists of five rather large white petals, with two small yellow spots near the base of each. The anthers are orange-coloured. It is also found in Scotland, Ireland, and but rarely in the North of England. The variety *comosa* has most frequently one flower, and a panicle formed by the crowding together of small leaves resembling bracts.

7. *Rubus chamæmorus*, Norwegian, Moltebær. Its leaves somewhat resemble those of the blackberry, to which genus of the rose tribe it belongs, and are 3 to 7 lobed. The large solitary white flowers, which have five petals, grow at the end of a stem about 8 inches high, and bear the stamens and pistils on separate plants. The fruit is first red, but turns yellow when ripe. Every traveller in Norway must have tasted this fruit stewed and served with sugar and cream.

FLOWERS YELLOW.

8. *Artemisia norvegica*, belonging to the Compositæ, has an upright, usually undivided stem from 2 inches to 1 foot high, which is furrowed and woolly, more especially towards the top. The divisions of the finely

divided leaves are narrow, of even breadth, and slightly pointed; they are hairy, especially underneath, and green on both sides. The lower leaves are stalked, the upper ones embrace the stem. The flower-heads are very large, and few in number, there being seldom more than six on one plant. They are drooping, and grow singly on woolly stems which spring from the axils of the upper leaves, and are 1 to 4 inches long. The involucre is hemispherical; its scales are oval or oblong, green at the back, hairy, especially at the base, and have a broad dark-brown border. The receptacle is smooth. The corolla is yellow and hairy; the root thick and strong. It flowers in August and September.

9. *Phaca frigida*, a mountain plant, belonging to the Leguminosæ or Pea and Bean Tribe. The smooth stem is upright, from 6 to 12 inches high, the lower part provided with egg-shaped broad scales. The leaves grow in pairs of 4 to 5, with large egg-shaped stipules, and oblong blunt leaflets, which are rather hairy, and of a bluish green underneath. The stalk on which the numerous flowers grow is about the length of the leaf-stalk. The yellow drooping flowers grow on much shorter dark-haired stalks. The standard (upper petal) is a little longer than the keels (lower petals) and wings (side petals). The drooping pod is covered with dark hairs; it is oblong and narrower at each end. It flowers in July.

10. *Papaver nudicaule*. All the leaves are collected together at the root, are covered with stiff hairs, are stalked, and are unevenly divided into egg-shaped divisions which point forward. There are one or more upright stems, which are covered with stiff hairs, are

from 2 to 8 inches long, and bear one flower each. The sepals are oval, and thickly covered with stiff dark-brown hair. The petals are yellow, inversely egg-shaped, $\frac{1}{2}$ to $\frac{3}{4}$ inches long, nearly twice as long as the sepals. The seed-vessels are oval, about $\frac{1}{2}$ inch long, and thickly covered with brown stiff hairs. The seeds are crescent-shaped, blunt at both ends, and striped lengthwise. It flowers in July.

FLOWERS BLUE.

11. *Oxytropis lapponica*, a mountain plant, belonging to the Leguminosæ. The leaves are unequally pinnate, growing in from 8 to 12 pairs, leaflets narrow and pointed, with white hairs on both sides. The root is strong and tough, and sends out numerous spreading upright hairy stems from 1 to 2 inches long. The stalk on which the raceme of flowers grows is very long. The flowers are nearly sessile (without stalks), and of a dark-blue colour. It flowers in July and August.

Of the eight species of gentians found in Norway three are selected for description here, one of which will be found amongst the flowers with red corollas.

12. *Gentiana nivalis* has a square, upright stem from 1 to 6 inches high, usually branched from the base. The stalks are also upright, and of about the same length as the stem. The root-leaves grow in a rosette, and are oval and blunt, the stem-leaves opposite each other, and are entire and egg-shaped. The flowers grow singly at the end of the stem and stalks. The calyx is divided to about the middle, into five narrow pointed sepals. The corolla is from $\frac{1}{2}$ to $\frac{3}{4}$ inches long, with five entire petals which stand out horizontally. The corolla,

especially in the inside, is a pretty bright blue. It flowers from June to August.

13. *Gentiana tenella* much resembles the last in form of growth, but the calyx is divided almost to its base into 4 to 5 sepals, which are shorter than the throat of the corolla. The corolla is *pale* blue and $\frac{1}{2}$ inch long, and consists of 4 to 5 petals. The white variety is rare. It flowers in July and August.

14. *Aconitum septentrionale*, belonging to the Ranunculaceæ. The upright hollow stem is from 4 to 6 feet high, and covered with soft hairs. The leaves are palmate with 5 to 7 divisions, and covered with soft hairs. The divisions are narrower and entire at the base, but divided at the upper end. The lower leaves are very large and stalked, the upper ones are less deeply divided and without stalks, the highest of all are narrow. The numerous 5-cleft flowers are covered with soft hairs, and grow in a terminal raceme on upright stalks (which are also covered with soft hairs) of about the length of the flowers. The follicle (seed-vessel) is smooth. The flowers are dark blue in colour, rarely white, and somewhat resemble those of the larkspur. It flowers in July and August.

FLOWERS RED.

15. *Gentiana purpurea*. The whole plant is smooth. The root is strong and thick, and of a very bitter taste. The round upright stem is undivided, leafy, and from 1 to $1\frac{1}{2}$ feet high. The pointed, entire leaves are from 5 to 6 inches long and $1\frac{1}{2}$ inches broad, and have five curved

veins. Those from the root are stalked; those from the stem are entirely or nearly without stalks, and grow opposite each other; those from the flowers are egg-shaped. The flowers grow without stalks from the upper leaf-axils, and in a terminal 3 to 6 flowered cyme, surrounded by egg-shaped leaves. The corolla is large ($1\frac{1}{2}$ inches long), salver-shaped (same shape as the primrose), rather yellow in the inside, dark red on the outside, with 5 to 6 blunt entire petals. It flowers in August, and is only found on the mountains in the south-west of Norway.

FLOWERS PINK.

16. *Linnæa borealis*, belonging to the Caprifoliaceæ or Woodbine Tribe. A pretty little plant with thin, trailing, reddish, hairy, and leafy stems, which are 1 to 3 feet long, and upright stalks 2 to 4 inches long, which are leafy in the lower part, and usually bear two drooping flowers. The evergreen leaves have short stalks, are nearly round or oval, are roundly toothed, and hairy on the upper side and at the edges. The

GENTIANA PURPUREA

flowers grow on short hairy stalks, which are of about the same length as the flower, and at the base of which are two tiny narrow leaves. Sometimes each stalk bears three to four flowers. At the base of each flower are

LINNÆA BOREALIS.

four hairy leaves, which apparently form an outer calyx, and enclose the seed. The bell-shaped corolla is white, but the pink stripes on the inside give it a decidedly pale pink appearance. It smells like almonds, and flowers from June to August. It is found in fir woods in all parts of Norway.

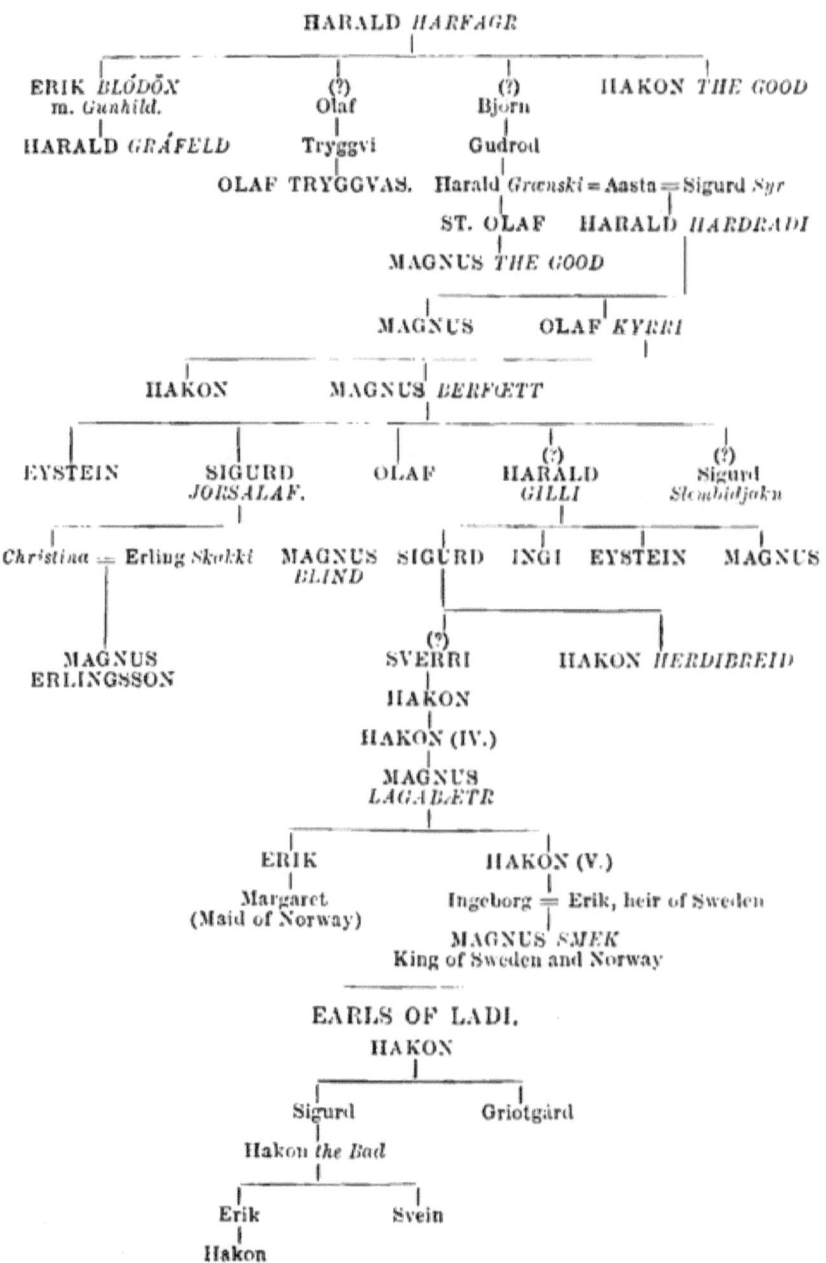

INDEX.

GEOGRAPHICAL INDEX.

Aalesund, 178.
Agder, 147, 149.
Akers Stream, 252.
Aldeigjuborg (Ladoga), 241.
America, 87.

Bergen, 59, 152, 161, 187, 263, 278, 284, 285, 309.
Bergenhus, 21, 349.
Bkeking, 147.
Bohuslän, 37, 61, 316.
Borgar Thing, 298.
Borgund, 267.
Brattalid, 85.
Bremanger Island, 187.
Brestad (*Sweden*), 38.
Brunkebjerge, 310.

Caithness, 70, 84, 217.
Calmar, 303.
Canal, Norwegian, 17.
Cape Stad, 18.
Cattegat, 144.
Christiania, 37, 252, 266, 335, 359.
Christianiafjord, 18, 20, 275.
Clontarf, 138.
Copenhagen, 318.

Dalecarlia, 226.
Dovrefjeld, 11, 19, 29, 208.

East Agder, 21.
Eidsvold, 144, 298.

Faroes, 83, 84, 142, 186, 291.
Finmark, 20, 339.
Fjärlefjord, 26.
Fjord districts, the, 230.
Folgefond, 10, 25, 26.
Frædarberg, 159.
Frædö, 159.
Frederikshald, 316.
Frederikstad, 316.

Gardariki, 169 *sqq.*, 304. See *also* Greater Suithiod, Russian Sweden.
Glaciers, Norwegian, 25.
Glommen River, 144.
Gokstad, 62.
Göta River, 212, 242, 274, 316.
Grænland, 21.
Greater Scandinavia, 88.
Greater Suithiod, 86, 169 *sqq.*, 241.

Greater Sweden, 246.
Gredungsbræ, 11.
Greenland, 85, 87.
Grönaas, 3.
Gudbrandsdal, 20, 21, 147, 208.

HADALAND, 208.
Hafirsfjord, 149, 240.
Halland, 147.
Halogaland, 20, 144, 186, 217, 230.
Hansa towns, 306.
Hardanger, 149.
Hardangerfjord, 12, 13, 26, 53.
Hardanger Vidde, 19.
Hauge, 152.
Hebrides, 69, 84, 292.
Hedemark, 21, 208.
Helge-Aar, 222.
Hellesylt, 3, 178.
Hitterdal, 267.
Hitterdalselv, 267.
Hladir. *See* Ladi.
Holmgaard (Novgorod), 86, 171, 240, 246.
Holmensgraa, 273.
Hördaland, 21, 147, 230.
Horedö, 275.
Horland. *See* Hördaland.
Hornélen, 187.

ICELAND, 83 *sqq.*, 122 *sqq.*, 134, 186, 211, 218, 290.

JÆDERENS REF, 149.
Jemtland, 226, 282.
Jomsborg, 87, 195, 243.
Jörundfjord, 178.
Justedalsbræ, 10, 11, 25, 26, 58.
Jötunfjeld, 11, 19.
Jotunheim, 29.

KARMÖ, 158.
Karmö Island, 152.
Kaupstad, 192, 262.
Keel, the, 19, 29, 144, 278.
Kiel, 318.
Kjendalsbræ, 11.
Kjölen, 19.
Kongsberg, 53, 267.
Konsghalle, 274.
Koppang, 29.

LADEHAMMER, 192.
Ladi, 147, 153, 165, 185, 194, 205, 208, 239, 254, 270.
Ladoga, 81. *See also* Aldeigjuborg.
Lærdal, 176, 267.
Largs, 294.
Laurvik, 210.
Leire, Kingdom of, 147.
Lindisnæs, 340.
Lofoten Islands, 8, 186, 349.
Lübeck, 307 *sq.*
Lund, 317.
Lyrskog Heath, 244.
Lysterfjord, 26.

MÆRA, 184-5.
Mjösen, Lake, 144, 208, 283.
Molde, 187.
Moldefjord, 159.
Möre, 148, 157, 205.

NESSJAR, 210.
Nidar, 192.
Nidarös (Throndhjem), 187, 192-3, 262, 263, 278, 282-3.
Nigardsbræ, 11.
Nordfjord, 187.
Nordlandsamt, 20.
Norwegian Canal, 17.

Novgorod, 81. *See also* Holmgaard.

ODDE, 53.
Odensjö, 97.
Odinshüg, 97.
Opslo or Oslo, 252, 262, 266, 275, 278, 288.
Ore, 145.
Orkneys, 69, 70, 84, 103, 138, 142, 146, 165, 186, 211, 217, 268, 291, 294.
Osterdal, 21.

RENNEBO (in Orkedal), 45.
Ringariki, 21.
Rogaland, 149, 183, 230.
Römariki, 21, 147, 208.
Romsdal, 20, 21, 46, 58, 158, 205.
Röraas, 29.
Rügen, 195.
Russia, 225, 228.
Russian Sweden, 169 *sqq.*
Rydiokul, 277.

SALTENFJORD, 186.
Sarpsborg, 144, 266, 316.
Sätersdal, 144.
Seim, 152.
Shetlands, 69, 70, 83, 103, 146, 165, 186.
Sjövik, Lake, 222.
Skagerrak, 18, 144.
Skane, 147.
Skjærgaard, 8, 12.
Sköne, 35.
Sleswick, 244.
Smaland, 147.
Sogn, 21, 238.
Sogndalsfjord, 26.

Sognefjord, 13, 18, 26, 176, 267, 285.
Sondre-Möre, 21.
South Möre, 178.
Stad, Cape, 18.
Stamford Bridge, 250.
Stangebro, 313.
Stavanger, 149, 152, 161, 266, 268, 349.
Stavangeramt, 183.
Stavangerfjord, 8.
Stiklestad, 229 *sqq.*, 245.
Stockholm, 311.
Stordö, 161.
Sudreyar, the, 69, 292.
Suithiod, 147.
Suithiod, Greater, 86, 169 *sqq.*, 241.
Sulen Islands, 249.
Svold, 196, 209, 260.

TANUM (*Sweden*), 38.
Thelemarken, 53, 144, 282.
Thoten, 208.
Tönsberg, 337. *See also* Tuna.
Troldfjord, 59.
Troldkirketind, 58.
Troldstol, 58.
Troldvand, 58.
Trollabrug, 59.
Trollhättan (*Sweden*), 38.
Trolltinder, 58.
Tromsöamt, 20.
Trondhjem, 20, 59, 144, 145 *sqq.*, 158, 165, 180, 230, 254, 262, 263, 266, 268, 278, 282, 288.
Throndhjemfjord, 185, 340.
Throndhjemsamt, 20.
Tun, 62.
Tuna, *or* Tünsberg, 145, 152.

UPLANDS, THE, 21, 144, 217.
Upsala, 97.

VALDERS, 208.
Vendland, 193.
Verdal, 226, 228.
Vesteraalen Islands, 349.
Viken, 145, 148, 165, 177, 211, 223.

Village community, 50.
Vingelmark, 21.
Vingulmark, 147.
Vinland, 86.

WESTFOLD, 21, 144, 147, 148.
Wisby, 306.

HISTORICAL INDEX.

AASTA, 206, 226, 245.
Adrian IV., Pope, 276.
Agantyr, 111.
Agriculture, 341, 344 *sqq*.
Afarfasti, 233.
Albert of Mecklenburg, 302.
Alexander II., K. of Scotland, 293.
Alexander III., ,, ,, 294.
Alfifa, 240.
Alfred *the Great*, 72, 80, 89.
Allogia, 169.
Alphabet, runic, 34.
Amter, 325.
Ankerstrom, 317.
Arnliot Gellini, 233.
Asgaard, 105.
Astrid, 167, 170, 184, 187.
Atila, 117.
Aud *the Wise*, 84, 129, 139.

BAGLERNE, THE, 288-9.
Balder, 101, 116.
Bergthora, 133.
Bernadotte, 318.
Birkibeinar, the, 279 *sqq*.
Björn the Marshall, 213, 235.

Björn (son of Harald), 152.
Black Death, the, 309.
Blood-bath of Stockholm, 311.
Borgar Thing, The, 144, 298, 316.
Borgemester, 326.
Bragi, 105.
Breakspeare, Nicolas. *See* Adrian IV., Pope.
Bui, Leader of Joms Vikings, 178.
Burislaf, 193.

CALMAR, Union of, 303, 309.
Carl Cnutson, 310.
Carlus (ship), 260.
Charles IX., 313.
Charles XI., K. of Sweden, 317.
Charles XII., ,, ,, 99, 314, 316-17.
Charlemagne, 67.
Christian II., K. of Denmark, 311.
Christian IV., ,, ,, 314.
Christian V., ,, ,, 317.
Christina, 275.
Church, the, 301, 312.
Cnut Svendsson, K. of Denmark and England, 172, 206 *sqq*., 229 *sqq*., 238.

Common Land, 340.
Communes (Bygdealmenninger), 350.
Constitution of Norway, 320.
Conveyance, 353.
Costume, 354.
Crane (ship), 195 *sq.*, 200.

DAG HRINGSSON, 232, 234, 236.
Der Straler Sund, 196.
Diet, 356.
Digri, 211. *See* Olaf, St.

EDMUND, ST., of England, 238.
Education, 330 *sqq.*
Edward the Confessor, 254.
Edwine, E. of Northumbria, 250.
Egil, 159.
Egil Skalagrimsson, 187.
Eidvold Thing, 298.
Einar, E. of the Orkneys, 348.
Einar Tambarskelfir, 201, 209, 219 *sq.*, 240, 270.
Eormanrik, 117.
Erik *Blódöx*, 119, 152 *sqq.*
Erik, Duke of Sondermanland, 302.
Erik, K. of Hardanger, 149.
Erik, Earl of Ladi, 260.
Erik Hakonsson, 177 *sqq.*, 194 *sqq.*, 206 *sq.*
Erik, K. of Sweden, 173.
Erik of Pomerania, 303.
Erik *the Priest-hater*, 301.
Erik *the Red*, 85.
Erik's Sons. *See* Gunhild's Sons.
Erling *Skakki*, 275.
Erling Skjalgsson, 184, 209, 219 *sq.*, 224, 270.
Erling, son of Thorfinn, 250.
Etzel, 117.

Eystein, Archbp. of Trondhjem, 276, 288.
Eystein Haraldsson, K. of Norway, 273-4.
Eystein *Meyla*, 279, 282.
Eyvind, 162.

FENRIR, 114.
Finn Arnason, 225 *sq.*, 229 *sqq.*, 270.
Fishing, 341 *sqq.*
Forestry. *See* Wood-cutting.
Formandskab, 326.
Frederick IV. of Denmark, 317.
Frederick VI., K. of Denmark, 318.
Frey, 98 *sq.*, 115, 148.
Freyja, 106.
Frigg, 106.
Frosta Thing, The, 144.

GAMLE ERIKSSON, 160.
Garm, 115.
Gauka Thorir, 233.
Gissur Gulbraa, 234.
Gissur *the Black*, 213.
Gissur *the White*, 187.
Glacial Age, 4 *sq.*
Glum, 132.
Godfred (*Dane*), 67.
Godwin, 254.
Gola Thing, The, 144.
Gorm *the Old*, 157.
Gregorius Dagsson, 274-5.
Grettir, 129.
Grim, 134 *sqq.*
Griotgaard, 165.
Groa, 109.
Gudbrand, Hersir, 147.
Gudleif, 186.
Gunhild, 120, 153 *sqq.*

Gunhild's Sons, 157 *sqq.*
Gunnar, 133.
Gunnar of Litharendi, 122.
Gustavus Adolphus, 99, 313.
Gustavus Vasa, 311.
Guthorm (*Dane*), 181.
Guthrum (*Dane*), 72.
Gyda, Sister of Earl Ulf, 254.
Gyda, Sister of Olaf Quaran, 175.
Gyda, Wife of Harald, 148.

H.EREDER, 325.
Hakon IV., 141, 289 *sqq.*, 359.
Hakon V., 302.
Hakon, E. of Ladi. 166 *sqq.*, 176 *sqq.*
Hakon Eriksson, 208, 224, 239.
Hakon *the Good*, 22, 120, 156 *sqq.*
Hakon *Herdibreid*, 274-5, 280.
Hakon Sverrason, 289.
Halfdan *the Black*, 147 *sq.*, 154.
Halfred Vandrædaskald, 121, 189.
Hallgerda, 132 *sqq.*
Hansa, The, 263, 305.
Harald *Bluetooth* (*Blaetand*), K. of Denmark, 157, 167, 176, 182 *sq.*
Harald *Fairhair*, 85, 119, 129, 147, 280.
Harald Gilli, 271, 276, 280.
Harald Godwinsson, K. of England, 249 *sqq.*, 250, 254.
Harald (Gold), 167 *sq.*
Harald *Grænske*, 206.
Harald *Grafeld*. *See* Harald *Greyskin*.
Harald *Greyskin*, 165 *sq.*
Harald *Hardradi*, 226, 245 *sqq.*, 262, 266, 315.
Harald *Harfagr*. *See* Harald *Fairhair*.
Harald Sigurdsson. *See* Harald *Hardradi*.

Hardacnut, K. of Denmark and England, 239, 242.
Harek of Thiottö, 230 *sqq.*
Hasting, 247.
Hättar, 317.
Hauskuld, 132.
Heimdal, 106, 115.
Hel, 101.
Helgi, 134 *sqq.*
Hermödhr, 106.
Hersar, 143.
Hervör, 111.
Hjalti Skaggjason, 187, 213 *sqq.*
Holdernessætter, 300.
House-building, 41 *sqq.*
Hrolf. *See* Rolf.
Hrut, 132.
Husmænd, 337.

IDUN, 106.
Ingegerd, Swedish Princess, 214, 246.
Ingiborg, 302.
Ingi Haraldsson, 273.
Internal Administration of Norway, 325 *sqq.*
Iron Beard (ship), 200.
Ivan the Terrible, 315.

JACOB. *See* Onund.
Jarisleif (Yaroslav), 170, 173, 246, 315.
Joms Vikings, The, 87, 142, 174, 177 *sqq.*, 206.
Jormungandr, 115.
Jotnar, 95.
Jotunheim, 108.
Jötuns. *See* Jötnar.

KALF ARNASON, 224 *sq.*, 228, 238, 240.

Kalf, relative of Kalf Arnason, 235.
Kark, 180.
Ketil *Flatnose*, 84.
Kiotvi *the Rich*, 149.
Kjartan Olafsson, 187 *sqq*.
Klærkon, 170, 171.
Kolbjörn, 203-4.

LAGABÆTIR. *See* Magnus the Law Reformer.
Lagamadhr, The, 214, 298.
Lag-man. *See Lagamadhr*.
Land tenure, 300, 337.
Law, 298.
Lendermen, The, 287, 300.
Lensmand, 327.
Lewis, *The Debonair*, 75.
Loki, 102, 106, 114.
Long Serpent (ship), 192, 193 *sqq*., 259.
Lund, 317.

MAGNUS *Bareleg*, 269, 271, 273.
Magnus Erlingsson, 275, 277.
Magnus Haraldsson, 273.
Magnus, St., 268.
Magnus *Smek*, 302 *sq*.
Magnus *the Good*, 240 *sqq*., 248.
Magnus, *the Law Reformer*, 295, 297.
Malcolm *Canmore*, 249.
Margaret, Maid of Norway, 302.
Margaret, the Great Queen, 302.
Menglöd, 109 *sq*.
Midsummer Fires, 55.
Morality, 329.
Morcar, 250.

NANNA, 106.
Napoleon, 318.

Nattmössor, 317.
Nelson, Lord, 318.
Nicholas Arnason, Bishop, 288.
Niordhr, 106.
Njal, 129, 133, 186.

Odalsret, 337.
Odin, 97 *sqq*., 102 *sqq*., 112 *sqq*., 153.
Œger, 106.
Olaf (Haraldsson), 210 *sq*.
Olaf, K. of Sweden, 194.
Olaf *Kyrri*, 264.
Olaf Quaran, 175, 181.
Olaf, relative of Kalf Arnason, 235.
Olaf, St., 22, 120, 172, 184, 206 *sqq*., 211, 240, 243, 260, 262, 266, 280.
Olaf *Skattkonung*, K. of Sweden, 209, 212 *sqq*., 173.
Olaf, son of Magnus, 302.
Olaf *the White*, 84, 139.
Olaf Tryggvason, 22, 71, 120, 141, 167, 169 *sqq*., 180, 209, 217, 260, 262, 280, 291.
Onund, K. of Sweden, 216, 221 *sqq*.
Ore Thing, The, 145.
Ottar *the Black*, 213.

PALNATOKI, 87.
Parliament. *See Storthing*.
Paul, E. of Orkney, 250, peat-cutting, 348.
Peter the Great, 315.

Raadmand, 326.
Ragnarök, the Doom of the Gods, 114 *sqq*.
Ragnhild, 148.
Rani, *the Far-travelled*, 206.

Index

Reformation, The, 312.
Religion, 328 *sqq.*
Repræsentantskab, 325.
Rock-carvings in Bohusläu, 37.
Rögnvald Brusason, E. of Orkney, 218, 245 *sq.*, 315.
Rögnvald, E. of W. Gothland, 212, 214 *sqq.*
Rolf or Rollo, 81.
Runic Alphabet, 34.
Russia, rise of, 314.

Sæters, 346.
Schools, 331 *sqq.*
Schools, High, 335.
Ships, Prehistoric, 39.
Ships, Viking, 39, 61 *sqq.*, 258.
Short Serpent (ship), 192, 195 *sqq.*, 200.
Siegfred. *See* Sigurd.
Sigismund, K. of Sweden, 313.
Sigmund, 134, 136 *sq.*
Sigrid *the Haughty*, 192.
Sigröd. *See* Sigurd.
Sigurd, 110, 117.
Sigurd, Earl, 165.
Sigurd Haraldsson, 273-4.
Sigurd Arund, 280.
Sigurd *Slembidjakn*, 272, 281.
Sigurd, son of Bui, 179.
Sigurd *Syr*, 206, 208, 226, 245, 257.
Sigurd *the Crusader (Jorsalfari),* 141, 253, 269, 271-2.
Sigvald, chief of the Joms Vikings, 174, 177 *sqq.*, 194.
Skarphedinn, 134 *sqq.*
Skiolld, 136 *sq.*
Skirnir, 106, 110.
Skuli, Earl, 141, 289.
Sten Sture the Elder, 310.

Sten Sture the Younger, 310.
Storthing, The, 321.
Stralsund, 196.
Stratsraad, The, 320.
Suiones, The, 35 *sq.*
Sulki, 149.
Sumerleda, 292.
Surt, 115.
Svein, Earl of Ladi, 208, 209.
Svend Estridsson, 240, 242 *sqq.*, 248.
Svend, son of Cnut, K. of Denmark, 240.
Svend, K. of Denmark, 172, 174, 192 *sqq.*, 239.
Svente Sture, 310.
Sverdrup, 323.
Sverri, 280 *sqq.*
Svipdag, 109 *sq.*
Svold, 196, 262.
Syssel-men, The, 287.

Thangbrand, Saxon priest, 186 *sq.*, 291.
Theodoric, 117.
Thing, The, 143.
Thirty Years' War, 313.
Thökk, 102.
Thor, 96 *sqq.*
Thorarin, 132.
Thorberg Arnason, 237.
Thorfinn, E. of Orkney, 218, 245.
Thorfinn Munn, 234.
Thorgeir of Kviststad, 232, 234.
Thorgils, 170.
Thorgisl, Viking leader, 70, 79.
Thorgnyr, a Lawman, 214.
Thorir Hund, 230 *sqq.*
Thorkil Leire, 179.
Thorolf, 170, 171.
Thorstein Knarrarsmed, 230, 235.
Thorstein *the Red*, 84.

Thursar, 58, 95.
Thyri, 193.
Tostig Godwinsson, 249 *sqq*.
Trolle, Primate of Sweden, 312.
Tryggvi, a Pretender, 240.
Tryggvi Olafsson, 165, 167.
Tyr, 98, 101, 115.

UDAL TENURE, 337.
Ulf, E. (Dane), 242.
Ulf *the Red*, 199.
Ulf (*Tellander*), 83.
Union of Calmar, 303.
University of Norway, 335, 359.

VALDEMAR OR VLADOMIR, 169 *sqq*.
Valhöll (Walhalla), 105, 114, 119.
Valkyriur, The, 104 *sq*.

Vegtam, 112.
Vends, 243.
Vierendehler Strom, 196.
Viking Age, The, 305.
Viking ships, 39, 61 *sqq*., 258.
Vikings, The, 60 *sqq*., 97, 146, 304-5.

WALDEMAR *Atterday*, 302, 307 *sq*.
Walhalla. *See* Valhöll.
William of Normandy, 249, 252.
Woden. *See* Odin.
Wood-cutting, 341, 348 *sqq*.

YNGLINGS, The, 100, 148.
Yngvi, 100.

ZOE, EMPRESS, 247.

LITERARY INDEX.[1]

ARI *Frodi*, 139.
Arne, 364.
Arnljot Gelliné, 365.

Bang, 362.
Beowulf, 9 *sq*.
Björnson, Björnstierne, 324, 361, *sqq*.
Brand, 140.
Brand, 367, 372.
Bugge, 362.

Cataline, 367.

Den Engilske Lods, 360.
De Nygifte, 365.
Descent of Odin, The, 112.
Det flager i Byen og paa Havnen, 365.
Det Norske Folks Historie, 362.

De Unges Forbund, 368.
Digte og Sange, 365.

EDDA, 90 *sqq*.
Edda, Prose, 101, 141, 205.
Egils Saga, 129.
Eiriksdrapa (quoted), 119.
Encomiæ or Laudatory Ballads, 118.
Et Dukkehjem, 366, 369.
En Fallit, 365.
En Folkefiend, 369.
En Glad Gut, 364.
En Hanske, 365.
En Malström, 373.
Eyrbryggia Saga, 129.
Erik Oddsson, 140.

Færeyinga Saga, 142.

---

[1] The names in italics are those of works referred to in the text.

Fiskejenten, 364.
Fjölsvissmál, 109.
Fruen fra Havet, 369.
Fru Inger til Ostcraad, 311, 368.

Garman og Worse, 373.
Genganere, 370.
Geografi og Kjærlighed, 365.
Gildet paa Solhung, 368.
Gisla Saga Súrsonnar, 128.
Grettis Saga, 129.
Grougaldr, 109.
Gull-horis Saga, 127.
Gunnlaug the Monk, 141.
Gunnlaugs Saga Ormstungu, 128.
Gylfaginning, 93, 141.

Hansa-horis Saga, 127.
Hærmændene paa Helgeland, 368, 372.
Halte Hulda, 364-5.
Hardar Saga, or *Hólmsvega Saga*, 127.
Háttatal, 142.
Hedda Gabler, 366, 370.
Heimskringla Saga, 141.
Hervarar Saga ok Heidreks, 111.
Holmboe, 362.
Thorsteins Saga Sidu Halls Sonar, 128.
Hrafnkels Saga Freysgoda, 128.

Ibsen, Henrik, 289, 311, 324, 329, 357, 361-2, 365, 371 *sqq*.
Islendinga-bók, 140.
Islendinga Saga, 142.

Jarla-Sögur, 138, 245. See *Orkneyinga Saga*.
Jomsvikinga Saga, 142.

KARL JONSSON, 140.
Keiser og Galitæer, 369.
Kjærlighedens Komedie, 368.
Kjelland, Alexander, 373.
Kolskegg Asbjornsson, 140.
Kongs Emnerne, 289, 368.
Kong Sverri, 364.
Konunga-bók, 140.
Kormaks Saga, 127.

Landnama-bók, 140.
Laxdæla Saga, 129.
Lie, Jonas, 373.
Lodsen og hans Husfru, 373.

Mallem Dralmingerne, 364.
Maria Stuart i Skotland, 364.
Moe, Jorge, 361.
Munch, Andreas, 361.
Munch, Peter Andreas, 362.

NIBELUNGEN, 117.
Njala, 122, 129, 135 *sqq*.
Njals Saga, 186.
Norges Dæmring, 361.

Odd the Monk, 141.
Olafs-Saga (the Longer), 170.
Orkneyinga Saga, 142, 245.

Paa Guds Veje, 365.
Peer Gynt, 367, 372.
Peter Wergeland, 360.

Redaktoren, 365.
Rosmersholm, 324, 370.
Rutland, 373.

SÆMUND *Frodi*, 140.
Sagas, The, 122 *sqq*.
Samfundets Støtter, 370.

Sars, J. E., 290, 362.
Schive, 362.
Sigurd Jorsalfari, 364.
Sigurd Slembe, 364.
Skalds, 119.
Skaldskaparmál, 142.
Skipper Worse, 373.
Skirnisför, 110.
Skjoldunga Saga, 142.
Snorri, 101, 274.
Snorri Sturluson, 94, 141.
Storm, 362.
Sturla Thordsson, 142.
Sturlunga Sögur, 142.
Svarfdæla Saga, 128, 131.
Synnöve Solbakken, 364.
'Syttendemai Poesi,' 360.

Thorgils Saga, 142.
Trœmasteren Fremtiden, 373.

Udsight over det Norske Historie, 362.
Unger, 362.

Vapnfirdhinga Saga, 128.
Vatnsdala Saga, 128.
Vegtamskridha (quoted), 112.
Viga Glums Saga, 128.
Vildanden, 370.
Völsung Cycle of Poems, 110.
Völuspá, 113 sqq.
Welhaven, 360 sq.

BOTANICAL INDEX.

Aconitum septentrionale, 392.
Alsine nirta, 382.
Alsine stricta, 382.
Anagallis scutellata, 380.
Arabis petraea, 386.
Arenaria ciliata, 382.
Artemisia norvegica, 382, 389.
Astragalus Oroboedes, 382.

Campanula rotundifolia, 374.
Campanula uniflora, 382.
Calluna, 384.
Carex arctica, 385.
Carex arenaria, 379.
Carex misandra, 382.
Carex rupestris, 381.
Carex rupina, 392.
Catabrosa algida, 379.
Cephalanthera rubra, 385.
Carex chordorhiza, 380.

Cirsium acaule, 385.
Cirsium heterophyllum, 384.
Convallaria polygonatum, 384.

Daphne Mezereum, 384.
Dentaria bulbifera, 384.
Draba alpina, 382.
Draba nivalis, 382.
Dryas octopetala, 381, 387.

Echinospermum deflexum, 385.
E. Lappula, 385.
Empetrum, 384.
Epipactis palustris, 380.

Fragaria collina, 385.

Gentiana nivalis, 391.
Gentiana purpurea, 392.
Gentiana serrata, 385.
Gentiana tenella, 386, 392.

Hippophaë rhamnoides, 386.

Iris pseudacorus, 379.

Kœnigia Islandica, 382, 387.

Latabrosa algida, 382.
Libanotis montana, 385.
Linnæa borealis, 393.
Luzula arctica, 382.

Mulgedium alpinum, 384.
Myricaria Germanica, 386.

Naumburgia thyrsiflora, 380.

Ononus campestris, 385.
Orobus vernus, 385.
Oxytropis lapponica, 381, 391.

Papaver nudicaule, 382, 390.
Parnassia palustris, 379.
Peristylis viridis, 385.
Phaca frigida, 382, 390.
Phleum phalanoides, 385.
Plantago borealis, 385.
Poa stricta, 382.
Potentilla nivea, 381-2.
Primula Sibirica, 385.
Primula stricta, 382.

Ranunculus aconitifolius, 384, 387.
Ranunculus gracialis, 375, 388.
Ranunculus nivalis, 375, 382.
Rhododendron lapponicum, 382.
Rubus chamæmorus, 389.

Sagina nivalis, 382.
Salix daphnoides, 386.
Salix polaris, 382.
Salix reticulata, 381.
Saussurea alpina, 385.
Saxifraga cotyledon, 388.
Saxifraga hieracifolia, 382.
Saxifraga oppositifolia, 375.
Saxifraga stellaris, 382, 389.
Sedum villosum, 385.
Stellaria numifusa, 385.

Thalictrum alpinum, 381.
Trifolium montanum, 385.

Vaccinium, 384.
Vahlbergella affinis, 386.
Veronica Beccabunga, 380.
Veronica saxatilis, 381.
Vicia pisiformis, 385.
Viola tricolor, 374.

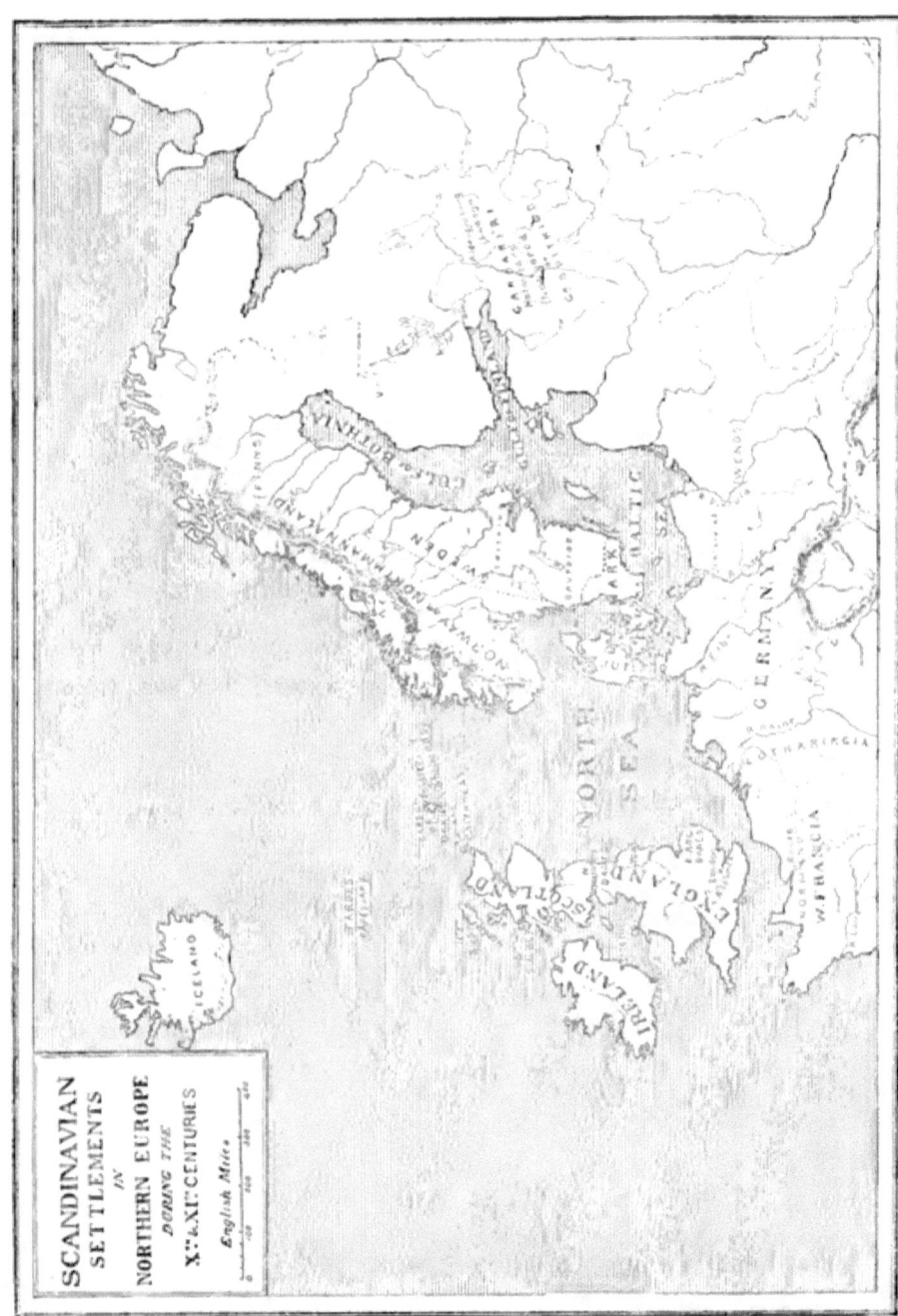

www.ingramcontent.com/pod-product-compliance
Lightning Source LLC
Chambersburg PA
CBHW050845300426
44111CB00010B/1133